SOCIALIST STRATEGIE

SOCIALIST STRATEGIES

edited by
David Coates and Gordon Johnston

MARTIN ROBERTSON · OXFORD

First published in 1983 by Martin Robertson &
Company Ltd.,
108 Cowley Road, Oxford OX4 1JF.

British Library Cataloguing in Publication Data

Socialist strategies. – (A Socialist primer)
  1. Socialism
  I. Coates, David   II. Johnston, Gordon
  III. Series
  335   HX73

  ISBN 0-85520-652-7
  ISBN 0-85520-653-5 Pbk

Typeset by Oxford Verbatim
Printed and bound in Great Britain by
Billing and Sons Ltd., Worcester

CONTENTS

Contents

NOTES ON CONTRIBUTORS

DAVID BAILEY (Ch. 6)
Member of the International Marxist Group from 1969 to 1980, currently working on a history of popular revolt in twentieth century Europe. He lives in Cambridge.

SARAH BENTON (Ch. 5)
Journalist on the *New Statesman*. She edited the Communist Party journal *Comment* between 1978 and 1980, and left the Party in 1981. She lives in London.

LIONEL CLIFFE (Ch. 1)
Senior Lecturer in Politics at the University of Leeds. He was a founding editor of the *Review of African Political Economy*, and is the author of a number of books and articles on East and Central Africa, on liberation movements and on the peasantry. He worked in Africa for twelve years, and now lives in Sheffield.

DAVID COATES (Chs 2 and 9)
Senior Lecturer in Politics at the University of Leeds. He has written extensively on the Labour Party and the question of socialism. A former member of the International Socialists, he is now active in the peace movement and the Socialist Society. He lives in York.

GEOFF HODGSON (Ch. 4)
Principal Lecturer in Economics at Newcastle upon Tyne Polytechnic. He was Labour Candidate for Manchester Withrington in 1979. His books include *Socialism and Parliamentary Democracy*, Spokesman, *Labour at the Cross-roads*, Martin Robertson, Oxford, 1981, and *Capitalism, Value and Exploitation*, Martin Robertson, Oxford, 1982.

Contributors

GORDON JOHNSTON (Ch. 3)
Lecturer in Politics at Leeds Polytechnic, currently researching labourism, socialist thought and the British Labour Party. He lives in Leeds.

ROBERT LOOKER (Ch. 9)
Lecturer in Politics at the University of York. His publications include *Rosa Luxemburg: selected writings*, Jonathan Cape, London, 1971.

SARAH PERRIGO (Ch. 7)
Lecturer in the Department of Peace Studies at the University of Bradford. She has taught courses on women and society for several years. She is an active socialist feminist, a member of the Labour Party and is currently researching the history of women in the Labour Party.

RICHARD TAYLOR (Ch. 8)
Lecturer in Politics and Modern History in the Department of Adult Education at Leeds University since 1970. He has written widely in the areas of peace studies, politics and social work, and has been an activist in the peace movement and in a variety of socialist organizations.

KEVIN WARD (Ch. 8)
Currently lecturer/co-ordinator for the 'adult education and the unemployed' project at the University of Leeds. He was previously a lecturer in social policy and community work at the University of Leeds, and before that a community worker with the Batley Community Development Project.

EDITORIAL INTRODUCTION

This is the second of a series of volumes issued under the general title of *A Socialist Primer*. Though each volume stands alone, and will – we hope – be of value and interest in its own right, each too should gather extra force from its place in the series as a whole. That series arose out of the recognition of a need on the Left for intellectual material of a certain kind: material that would place in the hands of left-wing activists the arguments, theories and information with which they could more easily construct the case for socialism in their discussions with others, and that was both concise and compact in its presentation, and as rigorous and exhaustive in its quality and range as we could make it. Our sense, in initiating this series and in steering it towards publication, has not been that such intellectual efforts on their own would shift the balance of class forces and power in contemporary capitalism in any significant way. Of course not. Such a view would grossly exaggerate the force of ideas in the struggle for social change. Our sense was much more modest – that that struggle for socialism has, as one of its prerequisites, the production and dissemination of a certain kind of literature. If socialism is ever to be 'an idea whose time has come' then socialism as a project has now to be deepened and widened by thought, discussion and planning, and socialist ideas need to spread out into the labour movement and beyond, there to become widely known and respected as the radical common sense of the age. Yet that will never happen unless the case for socialism is put together in a form that is easily accessible to those who have to argue and struggle for it on a daily basis. Nor will that argument and struggle succeed unless the case to be put is at least as sophisticated and multifaceted as are the alternative explanations and scenarios with which the idea of socialism is in competition. With Thatcherism rampant, unemployment rife, and the gains and arguments of the Left everywhere under threat, socialists in Britain need to harness their forces and launch their counter-attacks as never before, and the confidence that can come from the visible strength and superiority of a well-made socialist case is needed now on the Left more than it has been for at least a generation.

In designing and commissioning the series of which this volume is a part, we were prompted by a belief in the particular responsibility and distinct if limited role of socialist intellectuals in such a rekindling of the Left. If the 1980s are to see a revival of socialist support on any scale in Britain, it seems to us that one of the things the labour movement will need is a sophisticated and widely understood counter-culture. To build that the labour movement will, among other things, have to bridge the gap between its intellectuals and its activists, make more readily available its theories, and place in the hands of its militants the intellectual means by which they can grasp, build and sharpen the arguments on which the battle for the minds and support of the British working class can be won. The series as a whole sees itself as one small contribution to that particular project.

In the first volume, *Socialist Arguments*, we asked our contributors to address themselves to that first level of criticism and rebuttal experienced by socialists – to that range of 'explanations' of the present crisis of British capitalism that discredited socialism by focusing 'responsibility' for the crisis on those who suffer most from it. So the first volume brought together in one place socialist counter-arguments to those who claim that inflation and unemployment are the fault of workers and their unions, that job scarcity is caused by immigration, that low productivity is enhanced by too soft a welfare state and too burdensome a level of taxation, that the police, the media and the democratic state itself are neutral in the struggle between classes, and that socialism is bound to be violent and totalitarian and is, therefore, no answer in any case. It is our belief that the responses mobilized in volume 1 effectively discredited the orthodox arguments within which the present crisis is normally discussed, and by so doing created the space again within which socialists could offer an alternative explanation of our present difficulties and a set of strategies for their effective resolution. It is to the filling of that space that the contributions in this volume are now directed.

The chapters that follow attempt to do a number of things. The first three present socialist explanations of what is happening around us today – of the world recession, the decline of the British economy, and the dominant trends in contemporary British politics. This part of the volume is intended to be of value in two ways. We hope first that these arguments can be used by socialists to persuade others that a full explanation of our present situation can come only from such a socialist perspective, and that as a result, it is to the Left that they should look for guidance here, and not to the rag-bag of conventional wisdoms to which they are normally exposed by a capitalist press and conservative politicians. We hope too that these first three chapters will provide an internal benchmark against which the reader can assess the relative strengths and weaknesses of the various currents on the Left, currents that are canvassed and discussed in the two sections of the volume that follow.

Socialists continue to disagree amongst themselves about many things: about strategy, organization, programme, and even about goals. Those divisions are themselves a source of weakness and a barrier to recruitment by the Left. Yet they persist because the task which the Left sets for itself is such an enormous one, without obvious and simple solution. They persist because, in the pursuit of that solution, individuals and organizations come to invest immense amounts of their own personal credit and time in particular positions and patterns of behaviour and come to feel, as a result, that fundamental revisions of strategy and attitude would cost them dear in self-respect and status. The divisions persist also because no particular answer to the Left's perennial problems is able now, after all the traumas of twentieth century socialist politics, to point to its own record as evidence of unambiguous success. On the contrary, none of the traditions currently active on the Left is without its problems, nor is any free from vulnerability and failure. In fact, the Left in Britain today is as uncertain and unsure of itself as at any time this century. The Communist Party can no longer offer its politics as the obvious guide to the perfect society, as it could for many in the 1930s. The track record of Labour governments since 1964 has been so bad that no parliamentary socialist can easily offer that party as an unproblematic alternative. The small Trotskyist and semi-Trotskyist sects remain just that – small and often sectarian, more adept at spotting the sins of others than of winning the support of large numbers of people. Indeed, the very paradox of our present situation, of the deepest capitalist recession for half a century producing no mass turn to socialist politics, makes this a critical time for the Left – one in which an honest examination of alternatives, a dialogue between traditions, the encouragement of mutual support and the weighing of strengths and weaknesses can only help to clarify for all of us the way forward for the socialist project in the 1980s.

In designing the second and third parts of this volume with that recognition in mind, we were conscious that people approaching the Left for the first time are always struck by, and often need guidance through, the multiplicity of detailed programmes, organizations and revolutionary positions being canvassed. But we were conscious too that behind that clash of programmes and groups lay more basic disagreements on broad strategy, and on the general form that socialist politics must take. So we have left to the third volume of this series any detailed specification of organizational positions, and have instead asked people writing in this volume to address themselves to those more general and underlying choices. Under 'Socialist Strategies' you will find Geoff Hodgson advocating a particular interpretation of the relationship between parliamentary and extra-parliamentary struggles in the pursuit of socialism, and stressing the associated need to build that relationship through sustained activity within the Labour Party. Sarah Benton chronicles and explains the Communist Party's preoccupation with the creation of a broad coalition of popular forces under left-wing leadership. David Bailey presents again the case for revolutionary politics and a revolutionary party, and that case is developed further in the Conclusion (chapter nine) by Robert Looker and David Coates. But before that, and in the last two chapters in the second part of this volume, Sarah Perrigo explores the relationship between socialism and feminism, and Richard Taylor and Kevin Ward assess the strengths and weaknesses of single-issue campaigning in fields as disparate as bombs and housing. The Conclusion contains, in the end, a defence of the revolutionary position, but it only does so after an extensive survey of the twentieth century experience of all the Left positions canvassed here, a survey which is designed to leave you free to weigh the balance in your own way, and to come to your own personal political conclusions. We have attached a list of organizations, their addresses and their journals, so that you can easily contact them if you wish; and in volume 3 we will use that list to bring together in a concise way a description of where each organization stands on the questions of strategy, organization, programme and goal discussed here in more general terms by our contributors. We should say too that we regret the absence of a chapter here discussing the connection between black struggles and socialist politics, and hope that can be remedied in the volumes to come.

David Coates
Gordon Johnston

THE PRESENT CRISIS

Chapter one

MODERN WORLD CAPITALISM AND ITS CONTEMPORARY CRISIS

Lionel Cliffe

The most compelling feature of present-day capitalism is that it has not proved to be crisis free. Indeed, on many counts our present troubles bear comparison with the Great Depression. More people are now out of work in Britain than at the depth of the slump in the 1930s. Like then, whole industries are shutting down, whole regions are submerged by the blight of unemployment and short-time work, and a whole generation is growing up with no prospect of a job.

It is worth remembering, too, that this grim picture is not just true of Britain. We are almost, though not quite, the worst hit of the countries in the EEC which has, altogether, 11 million jobless. The USA alone has an even greater number, and all the industrialized countries have experienced an end to steady growth. The socialist countries of Eastern Europe have also been affected by the general global crisis; and for most of the developing countries, if they have no oil, the consequences have been catastrophic, as we shall see. In the developed North, large firms have gone bankrupt and major banks run scared of default, but in the South whole countries teeter on the brink of being declared insolvent. There, the problem of survival is not whether production levels and standards of living are eroded but whether whole segments of the population will have enough to sustain life itself.

Profound political implications for socialists in Britain stem from the fact of crisis, and from its international character. For socialists must not just bewail the system's ills, but must try to *explain* its chronic condition – as a prelude to confronting it. With that in mind, it is clear that any explanation of the crisis that is restricted to characteristics of these islands, or indeed any solution which is purely national, will be inadequate. The 'Iron

Lady' Margaret Thatcher may have made matters worse in the UK than they need be but even she did not 'cause' the depression. Tory 'monetarist' policies may have a more catastrophic consequence for the working class than others that could be pursued, or that are being pursued, for instance in Scandinavia, but they are not the origin of the problem. It is true that Britain is experiencing deindustrialization, a decline that may well be irreversible, but the shift in Britain's relative position is not the origin of our woes. It is rather an element in, and a consequence of, the general crisis. Attention must then be directed, if it is explanations that we want, to an international perspective, to look not just at what is particular to Britain but at what is *common* to the crisis confronting all countries and to the *interconnectedness* of the several national predicaments.

If the international character of the present crisis rules out solutions premised simply on a change of government or of policy in Britain, it should also make everyone on the Left realize that what we face now is a general crisis of capitalism as a system. This realization in turn ought to have finally laid to rest any idea that modern capitalism had been 'reformed' and was no longer 'anti-social'. Such ideas were common currency in the twenty years of the long boom after World War II. The most widely read economics textbook of all time, Samuelson (Eleventh Edition, 1958) solemnly proclaimed that 'by means of appropriately reinforcing monetary and fiscal policies, our mixed-enterprise system can avoid the excesses of boom and slump and can look forward to healthy progressive growth'[1]. At the same time, Anthony Crosland[2] sought to persuade the labour movement that the old-fashioned struggle for socialism was no longer necessary. Capitalism was a reformed beast. It was no longer crisis-ridden; it could be managed. It was no longer motivated by a selfish, anti-social grabbing after profits. All that was required was a continuing expansion of welfare and of policies of income redistribution, and equality of opportunity and universal prosperity would be here to stay.

Now that the enormity of the present depression has exploded the myth that a regulated capitalism could go on producing uninterrupted growth, it is tempting to simply dismiss such

1 P. Samuelson, *Economics; An Introductory Analysis*, 11th ed. McGraw Hill, New York, 1958, p. 360.
2 See his famous text: C. A. R. Crosland, *The Future of Socialism*, Cape, London, 1956.

arguments as facile. Certainly, Crosland was completely wrong
in some of his analyses of modern capitalism: the notion that the
power of the monopolies was somehow diminished, for instance
– they had simply developed and were now operating more internationally. In other respects, he drew unwarranted conclusions
from trends that were indeed occurring: the replacement of the
old-fashioned 'boss' by a managerial class. This class was indeed
divorced from ownership and the emergence of such managers
was politically significant, but their actions were no less dictated
by considerations of profit than had been those of their entre-
preneur predecessors. Indeed, if anything, the new managers
were even more prone to insist upon exact calculations about
longer-term maximization of profits. But it is still worth recal-
ling the other dimensions of change which lead people like
Crosland to argue that the system's social character had radically
changed, for changes there have certainly been. The state's role
in the economy, as a direct 'capitalist' producer, as benevolent
guarantor of minimum standards of living, as overall orchestrator
of the economy, was indeed a new feature common to all
capitalist countries in the mid-twentieth century. So too, apparently, was each capitalist state's pursuance of 'Keynesian'
policies of intervention in the economy, designed to manage the
level of demand for products to avoid periodic crises of over-
production. There has also occurred an unparalleled application
of science and technology to production that certainly constituted a second industrial revolution.

One simple way of dismissing Crosland and his kind is to say
that all these changes were in some way just superficial, and that
they did not affect the essential nature of the system. Such easy
dismissals often do not bother to explain what makes some
features 'essential', other than the convenience to their argument! But even if they do not beg that question, approaches that
relegate explanation to a reassertion of the basic and unchanging
nature of capitalism do little to explain the particular character of
this crisis. For the 1980s are distinct from the 1930s in many
ways – not least in the fact of inflation continuing alongside
stagnation. Politically, such differences could be crucial to
working out strategies (which later chapters explore) for combatting the crisis and confronting the system, for such strategies
need to be tailored to the times. We shall, indeed, go on to
consider a number of the other changed characteristics of late
twentieth century capitalism to which socialist analysts have

drawn attention. But first it is worth registering a further reason why such changed forms of capitalism must be explored: an alternative, socialist theory to those of orthodox economists or social democrats has to explain not simply the present crisis but also why the system did, in fact, perform so well for a generation from the 1940s.

Before we go on to look at some of the socialist explanations of capitalist boom as well as crisis and, in particular, of the contemporary crisis, a further political implication of this crisis must be registered to provide a starting point for discussion of explanations and strategies. We have stressed that this is a general, international crisis of the capitalist society that dominates our existing world. But what do we understand by 'crisis'? To translate this into an apocalyptic vision of a malfunctioning of the economic system so severe and irreversible that it will bring about the collapse (or explosion?) of capitalism under its own steam, as it were, is too simplistic and not useful politically. Nor are we today confronting an 'economic crisis' in the limited sense of the low point of the business cycle that has continued to mark, though in a dampened way, the fluctuating performance of capitalist economies, even in the post-war period. We are clearly experiencing not only a down-turn of what is termed a 'long wave'[3] and within that a recession of particular severity, but a 'structural crisis'. In a useful work on US capitalism, the French socialist Manuel Aglietta suggests that it is helpful to 'conceive crises as *ruptures* . . . (whose) resolution . . . always involves an irreversible transformation of the mode of production'[4]. Such a perspective envisages as one alternative, a *revolutionary* transformation: socialism is on the agenda. (I would be tempted to say that an assessment of the preparedness of the Left internationally makes a socialist transformation unlikely this time round, though such an assessment is the task of later chapters.) But such a view of crisis alerts us to the fact that if socialism is not to be the immediate outcome, then, neither will the capitalist system itself ever be the same again. In the process of seeking to 'solve' a crisis that puts the whole working of the system into jeopardy, major

3 On the so-called 'long-wave' or Kondratief wave, see E. Mandel, *Long Waves of Capitalist Development: Marxist Interpretations*, Cambridge University Press, Cambridge, 1981; J. J. van Duijn, *The Long Waves in Economic Life*, Allen and Unwin, London, 1983.
4 M. Aglietta, *A Theory of Capitalist Regulation: The U.S. Experience*, New Left Books, London, 1979.

structural transformation will be necessary. Castells, another French socialist, also writing on the USA, puts it well:

what defines a structural crisis is that it becomes impossible to expand or reproduce the system without a transformation or reorganisation of the basic characteristics of production, distribution, and management, and their expression in terms of social organisation.[5]

The resolution of this kind of crisis can be expected to change the system along several dimensions. It may redefine the competition between different capitals: the crisis at the end of the last century heralded the arrival of the great monopolies, recovery from the Great Depression saw the emergence of transnational corporations. What new forms of concentration of capital might now emerge? The present crisis may change the locations where capital produces and accumulates, and in the process redefine some countries' positions in the world economy – that may well be on the agenda for Britain. It may change the character of the state's involvement in the system – that may be the significance of 'monetarism', not just a policy pursued by some ruling parties but a general shift in practice that may characterize the coming decades. Most fundamentally, we can already discern ways in which the basic class relationship between capital and workers is being redefined. Structural crises such as the one we are living through are not just symptomatic of 'long waves' but mark the end of a particular stage or phase of capitalism and may herald a new one. An understanding of the possible new phase is necessary in order to be 'able to predict tendencies and act on them to *change the trend*', to quote Castells again – a crucial task for socialists.

EXPLANATIONS OF CRISIS

Many socialist analysts have sought to explain the recurrence of slump by asserting that it is a result of the inevitable working out of basic tendencies in the capitalist system. One such approach that has received much attention recently is to advance a theory of the 'long waves' that we have mentioned above. This resurrects ideas put forward by, Kondratief, a Soviet economist in the 1920s, who argued that as well as the well-known 'business

5 M. Castells, *The Economic Crisis and American Society*, Blackwell, Oxford, 1980.

cycle' of 9–10 years duration, the history of capitalism had been marked by another periodic cycle of some 50 years. In each period the upswing would be marked by more dramatic recoveries and generally bouyant conditions, only to be succeeded by a period of about 25 years wherein the recessions were sharper and conditions were more stagnant. For what it is worth, the facts, if one takes statistical series of output, employment, investment, etc. do seem to bear out some periodicity of this duration: our slump today comes 50 years after the Depression. As for explanation, Kondratief himself put it down to the particular pattern of investment that happened to occur. In the long downswings the investment that did occur made less impact on developing the productive capacity – it was spent on wars, on foreign investment or in railways or other equipment that would only have a long pay-off. His was an historical explanation. Contemporary writers have sought to offer a more theoretical explanation trying to link the long waves to the hints that Marx offers in his work to explain crises[6]. Essentially, without going into the technicalities, we are offered an explanation of crisis which roots it in some general law of operation of the capitalist system. What causes the crisis? The answer: capitalism, which is always subject to 'long waves'.

A more common approach in recent socialist writings situates an explanation of our present plight in more conventional Marxian 'crisis theory'[7]. Presumably 'crisis' would here correspond more to the shorter business cycle. But the logic of the various arguments is similar in that they explain the crisis of the 1980s in terms of the general tendencies of a system that is crisis-ridden. Different analysts give pride of place to a different feature that they derive abstractly from the basic model of capital that Marx sets out in his main work. Indeed there is a vigorous debate between these protagonists who each assert the explanatory primacy of a particular 'law' of capitalist development. They are also prone to assert that theirs is the 'correct' reading of Marx, which alone will be the guide to correct political practice in the predicament that faces us.

---

6 See, especially, Mandel, *op. cit.* and also his *The Second Slump: A Marxist Analysis of Recession in the Seventies*, New Left Books, London, 1978.
7 For a useful summary of this literature E. Olin Wright, 'Alternative Perspectives in Marxist Theory of Accumulation and Crisis' in J. Schwartz, (ed), *The Subtle Anatomy of Capitalism, Selected Readings*, Goodyear, Santa Monica, 1977, also in his *Class, Crisis and the State: the Limits of the Mixed Economy*, New Left Books, London, 1978.

Modern capitalism and its crisis

One school of general crisis theorists argues that the crisis is one of profitability. Fundamental, they argue, is the 'law of the falling rate of profit' that Marx wrote extensively about in *Capital* and which is manifest in the crisis. Briefly, this tendency occurs, in Marx's view, because labour was the only 'creative' component of production that could impart more value into a finished product than was intrinsic in it (unlike raw materials, or machinery) and was thus the sole source of profit. But the typical pattern of investment under capitalism would be to substitute machinery, what he called 'dead labour' (the product of past labours), for 'living labour'. So as capital accumulates, a decreasing proportion of it is expended on the creative, living ingredient of production. Thus, the tendency over a period would be for the *rate* of profit that each unit of (an expanding) capital could call forth to slow down.

Any crisis theory aims to put forward an explanation of the blockage which halts the steady and continuous process of capital accumulation. In the works of Yaffe, Mattick, and Cogoy[8], the one impediment is the tendency of a falling rate of profit inherit in capital accumulation itself. But their theory goes on to argue that the economic crisis 'restructures' capital and the conditions for accumulation so that more profitable investment can occur. Their views are challenged on both theoretical and empirical grounds. Their critics remind us that although such a tendency can be derived from Marx's model, Marx himself offered a list of 'countervailing tendencies' that could in practice reverse the falling profit rate, such as increased exploitation of workers, or of foreign investment yielding 'super-profits'. They also challenge the assumption that the pattern of investment will be as forecast, will be labour-saving. Without going into the complex technicalities of the debate, it seems fair to say that although there *could* be a falling rate of profit, 'no general law can be assumed at an *a priori* level on the relationship between technology [whether labour-saving], productivity and value distribution [especially profits]'[9]. The empirical evidence of *actual* profit rates seems also inconclusive.

8 The works referred to are: P. Mattick, *Marx and Keynes: the limits of the mixed economy*, Merlin, London, 1969; D. Yaffe, 'The Marxian Theory of Crisis, Capital and the State', *Economy and Society*, Vol. 2, No. 2, 1973; M. Cogoy, 'The Fall of the Rate of Profit and the Theory of Accumulation', *Bulletin of the Conference of Socialist Economists*, Winter, 1973.
9 Castells, *op. cit.* p. 23.

Another alternative explanation is to see the basic blockage occurring because capitalists cannot sell all that they produce. There is a problem of 'under-consumption' or 'over-production'. This may be for two possible reasons. The exploitation of workers required by the profit-motive does not allow the working class to spend at a level that will provide a sufficiently expanding market. Or the problem may be the more complex one of 'disproportions' between production of consumer and capital goods. The former may not be expanding enough to buy all the machines produced by the latter. Again on *a priori* grounds one can grant that either of these may be a problem but that they should inevitably and periodically provide the crucial bottleneck is not so easy to prove.

Some critics of these two explanations, most notably Glyn and Sutcliffe[10], say that such arguments forget the essential role of 'class struggle'. The crisis of profitability that recurs is due to successful pressures for higher wages at the expense of profits. Other perspectives have been less monocausal and have sought to see these several factors inter-related in a more complex view of crises. Undoubtedly, the most sophisticated attempt to do this can be found in the works of Ernest Mandel[11]. He also attempts to explain crises not just by derivation of general laws from abstract models of the capitalist mode of production but to offer an explanation of particular crises in their historical context. Indeed, Castells makes one general criticism of all the different 'crisis theories' considered here when he accuses them of a 'social naturalism'. Their explanations are located in terms of 'the immutable essence of capitalism and . . . the necessary nature of its crisis'[12]. Such perspectives in fact run the risk of explaining nothing: 'What causes the crisis?' 'Capitalism'. 'How?' 'It's the nature of capitalism'. In contrast he offers what would seem to be a more illuminating perspective on crisis. Instead of seeing our ills – unemployment, deindustrialization, falling living standards, increased repression – as results of a disease called 'crisis', which in turn is 'caused' by something out there called capitalism, he reverses the interactions. It is the existing system of capitalism that is experiencing the crisis and that is because it is being

10 A. Glyn and B. Sutcliffe, *British Capitalism, Workers and the Profit Squeeze*, Penguin, Harmondsworth, 1972.
11 Among Mandel's most relevant works are *Late Capitalism*, New Left Books, London, 1975 as well as his *The Second Slump* and *The Long Waves of Capitalist Development*, *op. cit.*
12 Castells, *op. cit.*

Modern capitalism and its crisis

challenged by people's actions on several fronts: 'we are living in an economic crisis caused by a general process of social disruption in most advanced countries, [and, one might add, throughout the capitalist world] which has called into question the structure of social relationships underlying the pattern of capital accumulation'[13].

HISTORICAL EXPLANATIONS OF BOOM AND CRISIS

Castells' approach is characteristic of many that do not simply explain the crisis as the inevitable manifestation of a fundamental law. At the same time, they can be contrasted with those who eschew theory to the point where our woes are attributed to one or more particular historical occurences that are seemingly 'accidental'. There is no shortage of such critical events that are given the blame: the massive oil price rise of 1973 is one favourite; a somewhat more general catastrophe that brought much else in its wake was the breakdown of the accepted system of international payments, based on the dollar, in the early 1970s. Some on the Left relate everything back to the defeat of the USA in the Indochina War. Important as these events were, to see them as 'prime causes' rather than just dramatic episodes, perhaps with amplifying effects, is inadequate, if only because these events are themselves then not explained. One group of socialist writers, like Castells, Aglietta and Arrighi[14], instead try to use theoretical insights to offer a view of the actual working of capitalism in various countries and globally, as a total entity in which key historical events are inter-related. Moreover, their approach forces us to start analysis of the present slump with the long, preceding boom of the post-war years. The system that is now in crisis is the modern world capitalism that was cobbled together in the 1940s as a response to the last crisis of the depression of the 1930s, the breakdown of world trade that resulted and the war that followed.

The main lines along which the system of capitalism was restructured after World War II and which provided the basis for the boom can be summarized as follows. On a global level, an

13 *Ibid.* p. 5.
14 In addition to the works of Aglietta and Castells already cited, see G. Arrighi's contribution in S. Amin, G. Arrighi, A. G. Frank and I. Wallerstein, *Dynamics of Global Crisis*, Macmillan, London, 1982.

17

inter-related network of national economies was pieced together as the 'free world'. The initiative for this reorganization of international transactions along new lines and the revivifying of the European and Japanese national economies was taken quite deliberately by the US Government which remained the main orchestrating influence. US domination was achieved by a range of mechanisms, the most crucial being financial and military. To replace the protectionism and the breakdown of the gold standard of the 1930s, a new international monetary system was set up at Bretton Woods at the end of the War, in which all countries adopted the dollar as an international means of payment. Thus the dollar became one instrument of control of other national economies and had the further advantage in that the USA could later live with increasing trade deficits by simply printing more dollars which other countries had to accept. Any threat to US dominance was met, especially in the Third World, with direct military intervention or a range of indirect political string-pulling by the CIA as the imperial policeman.

It should be stressed that, of course, the capitalist system has always operated, and thus must be understood, at a level beyond that of the *national* economy. What was new about the post-war period was the increased extent and new forms of internationalization of capital. Crucial to the very origins of capital was trade to the Orient. The initial accumulation of capital that financed capitalist industry was the pillage of India and the Indies and the slave trade from Africa and slave plantations in the New World. The industrial revolution depended on foreign markets for manufactures secured through 'free trade' within a Euro-centred world system underwritten by Britain. This dominance was challenged as rival imperialist states, prodded by their national cartels, struggled for power and thereby destroyed global political and economic structures and threw up new ones. The early part of this century was marked by titanic struggles between states, each asserting fuller control of their national economies – a system marked by what Bukharin[15] referred to as increased ordering of national economies while anarchy still characterized the world economy. But if part of the pattern of working, in that period at any rate, was strife, a pattern there certainly was. Most obviously, there was a world market, built up over centuries through an ever more extensive international transport network. Capital has

15 N. Bukharin, *Imperialism and the World Economy*, Monthly Review, New York, 1973.

been invested overseas for centuries but by the turn of this century its cartelization was beginning to transcend national boundaries. International migration of labour was also common – to the New World, to the colonies from Europe, and from one part of the Third World to another. As well as the traffic in slaves, indentured labour went from India, China and Indonesia to Malaya, South and East Africa, the West Indies and North America. But most fundamental to the pattern of the world economy had been the growth over one hundred years or more of a distinct, 'colonial' international division of labour: industry sited in Europe, North America and Japan, a Third World of raw material producers. All these patterns were now subject to change.

The economic character of this hegemony of US capital was different, however, from that which Britain had used to rule the waves in the nineteenth century. In place of direct colonies, free trade to provide markets for manufacturers, and 'portfolio investments' by British banks lending to foreign governments, municipalities and companies, modern US hegemony has been characterized by direct investment in productive activities overseas by what we now all refer to as 'multinational corporations'. Indeed, US aid for reconstruction in Europe was as much premised on providing openings for US multinational corporations (MNCs) as stimulating trading partners. This pattern of MNC subsidiaries acquiring or creating industrial production also stretched to include certain selected Third World countries, like Brazil, Hong Kong, Korea – the 'Newly Industrializing Countries' – though the more typical pattern of MNC investment in underdeveloped countries was in resource extraction[16]. By and large, the consequences for most poor countries were new forms of dependence, on the USA, the MNCs and the international economic institutions, in place of the metropolitan colonial power, and continued and intensified extraction through unequal trade. Thus, instead of 'free trade', the major imperative behind US control of the rest of the world was an 'open door' policy with respect to foreign investment. Indeed overseas production by MNCs based in the USA is now half as much again as the total of US imports and exports, West German companies operating abroad employ a labour force equal to 20

16 For recent changes see F. Fröbel, J. Heinricks and O. Kreye, *The New International Division of Labour*, Cambridge University Press, Cambridge, 1980.

Socialist strategies

per cent of the total labour force in manufacturing industry in Germany. A survey of 298 of the largest US corporations showed that by 1970 they obtained 70 per cent of their profits abroad. The US-dominated restructuring of the capitalist system formed the basis for an unparalleled explosion of new technological means of production. This led to growth in the European and Japanese economies that eventually became greater than that in the USA. These countries' own MNCs were fostered and the companies embarked on the same interpenetration of each others' economies and the same formation of subsidiaries in the Third World. In this latter process, however, lay the seeds of one of the challenges to the structure that gradually emerged through the increasing assertiveness of non-US MNCs and their national economies. The culmination of these tensions was the final rejection of the dollar as the international currency and the breakdown (and just as significantly the *non*-replacement) of the Bretton Woods monetary system[17]. But this episode involved more than inter-imperialist rivalry and we shall return to it.

Challenges also increasingly emerged in the 1960s to the pattern forced upon the Third World of unrepresentative and illegitimate regimes which watched over an open economy and a cheap and defenceless labour force. National liberation struggles in all continents challenged this pattern and sapped the strength of those forces that sought to underwrite the system. The greatest blow was experienced by the USA in Indochina, with the liberation of Vietnam, Laos and Cambodia. But this was not the only form of challenge. A variety of regimes not dominated by socialist or liberationist elements sought to implement a range of policies of 'economic nationalism'. But again we are running ahead of our story.

First we must note another distinctive feature of modern capitalism that has shaped its international as well as its national working – the central role of the state in the economy. At one level, the state's role has been one of overall steering of the economy – until recently by what we all referred to as 'Keynesian' policies. A variety of means, fiscal chiefly but also monetary tools, such as the manipulation of interest rates and the availability of credit, have been used by governments to provide stimulation or curbs to demand, with the object of ensuring steady

17 F. Block, *Origins of International Economic Disorder: A Study of United States International Monetary Policy from World War II to the Present*, University of California Press, Berkeley, 1977.

20

growth. Some states in advanced capitalist countries, especially France, have taken this directive role further and attempted an exercise in 'indicative planning' of the economy. This meant specifying production levels for the economy as a whole and for major sectors and attempting to reconcile these, but only in terms of monetary measures, not targets of actual quantities of goods as in socialist planning.

These Keynesian measures did have some success in avoiding extremes in business fluctuations for some years after 1945, though that is not the same as saying that they were alone *responsible* for the long boom. Rather, as has been suggested by Aglietta[18], the effectiveness of international arrangements and the growing internationalization of the capitalist economy may have made Keynesian measures work, in that any particular country experiencing a down-turn could 'externalize' recession by measures to improve its trading position. But Mandel[19] has argued convincingly that, after a time, internationalization had reached a further point where it began to reduce the possibility for Keynesian manipulations. The capitalist world economy was now so integrated that national economies no longer experienced their cycles of boom and recession out of phase, so that one could off-set the other. Instead the rhythm was now synchronized so that recession was general.

We have already noted the other important tendency which curtailed the power of national states to direct their economies – the rise of the multinationals. Traditionally, central banks have bought their own currencies to keep up the exchange rate when it was threatened by an economy showing signs of weakness, at which point the currency speculators would move in and amplify any such tendencies. But now even national banks did not have the monetary resources at their disposal to counter the largest speculators, the MNCs, who hold enormous balances of all currencies[20].

The role of the state – in all capitalist economies – was not, however, confined to these attempts at overall orchestration. The post-war period saw public ownership of major industries be-

18 Aglietta, *op. cit.*
19 Mandel, *The Second Slump, op. cit.*
20 See R. Murray, *Multinationals Beyond the Market, Intrafirm Trade and the Control of Transfer Pricing*, Harvester, Brighton, 1981. He had already made the point in his article, 'Internationalisation of Capital and the Nation-State', *New Left Review*, No. 67, 1971.

come a characteristic of most capitalist economies. Objectively, the chief function of the state taking over productive industries has been to socialize production of key materials, especially producer goods, so as to make them available more cheaply to capitalist producers of other goods. There has, of course, been a parallel process of socialized production, and thus a cheapening, of 'collective wage goods' – to use the current economic jargon the Left uses for the social services. But the effect of the resultant narrowing of the base of production for private profit, coupled with an ever-increasing provision of social services, needed if only as the price of incorporating the working class, has been to reduce the state's field for raising revenue to pay for the services. The impoverishment of state coffers is made more severe by the ability of MNCs to avoid paying tax. Thus is generated another dimension of crisis – what some socialist writers, in interesting debates[21], have termed the 'fiscal crisis of the state'. There are signs, now, that in so far as capital is successful in restructuring economies to find a way out of crisis, the domain of the state in national economies may be redefined. A part of collective welfare provision and some profitable sections of nationalized industry may be hived off, thus easing both the state's financial crisis and also meeting capital's desperate need to expand the area of production in society from which profit can be extorted. Such measures would also cheapen the real cost of labour and thus make for greater profitability at the expense of workers' living standards.

In trying to come to terms with such changes, socialists are having to begin to reformulate their whole conception of the state. However, theoretical conceptions often lag behind this changing reality. The state tends still to be relegated to a 'superstructural' level, where the political forms and ruling ideas are but reflections of an economic 'base'. The contemporary state ought instead to be analysed as very much part of the 'economy'. One valuable pointer to a more fruitful understanding of the state comes from the work of French socialists, notably de Brunhoff,[22]

21 J. O'Connor, *The Fiscal Crisis of the State*, St Martin's Press, New York, 1973, and for comments: H. Mosley, 'Monopoly Capital and the State: some critical reflections on O'Connor's 'Fiscal Crisis of the State'. *Review of Radical Political Economics*, Spring 1979 and I. Gough, *The Political Economy of the Welfare State*, Macmillan, London, 1979.
22 S. De Brunhoff, *State, Capital and Economic Policy*, Pluto Press, London, 1980.

who remind us that the state has always been an indispensable element in defining, guaranteeing and ensuring the reproduction of the social relations that make capitalism possible. In particular, they show that it has always been the job of the state to arrange for the 'production' of two ingredients essential to the whole system: money, which makes a 'market economy' go round; and 'labour' in the form of a working class obliged to sell it for wages.

We have already touched on the contemporary state's handling of money, but distinctive patterns of organizing the availability of labour have characterized the post-war period. One feature of this has been that all developed capitalist economies evolved in one form or another, and largely through some immigration, a new section or tier of the working class whose conditions, security and political rights were decidedly inferior to the more established workers. Then as the long boom conditions began to ebb, the state sought to cash in on the relative defencelessness of this stratum, casting it back, often literally to homeland or back into the home, into the reserve army of unemployed labour, but also to use it as the thin edge of the wedge to attack the standard of living of all workers and so to create conditions for increased profitability. Another dimension of state control of the reproduction of labour is its assumption of a defining role in relation to what constitutes the 'family', and hence the position of women. In the early stages of the boom, the state was relatively successful in its use of ideological persuasion as a means of getting many women who assumed war work back into the home. Then in the 1950s, many women were once more drawn into paid employment to fuel the boom, only later, as crisis began to bite, to be thrust back into the kitchen. But, this time, more drastic measures have had to be used. Redundancies among women have run far higher than among men. In Britain, the increase in the rate of unemployment among women has been five times that among men, even according to official figures which would not enumerate those women who do 'accept their role' as housewife when out of work and do not seek another job.

MONOPOLY CAPITALISM

A third major feature of contemporary capitalism, its monopolistic character, is inextricably linked to its international and statist dimension – to the extent, indeed, that some theorists associated with orthodox communist parties have, as we shall see, coined the term 'state monopoly capitalism' to describe the current stage of capitalist development[23]. Yet the epithet 'monopoly' to characterize a distinct phase of capitalism is by no means new. Lenin, Rosa Luxemburg and their contemporaries were making the same point at the turn of the century. Indeed a pattern where capitalist firms monopolized their sector of their national economy and had their national state to do their bidding, accurately epitomized the first half of the twentieth century. So what is there that is new and more monopolistic about developments in the second half of the century that might warrant another designation? We have already remarked that Crosland's fond belief that the monopolies had lost some of their power was mistaken. One shift was for capital to internationalize beyond the confines of the national economy, and beyond the confines and controls of the nation state too. But the trend toward multinationals was but one feature of a monopolization that was continuing apace within national economies, a trend which accelerated in Europe as the long boom ran out of steam in the 1960s. Thus, in Britain, the top 100 firms had only a 20 per cent share of net manufacturing output in 1949, but twenty years later that share had doubled. The concentration of production in the hands of a few firms was such that only in one major sector of British industry, non-electrical engineering, did the top four firms control less than two-thirds of the sector's output by 1969. In Britain, this level of concentration was reached in part through the great merger movement of the late 1960s; in 1968 the intensity of mergers was such that expenditure on acquisitions was almost double the net domestic fixed capital formation, and over a quarter of all the capital stock of all companies was subject to takeovers in that year[24].

What should concern socialists is not just the fact of monopoly or the extent of it but what difference it makes to the working of the system. One consequence of monopoly becoming the 'typical'

---

23 For an extended review and evaluation of the concept 'state monopoly capitalism' see B. Jessop, *The Capitalist State: Marxist Theories and Methods,* Martin Robertson, Oxford, 1982, and for critique see M. Wirth, 'Towards a Critique of the Theory of State Monopoly Capitalism', *Economy and Society,* Vol. 6, No. 3, 1977.
24 The information in this paragraph is from K. Cowling, *Monopoly Capitalism,* Macmillan, London, 1982.

form of capitalist organization and thus defining the system, stems from the fact that monopolies tend to be what the American radicals, Paul Baran and Paul Sweezy[25], termed 'price givers', not 'price takers' as are firms in a competitive economy. General price levels thus tend to be 'sticky upwards' – easily pushed up but not so responsive to forces working in the opposite direction – suggesting how monopoly contributes to our persistent inflation. It is further suggested that this ability of monopolies to pass on cost increases through price rises is one mechanism whereby any short-run wage gains are not sustained. An increasing degree of monopoly will tend to imply a diminishing share of wages in the national economy at the expense of the profit share[26].

Clearly, monopoly always implies the possibility of above average profit rates but whether profits and the overall profit share do actually increase will depend on whether the processes of capital accumulation and growth in production go on uninterrupted. In fact we know this has not been so since the 1960s, and subsequent recessions may have been intensified by contradictory effects the monopolies have on these processes. Monopolies may promote investment up to a point, as part of their strategy of building excess productive capacity which they can threaten to bring into production to scare off competitors, but in so far as this happens it also builds into the system a tendency for unutilized capacity. Baran and Sweezy see an even more general 'over-production' problem: the monopolies guarantee super profits but only at the expense of artificially holding back production levels. Given such curbs on production, how then to get rid of the ever-expanding 'surplus' that is generated? Partial and, in the end, counter-productive solutions might lie in the great emphasis on sales promotion – advertising itself absorbs surplus (unproductively) but also generates consumption – and other forms of 'waste', like in-built obsolescence. Export sales dumping might have been another answer, at least for the US economy during its period of unchallenged dominance up to 1968. State expenditures might offer another way out, but only certain *forms* of it. Only those that do not compete with private investment, increase the collective wage and thus eat into profits, or 'subsidize unemployment' and then reduce the workers' readiness to work, will suit capital. Thus 'capitalist interests will tend to

25 P. Baran and P. Sweezy, *Monopoly Capital: An Essay on the American Economic and Social Order*, Penguin, Harmondsworth, 1966.
26 The argument here is that of Cowling, *op. cit.*

prefer roads to public transport, and will be against welfare benefits and food subsidies'[27]. The ideal expenditure from this point of view is of course *military*. Thus, many socialist economists have come to see arms production and sales as endemic to contemporary capitalism[28]. But these perspectives on the logic of 'monopoly capitalism' also point to an underlying tendency for economic collapse should some of the artificial mechanisms for surplus disposal break down.

Before finally pursuing the actual breakdown, one final feature of the boom period of capitalism since World War II should be registered – the extent to which it was premised upon capital gaining greater dominance over the workers. Mandel, who tries to weld a series of factors into his explanation of how the system was restructured[29], gives pride of place to such a shift in the class struggle. In the 1930s, the working class had in most advanced capitalist countries taken a series of batterings – especially in those countries, Germany and Japan, that were to experience the most rapid post-war expansion. Thus, the basis was laid for capital to gain greater profit rates at the expense of labour. In similar vein, Aglietta[30] puts forward a view of a reconstituted system which relates all of the changes – the internationalization of capital, the role of the state, the technological revolution – to a shift in the form of the 'wage relationship' which is always at the core of capitalism. But instead of just the simple fact of a deterioration in the relative strength of the workers' ability to resist a worsening in their conditions, he points to a wider set of changes. On the one hand, there is a further transformation of the work process – the generalization of 'Fordism', which introduces a particular technology, one that raises the possibility for a minute control of human labour within the factory system to an even higher lever. Another dimension, though, involved the subordination of workers' consumer needs to the same processes of mass production, which was a crucial ingredient in fuelling the boom. It is precisely this set of relationships that may well be under challenge as capital seeks a way out of the present crisis: a

27 *Ibid.*
28 As well as Baran and Sweezy, see M. Kidron, *Western Capitalism since the War*, Penguin, Harmondsworth, 1970; S. Melman, *Pentagon Capitalism – The Political Economy of War*, McGraw Hill, New York, 1970; and N. Harris, of *Bread and Guns; The World Economy in Crisis* Penguin, Harmondsworth, 1983.
29 Ernest Mandel, *Late Capitalism. op cit.* p. 162
30 Aglietta *op. cit.*

further shift in the technological control of labour, and production less oriented to the satisfaction of working class consumption.

THE ONSET OF CRISIS

If we operate within a perspective that sets the class struggle at the centre of analysis, it fosters a view of capitalism not just as a structure – whether it be of a market or monopolistic production units, of a world system which puts national economies in a hierarchy, or of an economy whose working imposes its dictates on the way all social life should progress. Instead, it sees the system as one of relationships between groups of people – a set of relationships of conflict and opposition of interest that is only held in check with difficulty. From this perspective, the crisis can be understood as a series of challenges by oppressed and exploited groups – rebellions which undermine relations on which the continued profitability of the system depends. Many of these challenges began to emerge in the late 1960s. Major confrontations of the state and capital with various social movements occurred in one form or another in several capitalist countries.

The May events in France in 1968 and the strike movement in Italy sent out shock waves elsewhere in Europe whose reverberations called into question the basis of the post-war pattern – the incoporation of a quiescent working class. Less dramatic confrontations occurred in Britain in the early 1970s. But then the southern zone of Europe was shaken by the upheavals against fascism in Portugal, France and Greece and the emergence of the Italian communists on the fringes of rule in Italy. In the USA, a different but broad-based confrontation with the state developed on the basis of the anti-war movement. But it was the Vietnam war itself which was the single most important challenge to the US-dominated world system of open-door economies. The USA actually fought in Indochina, and after the 1968 'Tet' offensive when the Vietnamese National Liberation Front showed they could counter-attack against half a million US troops, ran the risk of defeat in its global role as guarantor of the 'free world' as an economic empire. Since then, its hegemony has been challenged in many parts of the Third World – in southern Africa, in Chile, now in Central America.

But a challenge also emerged from the other advanced capitalist centres. Europe and Japan had been more successful in their expansion of production, their adoption of new technologies and their share in trade, so their MNCs sought a greater share in new spheres of investment. These states pushed through a plan for a new international means of payment – a cluster of all their currencies, in the form of 'Special Drawing Rights' – to replace an ailing, and resented, dollar. But there was to be no orderly transition to a new monetary order. The impulses of the financial managers of the MNCs and the multinational banks in playing the currency market scotched such ideas. The USA seized the chance to claw back some relative financial hegemony by revoking the dollar's convertibility, and imposed restrictions on imports[31]. But, in the process, the post-war world economy was prodded further along the road to anarchy and protectionism by being deprived of a viable monetary system. A weakening system with mechanisms for exerting its control that were no longer effective was then taken advantage of and further weakened by the huge oil price rise engineered by the OPEC countries in 1973 – a reflection rather than a cause of crisis and a sign of it. The oil price rise of course improved the relative global position of OPEC countries but also did nothing to harm the profits of the largest MNCs – the oil giants. And as oil prices began to collapse, the oil companies were quick to reassert their control of the oil market.

The half-forgotten but familiar features of depression reappeared starkly in all the developed capitalist countries with the severe recession of 1974 – unemployment, over-production, stagnation, bankruptcies. There was a general crisis of profitability – the windfall of the oil MNCs notwithstanding – but one that cannot be attributed simply to the working out of some inevitable law of the system, for that 'explains' nothing. The manifold contradictions that could only in propitious circumstances be contained were no longer containable.

In noting some of the more crucial of these contradictions we should touch on two further arenas, from whence confrontations emerged that called the system into question but which also experienced the impact of the onset of the crisis in particular

31 On changes in the relative position of the USA in the 1970s see Block, *op. cit.* plus J. Petras and R. Rhodes, 'The Reconsolidation of U.S. Hegemony', *New Left Review*, 97, 1976 and the debate this article gave rise to in *New Left Review*, 101 and 102, 1977.

ways. First are the 'socialist' countries. The evidence is that though planned economies they are still prone to investment cycles. In recent years these fluctuations have become periodic with those of capitalist countries – a consequence of the increased trading links but even more crucially of the financial ties and the joint venture business that East European countries have established with the West. Poland, of course is the chronic case, hopelessly in debt to Western banks to the tune of $27 billion. Once it was clear that Poland was unable to repay these debts, imports dried up and industrial output plummeted, with serious knock-on effects for other COMECON economies and for the Western banking system. Political and social disturbances – the Solidarity movement in Poland and its suppression, yet another change of regime in China – have followed in the wake of economic crisis in the socialist countries. Yet despite an earlier period of political detente and of increasing economic interpenetration, the onset of the worst of the crisis has coincided with a dramatic intensification of the Cold War. This is not an accidental response to 'Soviet aggression', for even if the USSR's initiatives in Afghanistan, in the Middle East and the Horn of Africa from 1978 on could be so labelled, conditions on the ground in these areas were themselves a product of the weakening hold of the USA. The aggressive response of a US government now threatening 'linkage' in all regions, to 'roll back' communism and to contemplate a nuclear first-strike is, equally, not just attributable to a new administration. Just like the Malvinas/Falklands fiasco of the weak, old imperialist British lion (or for that matter Nazi rearmament in the 1930s), these are typical, militaristic searchings for a new restructuring that could herald a new capitalist order.

Perhaps the most shattering effects of crisis and possible reordering are discernible in the Third World. The conventional symptoms of unemployment and underutilized capacity often reach degrees not even envisaged in the severest slump in the capitalist centres. Those countries that have not been the sites of industrial relocation – the newly industrializing economies like Singapore, Korea, Brazil – and that rely on export commodities other than oil, have found that the harsher climate of world trade hits them most severely. To import a truck may now cost two and a half times the number of bales of cotton that had to be exported in 1970. Revenues from copper met two-thirds of Zambia's budget needs then; they now contribute a *negative* amount as government subsidizes copper mines to keep them open! How in these circumstances to balance the budget, or the foreign payments, especially when the oil bill is up four-fold, and the servicing of earlier doses of 'aid' is enormous? Countries can no longer pay for imports of raw materials and spares and thus Tanzania, for instance, can only operate the little industry it has at 30 per cent of its capacity. Food may often be the one item that cannot be procured and the effect will be catastrophic now, whereas it was not in the 1930s, as food self-sufficiency has been undermined by the encroachments of agri-business. Its dynamics are complicated[32] but the fact is that whereas crisis in the advanced capitalist economies may be associated with the over-production of commodities (i.e. goods produced for sale that cannot be sold), in the underdeveloped countries it gives rise to the 'underproduction of use-values' (i.e. goods needed for survival are just not produced).

In these circumstances, underdeveloped countries seek temporary respite for their beleaguered economies and budgets by seeking more loans – to pay their bills and pay previous interest. The ones with some valuable resources or some industry have been lucky enough to be able to borrow on the commercial money markets. Those that are at least handy political allies, like Zaire or Pinochet's Chile, can get their loans rescheduled even if they are broke and corrupt. The less fortunate are those that are not slavishly pro-West nor have important raw materials. They have had to put up with IMF prescriptions of severe deflationary policies, wage freezes, the cutting of all social benefits, massive devaluation and an end to all public development expenditure. In these appalling circumstances, the drift into recession has been widespread but so also has been that into militarist confrontations between Third World states themselves. The only items not subject to economy are the imports of weapons and the military budget – the more credit-worthy a country the more they increase. But the signs were, by 1982, that these trends could not go on indefinitely. Until then, multinational banks and aid agencies had gone on lending more and more to service earlier loans in an ever-spilling circle of indebtedness, at least to certain

32 On the 'food crisis' see S. George, *How the Other Half Dies: the Real Reasons for World Hunger*, Penguin, Harmondsworth, 1976 and B. Dinham and C. Hines, *Agribusiness in Africa*, Earth Resources Research, London, 1983; and for the generalization of this condition to the overall crisis see A. G. Frank, *Crisis in the Third World*, Heinemann, London, 1980.

countries. But even the most resource-rich, industrialized and credit-worthy, e.g. Mexico and Brazil, suddenly showed they could reach a point where they had to default on their loans. By this time, the lending of money to repay earlier loans was so widespread that it had become a cornerstone of the international banking system as well as an indispensable prop to Third World economies. Bank failures would be the second line victims of a 1980s Crash rather than the first to go as in 1929 – but the prospect is very real, with some 25 countries estimated as in serious risk of defaulting on their loans in 1983. Mexico and Brazil had to be saved but will all the others be propped up so as to avoid the whole system crashing down?

CONCLUSION

This is the situation in which contemporary capitalism finds itself. It cannot survive as it is. To survive at all it will require major surgery which will reduce the standard of living of workers, in their pay-packet and their social services, will undermine their ability to defend what they have, and will further marginalize the least strong groups, such as immigrants, blacks, and women. It will have even more catastrophic effects on the population of most developing countries where their very survival will be put in jeopardy. Forms of resistance to these pressures are already evident – not always in orderly political forms based on an explicit class consciousness but mediated through various nationalist, sectarian, religious, messianic, often spontaneous upheavals. All kinds of genocide and nuclear war may stem from capital's attempts to maintain its control and to recreate conditions for its resurgence. Socialists must seek to understand such processes to intervene to curb these manic excesses of the system but also in order to place an alternative future on the agenda. How well the Left is equipped for these tasks will be the subject of following chapters.

Chapter two

THE CHARACTER AND ORIGIN OF BRITAIN'S ECONOMIC DECLINE*

David Coates

I

The deepening crisis of the manufacturing and service sectors of British capitalism is often indicated by the use of two quite different but related sets of economic measures: those that record recession and those that measure relative international performance. To take the question of recession first, it is clear that the manufacturing and service sectors of British capitalism have now been incapable of sustaining any significant degree of economic growth since at least 1974, and that in the early 1980s, the severity of their recession was actually increasing. The index of industrial production fell 17 per cent in a two-year period after 1979. The official figures for unemployment moved from 331,000 in 1966 (1.4 per cent of the working population) to well over three million by December 1982 (14 per cent) and the latter figure might well understate the true level of unemployment by anything up to one million[1]. The rate of inflation, running at an annual average of 16 per cent between 1974 and 1978, and still nearly 6 per cent by December 1982, compared adversely with an annual rate of 2.6 per cent between 1953 and 1966.

To a degree, this reflects processes that were general to the advanced capitalist economies as a whole. As Lionel Cliffe has already observed, throughout the OECD countries, inflation rates rose sharply in the 1970s, and unemployment grew to over

* I would like to thank Gordon Johnston, Ray Bush, Doreen Massey, Lionel Cliffe, Bernard Stafford and Robert Looker for their comments on an earlier draft of this chapter.

1 On the missing million, see *New Statesman*, 27 March 1981, p. 4.

twenty million by the end of the decade. Nowhere was there a return to the rates of economic growth commonplace in the 1950s and 1960s, but what growth there was after 1974 was most advanced in Japan, Germany, Italy and France, and least evident in the USA and Britain. Indeed, this last fact reminds us that the experience of the post-1973 recession has been more serious in Britain than elsewhere in the advanced capitalist world, and that the competitive position of British capitalism has been eroded further than that of any other major industrial power.

There is nothing particularly new in that, of course. Even in the years of the long post-war boom, between 1948 and 1973, when all the capitalist economies enjoyed rates of growth and standards of mass consumption far in excess of any that they had achieved before, it was British capitalism that grew more slowly than the rest. The annual rate of growth of gross domestic products between 1951 and 1973 was only 2.8 per cent for Britain, but 9.5 per cent for Japan, over 5 per cent for West Germany, France and Italy, and even 3.5 per cent for the USA[2]. The growth of the manufacturing sector in Britain was even less impressive: 3.1 per cent as an annual average between 1955 and 1973, compared with 13.9 per cent in Japan, over 6.5 per cent in Italy, West Germany and France and 3.5 per cent in the USA[3]. The share of world trade between major OECD countries captured by Britain's slowly growing manufacturing sector fell dramatically, from 25.5 per cent in 1950 to 9.8 per cent by 1978[4] and the degree of penetration of the British home market by foreign manufactured goods increased in an equally dramatic way. Foreign manufactured goods made up only 6 per cent of total domestic sales in 1955, but 25 per cent by 1979[5]. By then the rate of foreign penetration of home markets had quickened significantly (from an average annual rate of growth of 5.8 per cent between 1968 and 1978 to one of 15.7 per cent for 1979 alone[6]) to create a situation in which, to take only one major example, foreign manufacturers commanded nearly 60 per cent

2 G. B. Stafford, *The End of Economic Growth? Growth and Decline in the U.K. since 1945*, Martin Robertson, Oxford, 1981, p. 8.
3 S. Aaronovitch and R. Smith (with J. Gardiner and R. Moore) *The Political Economy of British Capitalism*, McGraw Hill, New York, 1981, p. 57.
4 *Ibid.* p. 222.
5 G. B. Stafford, *op. cit.* pp. 91 and 105.
6 S. Aaronovitch, *The Road from Thatcherism*, Lawrence and Wishart, London, 1981, p. 8.

of the home vehicle market by 1980 whereas they had only had 4.5 per cent seventeen years before[7].

In part, that dwindling competitiveness at home and abroad was associated with a lower than average rate of investment in Britain in manufacturing plant and equipment. There are many ways of indicating this. If we take 1973 for example, at the peak of the long boom, the share of gross domestic product going into investment was 19.8 per cent in Britain. Of the major capitalist powers, only the USA had a smaller percentage (18.5). Japan was much larger, at 36.6 per cent, as were West Germany (24.6 per cent), France (24 per cent) and even Italy (20.9 per cent)[8]. Given the varying sizes of the gross domestic products involved, and the relative employment levels in the various manufacturing sectors, that meant that each worker in British manufacturing industry had considerably less new machinery to work with that year than did workers elsewhere: $751 worth in Britain compared with $1,224 in Italy, $1,658 in West Germany, $2,417 in Japan, $2,182 in France and $2,551 in the USA[9]. Not surprisingly then, the growth of labour productivity in the British manufacturing sector continued to lag behind as well, averaging each year only 2.3 per cent in the 1960s against 8.9 per cent in Japan, 6.5 per cent in Italy, 4.9 per cent in France, 4.8 per cent in West Germany and 2.6 per cent in the USA[10].

The figures for the 1970s are even more striking. Output per hour in manufacturing industry between 1973 and 1978 rose by only 0.2 per cent in Britain but by 5.1 per cent in West Germany, 4.8 per cent in France, 3.5 per cent in Japan, 2.6 per cent in Italy and 1.7 per cent in the USA. This left productivity levels in Britain at only 'about 30 per cent of those in the United States and . . . less than 70 per cent of those in competing countries such as France and West Germany'[11]. Moreover, there is evidence too, and this is important and we shall need to come back to it later, that the shortfall in productivity reflected not simply the inadequacy of total investment levels but also a lower rate of utilization of investment of whatever volume. So a comparison of the change in per capita GDP per unit of gross fixed capital invest-

7 N. Harris, 'Deindustrialisation' *International Socialism 7*, 1980, p. 79.
8 Aaronovitch and Smith, *op. cit.* p. 57.
9. G. B. Stafford, *op. cit.* p. 55.
10 Aaronovitch and Smith, *op. cit.* p. 57.
11 *Ibid.* p. 280.

ment between 1970 and 1977 gave Britain a score of only 0.52, but France 1.06, Italy 1.03 and West Germany 0.8[12].

The weakness of British manufacturing capital, slowly becoming more obvious towards the end of the long boom, was thrown into sharp relief by the world recession after 1973. The rate of economic growth in Britain after 1973 was lower than elsewhere: 1.1 per cent as an annual average to 1979, compared to 4.3 per cent in Japan, 3.9 per cent in Italy, 3.3 per cent in France, and 2.5 per cent in West Germany and the USA[13]. The inflation rate throughout the OECD countries as a whole averaged 7.6 per cent between 1968 and 1978, and 12.6 per cent in 1980. The comparable British figures are significantly higher, at 11.8 per cent and 19 per cent respectively[14]. The scale of deindustrialization in Britain has been much more dramatic than elsewhere. The fall in the number of workers employed in British manufacturing industry (from 8.6 million in 1961 to 7.4 million in 1976) is to be compared with the quite different trends in Japan, West Germany and Italy[15], and though all the OECD countries thereafter shed labour from their manufacturing sectors, the fall in Britain (to 6.8 million by 1979) was far sharper than elsewhere[16].

II

The question we must answer here is why British capitalism has proved so vulnerable to the world recession and why, as a result, employment levels, output figures, trade balances and standards of living have all been so adversely affected since 1973. There is, of course, no shortage of answers already available to that question. The excessive power of trade unions, on wages, working practices and levels of manning (and the associated propensity of British workers for idleness and restrictive practices), is a favourite of many commentators on the Right and Centre of British

12 *Ibid.* p. 281.
13 *Ibid.* p. 57.
14 Aaronovitch, *op. cit.* p. 9.
15 *Japan*, up from 8.5 million in 1957 to 13.5 million in 1976; *West Germany* rising from 3.4 million in 1955 to 9 million by 1961, and then a slight decline to 8.9 million in 1975; and *Italy* rising from 5.5 million in 1961 to 6.1 million in 1975.
16 See N. Harris, *op. cit.* pp. 72–3 and 76.

politics. So too is the thesis of excessive government activity. Modern monetarist doctrine often points to the way in which politicians overspend in the pursuit of votes, fuelling inflation as they do so, and helping to consolidate outmoded working practices by their 'artificial' maintenance of over-full employment and their 'cosseting' of workers through excessive welfare provision. Monetarists too tend to blame governments for protecting and subsidizing firms, and for making credit too easily available, all of which only lessens, in their view, the impact of those important market pressures which alone can spur essential innovation and rationalization in methods of industrial production, in product design and in marketing. There is also the argument, often seized upon by those with right-wing political leanings, that it is the excessive expansion of state employment that holds the key to Britain's relative economic decline (the Bacon–Eltis thesis[17]). This often joins other monetarist arguments as a justification for reductions in both the scale and range of government activity as a way of re-establishing the economy's competitive edge, no matter what the short-term costs may be (and they are invariably high ones) in public sector unemployment and the diminished provision of hitherto essential social services.

Explanations from the Centre of British politics tend to be gentler, emphasizing a whole range of relatively disparate factors as causes of economic decline: the low level of demand in the home market, poor quality management, inadequate provision of industrial retraining, deficiencies in our education system, the damaging impact of perpetually changing government policies, inadequacies in the machinery and personnel of governments, the excessive centralization of decision-making, or even the decay of those social values of thrift, discipline and a respect for authority that are widely thought to be crucial to the industrial renaissance of others. The Parliamentary Left, for its part, tends to emphasize low levels of industrial investment, the absence of economic planning and the persistence of social inequalities as causes of industrial decay. The Labour Left criticize the Thatcher Government for failing to reflate the economy, arguing that a low level of demand is itself a cause of stagnation and inefficiency. They are also highly critical of the financial institu-

17 R. Bacon and W. Eltis, *Britain's Economic Problems: too few producers* Macmillan, London, 1976.

tions of the City, especially the banks, the insurance companies and the pension funds, because of their encouragement of capital exports and their preoccupation with high exchange and interest rates. Parliamentary socialists tend to draw attention to the excessive concentration of ownership in manufacturing industry, and to its increasingly multinational character, and point to the problems of controlling and harnessing industrial activity behind nationally specified goals without an extension of public ownership, the tight supervision of private industry and some forms of import controls. And left-wingers too tend to stress the low quality and restricted social background of many leading figures in British industrial life, 'dead-wood in the board rooms' that in their view is maintained there by an archaic class structure and the absence of industrial democracy.

Sections of the extreme Left often bring the argument full circle, going beyond the theses of the parliamentary Left to recognize the way in which the strength of the British labour movement has provided a barrier to the effective restructuring of British capitalism. Much recent Marxist scholarship has conceded that since the war industrial capital here has been too weak to enforce significant industrial change on a strongly defensive working class, whilst that class has been too conservative politically to force through a socialist alternative to capitalist decay. From these arguments, as from all the others, very clear political programmes directly emerge, with the solution to the economy's ills necessarily dependent on the mobilization of forces strong enough to sweep away the impediments singled out for attention. For that reason if for no other, it will be necessary in the argument that follows to consider the strengths and weaknesses of each of these theses too; to build, that is, not simply an explanation of our current malaise but also a critique of the commentaries upon it. In this way this chapter will draw on arguments more fully developed in volume 1, *Socialist Arguments*, as it attempts to establish a common background for the discussion of socialist strategies to come.

III

The first thing to say on the general recession, as distinct from on British capitalism's poor performance within it, is that it is really no surprise. Crises are, and always have been, endemic to

Socialist strategies

capitalism, since they are both the major manifestation of the
contradictory relationship between wage labour and capital on
which the system rests, and the primary mechanism by which
those contradictions are temporarily reconciled to the advantage
of the stronger class, and of the strongest fractions within each
class[18]. What is more surprising is the length of time that
capitalism took to precipitate a world crisis again, after its last
general downturn in the 1930s had culminated in fascism and
war. The precise basis of the long post-war boom, and the
reasons for its collapse, have been documented fully elsewhere[19].
As Lionel Cliffe has argued in chapter one, it was a boom
predicated on US economic, political and military hegemony,
and hence on the widespread acceptance of the dollar as an
international unit of exchange. It was a boom built on the dissemination of technological advances initiated during the war,
and on the widespread defeat or co-option of labour movements
before and during the war and in the immediate post-war period
of reconstruction, a reconstruction that was then fuelled by the
availability of large reserves of labour for the new factories. It
was a boom made possible only by the rapid expansion of government spending and employment, and the concomitant state
supervision of ever greater supplies of private bank credit. And it
was a boom whose base was eroded by the emergence of West
German and Japanese challenges to US dominance and the
dollar, and by the shift in class power away from capital towards
labour produced by prolonged full employment and the exhaustion of easily available sources of cheap labour in the metropolitan centres of the world system. It was a boom, moreover, that
was destroyed in the end by the inflationary propensities of
excessive US military spending abroad, especially in Vietnam,
that US governments undertook in defence of their economic
and political hegemony; by the trading uncertainty that arose

18 For a full discussion of Marxist crisis theory, see E. O. Wright, 'Alternative
   perspectives in Marxist theory of accumulation and crisis' in J. Schwartz (ed),
   The Subtle Anatomy of Capitalism Goodyear, New York, 1977.
19 In the chapter by Lionel Cliffe in this volume; by E. Mandel in his *Late
   Capitalism* New Left Books, London, 1975, and *The Second Slump* New Left
   Books, London, 1978; in Aaronovitch and Smith, *op. cit.* chapter 13; in
   G. Arrighi, 'The roots of the present recession' *New Left Review*, 111,
   September–October 1978, pp. 3–24; in M. Itoh, 'The inflational crisis of
   world capitalism' *Capital and Class*, 4, pp. 1–10; and D. Coates, *Labour in
   Power? A Study of the Labour Government 1974–79* Longman, London,
   1980, chapter 4.

from the associated breakdown in the system of fixed exchange rates that had operated from 1944; and by the inflationary consequences of high state spending and employment that became evident only at that moment when the dissemination of existing technology was broadly complete and rates of growth of labour productivity began correspondingly to slow.

The steady erosion of the conditions underpinning the 25 years of economic expansion manifested themselves everywhere in the capitalist world by the late 1960s as a quickening in the rate of inflation, widespread working class militancy and shrinking corporate profits. They resulted everywhere in an intensification of competition between ever larger and increasingly multinational corporate units, and the beginning of a redistribution of productive activity on a world scale (a new international division of labour) as more and more companies merged and then engaged in an increasingly desperate search for temporary market advantage, cheaper labour and renewed profit levels. This was accompanied by the closer interconnection of all the western economies, ever more linked together by common structures of multinational ownership, complex sets of banking and credit arrangements, and a heavy dependence on each other as the major market for their manufactured goods. By the late 1960s, a new world trade cycle had come into existence, as all the major capitalist economies began once again to expand and contract in step with one another, to shift the terms of trade in favour of primary producers at a time of general boom, and to collapse together into serious recession in the face of the extra-inflationary thrust and balance of payments difficulties released by OPEC's reaction to the Yom Kippur war in 1973.

Given all that, it is not surprising that the British economy in the 1970s should have experienced increasing difficulties in its export markets and foreign penetration of its home base. It is not surprising that industrial output in Britain should have stagnated, profits collapsed and unemployment soared. Nor is it surprising that governments should have found themselves trapped between low economic growth and rising prices, and between militant labour movements and foreign financial pressure to reduce the provision of social services. For all that was broadly the agenda of economics and politics across the capitalist world in the 1970s, the legacy of contradictions implicit in the post-war settlement that had been hidden for 25 years by the buoyancy of profits and trade under US leadership.

The problems faced by British governments after 1973 were, in that sense, not solely of their making, nor of themselves simply a consequence of 'weaknesses' unique to British capitalism and its associated social classes. What the particular balance and character of class forces in Britain contributed was not the problems themselves but the inadequacy – in either capitalist or socialist terms – of the response to them, and the resulting *extra* severity of the recession here. It is that *differential* experience of recession that requires an analysis of features unique to the British situation, and to which we now must turn.

IV

It is, presumably, generally recognized that British industry has been undercapitalized for a very long time, and that it has never been able to restructure itself to the degree necessary to re-establish the kind of industrial dominance that it enjoyed before 1900. Instead, the competitiveness of its products has eroded in a cumulative fashion down the years, with existing inadequacies in investment levels, productivity and profitability then discouraging still further the investment and changes in working practices vital to break the circle. I will discuss this process of cumulative decline later. What has first to be established is when it began and why, and here it is clear that developments in the last quarter of the nineteenth century, when industrial capital first began to experience serious international competition, are of crucial importance.

It was in that period of industrial challenge, and in the years of world monopoly for British-based industrial capital that preceded it, that the balance and character of class forces in Britain settled into a particular form. It was in that period that there emerged a labour movement of a certain kind, which we will need to examine in detail in a moment. It was from that period too that the organization of industrial production in Britain emerged as too small in scale, too defensive in orientation and too anchored in old industries, methods of production and markets, to be able to withstand easily the growing scale, intensity and quality of foreign competition. But it was also in that period that we can locate the foundation of a particular relationship within the British ruling class between financial and industrial interests – a relationship which even today con-

Britain's economic decline

tinues to play an important part in the continuing political weakness and economic vulnerability of British-based manufacturing industry. In any proper explanation of that vulnerability, it is with the power of the City that we need to begin. Initially, British industrialists did not need bank capital to anything like the degree that characterized the fledgling industries of Germany and Japan. Britain's world monopoly position gave its industrial capitalists surpluses on which internally financed long-term investment could proceed apace. It also gave sterling a particular role in the nineteenth century world economy (broadly similar to that of the dollar between 1944 and 1971), and attracted to London foreign borrowers keen to draw on those surpluses for their own industrial take-off. From the 1870s the English banking system found it more profitable to finance foreign trade and to handle portfolio investment abroad than to seek out domestic industrial demand for long-term finance. This established both a distance between industrial and financial interests and an international focus for British banking practices that had no close parallel elsewhere. When challenged by the rise of German and US competition in the last quarter of the nineteenth century, this first capitalist class did not respond by a rapid and far-reaching restructuring of its domestic manufacturing base. Instead its industrialists turned increasingly to the security of protection within the markets of the Empire, and its bankers found even greater reasons for concentrating on the expansion of the overseas interests and role of British-owned capital. Between 1880 and 1914 those financial interests established a position of dominance for themselves in the councils of the state, so that by 1914 at the latest, because of the way in which 'early industrialization and subsequent internationalization of British capital under the umbrella of imperial power had [made] . . . it more profitable to expand abroad than to innovate and accumulate in Britain', nationally-based industrial interests found themselves facing 'a ruling class and a policy regime dedicated to the international interests of British capital rather than the development of the domestic economy'[20].

20 D. Currie and R. Smith, 'Economic trends and crisis in the U.K. economy' in D. Currie and R. Smith (eds), *Socialist Economic Review 1981*, Merlin Press, London, 1981, p. 10. For a full discussion of this subordination of industrial interests in Edwardian Britain to those of finance capital, see Tom Nairn, 'The Future of Britain's Crisis' *New Left Review*, 113–14, January–April 1979, pp. 51–56.

Socialist strategies

Initially, this fracturing of interests between nationally based industrial and internationally oriented financial capital was mutually beneficial. 'So long as Britain was the principal "workshop of the world" for both capital and consumer goods, this specialization did not constitute a serious obstacle to industrial accumulation in Britain but actually stimulated it through the creation of overseas demand'[21]. But once British domination of world trade and industrial production had gone, the interests of the two sections of British capital proved increasingly incompatible, and nationally based industrialists found themselves locked into increasingly outmoded industries and production methods, whilst at the same time being both disadvantaged in their access to long-term credit relative to their competitors, and subject to a political class in which financial interests had a disproportionately strong voice. Unlike their counterparts in Japan and Germany, British industrialists found their bankers geared to the export of capital, and preoccupied with maintaining the 'conditions in which exported capital was safe, sterling defended, and international commercial and financial operations could freely function'[22]. They found it difficult to persuade bankers to make long-term loans to industry on any scale, or to put up risk capital in sufficient quantities, and hence were driven back into a disproportionately heavy reliance on their own by now inadequate sources of internal funds to fuel the investment process.

Financiers for their part, because of their world-wide interests, lacked any great concern with the successful expansion of the domestic productive base, and instead used their considerable political leverage (which accrued to them through the City's centrality whilst sterling remained a reserve currency, and via the Bank of England's connections to the Treasury and, lately, the IMF) to hold successive British governments to policies that were vital to London's role as an international money market but detrimental to any restructuring of British manufacturing industry[23]. The defence of free trade before 1914, of a return to

21 B. Jessop, 'The transformation of the state in post-war Britain' in R. Scase (ed), *The State in Western Capitalism* Croom Helm, London, 1977, p. 30.
22 Aaronovitch and Smith, *op. cit.* p. 61.
23 The contrast with West German and Japanese experience is telling: 'in these countries the establishment of a powerful, technologically-modernised domestic base was the priority. Expansion into world markets was expected to start from that base and not as an alternative. And further, the banks and industry were closely connected, making long-term capital available at relatively low rates of interest and with longer term horizons' (Aaronovitch, *op.*

the gold standard in 1926, of a high exchange rate in the 1950s and 60s and of the high interest rates and deflationary policies with which the defence of sterling was associated, are all examples of the way in which financial interests had the political leverage to establish a popular connection between their needs and 'the interests of the nation as a whole' that actually eroded the capacity of the industrial sector to maintain economic growth, market-share, profits and jobs[24]. Then the resulting underperformance of that industrial sector became a force shaping investment patterns in its own right, reinforcing the banking network's antipathy to the risks involved in supporting industry, and encouraging them to continue to concentrate a high proportion of their considerable resources on government debt, property speculation, capital export and short-term small-scale

cit. p. 6). One piece of evidence that is often cited against the City is the sheer volume of capital exports. This was very marked before World War One. At 7 per cent of National Income by 1914, 'more capital was actually being exported than was invested at home' (*ibid.* p. 6). But that export of capital diminished in the 1930s, and has not returned to anything like the pre-1914 level. In the 1950s, for example, the scale of British investment in foreign plant and equipment (as distinct from portfolio investment) was only 13 per cent of investment levels in domestic manufacturing machinery. The outflow of capital latterly has been significantly more than that (as a percentage of domestic fixed capital formation, it was 19.9 per cent in 1972–73, jumped to 38.5 per cent in 1973–74 and remained very high, at 37 per cent in 1974–75); and Britain remained, into the 1970s, the second largest capital exporter. The USA was responsible for 52 per cent of the total, and the UK for 14.5 per cent as against France's 5.8 per cent, West Germany's 4.4 per cent and Japan's 2.7 per cent (see F. Longstreth, 'The City, Industry and the State' in C. Crouch (ed), *State and Economy in Contemporary Capitalism* Croom Helm, London, 1977, p. 187. However, given the inflow of investment in the post-war years, and the role the multinational companies have come to play in redirecting capital flows away from Britain, capital export itself should not now be taken as the major indicator of the detrimental effects of financial interests on industrial recovery. Instead, and as far as the *banking* networks and *finance houses* are concerned, it seems best to stress their indirect and cumulative role in weakening industrial capital: by their heavy capital export prior to 1914; by their failure to throw their activity and political weight behind national industrial restructuring over a long period; and by their associated defence of lending policies and government initiatives that actually militated against that industrial reconstruction.

24 'The City has, in other words, largely set the parameters of economic policy and its interests have generally predominated since the late nineteenth century. Its predominance has been so complete that its position has often been taken as the quintessence of responsible financial policy' (Longstreth, *op. cit.* p. 161–2).

Socialist strategies

industrial loans. In this way, it is now quite legitimate both for critics of the banking system to call for greater bank involvement in industrial investment[25], and for others to retort that more money is available within the City for industrial use than is currently being taken up by industrialists[26]. The arms-length relationship of financial and industrial interests that has persisted for so long, and the *political* dominance at critical moments of financial interests over industrial ones, have by now helped to establish a situation in which the simple logic of market forces and relative competitive performance keeps the banks and the factories apart.

V

One consequence of this is that British industry has for over 60 years been 'characterized by low investment, technical backwardness and an outmoded industrial structure'[27]. This weakness of industrial capital is thus an important contributory factor to the economy's present competitive difficulties, but it too needs careful delineation and explanation, not least because of the considerable disagreement in the relevant literature on both the problems of industrial capital and their origins.

Left-wing critics have often pointed to the low levels of investment in manufacturing plant and equipment as the crucial factor in Britain's economic decline – a pattern of under-investment by international standards that stretches back at least to 1900, and means that now 'the average life of all plant and machinery in Britain is 35 years, almost double that of France, Germany and the US'[28]. But other commentators, equally left-wing in their sympathies, have doubted the adequacy of this as an explanation and, hence, by implication, as a solution as well. For there is no simple and direct correlation between rates of economic growth and shares of gross domestic product going into manufacturing investment; and even where that correlation holds, it is by no

25 See, for example, H. Lever and G. Edwards, 'Why Germany beats Britain' *Sunday Times*, 2 November 1980, pp. 16–18; and the Labour Party statement *Banking and Finance*, London, 1976.
26 See, for example, D. H. Gowland, *Modern Economic Analysis*, Butterworth, London, 1979, chapter 4.
27 The Cambridge Political Economy Group, *Britain's Economic Crisis*, Pamphlet 44, Spokesman, Nottingham, 1974, p. 7.
28 Lever and Edwards, *op. cit.* p. 16.

means certain whether it is investment or growth that comes first. In any case, the undoubted gap between the British investment ratio and that elsewhere in the OECD countries has diminished lately without any concomitant equilization of growth rates. On the contrary, in the years immediately before 1973 'the proportion of GDP which the UK mobilised for investment rose fairly steadily . . . and the gap between the investment ratio in the UK and that in the other advanced capitalist countries *narrowed* to a difference of 2 or 3 percentage points . . . at precisely the same time as the UK was falling further behind them in the rates of growth of per capita income and real wages'[29]. What has persisted is a lower rate of *productivity* of investment in the UK relative to its foreign competitors, and it is the technical reasons for that, and the social conditions which produce them, which we particularly need to explore.

The weakness of British industrial capital here is now fully documented: 'that differences between the growth rate of the UK and eleven other advanced economies from 1955 to 1962 [were] much more associated with differences in the productivity of capital than with differences in investment ratios'[30]. The growth of output per unit of investment between 1961 and 1972 in Britain 'was only half that of Britain's major competitors such as France, West Germany and the USA and two-thirds that of Japan, whereas Britain's investment ratio was only marginally lower'[31]. This deficiency in capital's productivity has many causes. One is undoubtedly the defensive strength of the labour movement, to which we will come. Another, and much more important cause, to which we have alluded already, and to which we will return, can be found in the persistent deflation of levels of demand in the post-war economy made necessary by the prior commitment of government to the protection of sterling and the international role of the City. These causes worked in conjunction too with a whole cluster of other factors which varied in importance in different industrial sectors: factors such as inadequate levels of capital and its outmoded distribution between industries, technologies and products; the inability of particular industries and firms to exploit economies of scale because of

29 D. Purdy, 'The Left's Alternative Economic Strategy' in B. Hindess *et al.* *Politics and Power 1*, Routledge and Kegan Paul, London, 1980, p. 73.
30 G. B. Stafford, *op. cit.*, p. 40 (referring to a study by Wilfred Beckerman).
31 D. Purdy, 'British Capitalism since the war', *Marxism Today*, October 1976, p. 313.

Socialist strategies

limited production runs, too small a capital base, or too restricted a home demand; and the weakness of innovation and generally unadventurous style of management that is common across large sections of British industry.

This last feature seems vital, but is difficult to isolate or to quantify – a particular lack of intensity and innovative ruthlessness in large sections of British industrial management which has resulted in 'technological backwardness . . . leads lost, opportunities missed, markets relinquished that need not have been'[32]. Some parts of that managerial weakness may well be explicable in terms of long-established deficiencies in technical and managerial training (themselves, of course, in need of explanation); or by the way in which low rates of economic growth and capital accumulation even during the long post-war boom failed to create the market conditions and profit rates favourable to major technological and industrial change. Some part of the explanation for the quality and style of British management may lie with working class industrial strength or with the particularly easy competitive conditions experienced by British industry in the first ten years after the war, neither of which predisposed managements to rapid technological change or major shifts in the character and location of investment, and both of which helped to consolidate a complacency in managerial circles that was to be rudely shattered by the recession of the 1970s. But it is also clear that British management teams abroad have been quite capable of confronting labour movements and quickening the rate of exploitation of labour; and that suggests that the underlying reasons for the poor performance of domestic management lies much further back in the history of British industrial capitalism as a whole.

The fact that Britain industrialized first meant 'that British capital was locked into areas and techniques of production that became obsolescent as more advanced products and technologies were discovered'[33]. The long period of nineteenth century world monopoly consolidated industrial capital in Britain into small production units that were slow to cartelize in the face of competition from far larger overseas units of capital,

32 David Landes, quoted in S. Gomulka, 'Britain's slow industrial growth: increasing inefficiency versus low rates of technical change' in W. Beckerman (ed), *Slow Growth in Britain: causes and consequences* Clarendon Press, Oxford, 1979, p. 189.
33 Jessop, *op. cit.* p. 34.

and which accordingly lacked any strong central co-ordinating structure which could bring effective pressure to bear in their defence on the banking network and the state. More impressionistically, because they industrialized first, and did so in a political alliance dominated by the personnel and attitudes of a non-militarized aristocracy and an internationally oriented financial establishment, British industrialists lacked that 'growth culture' and aggressive nationalism vital to the class of industrial owners in second-wave capitalist countries (like Japan and Germany) who were bent on catching up already existing capitalist competitors by 'showing a high degree of openness to foreign expertise' and to promoting 'values and attitudes which helped to stimulate the process of pursuit of the world's technological leaders'[34]. It was for this reason that British education and government policies were never systematically geared to the adoption and dissemination of foreign innovations in technology (as happened particularly in Japan)[35]. Instead, British capital reacted to the rise of foreign competition in a defensive way, seeking protection in the markets of an expanding empire and remaining for too long tied to outmoded methods of production and declining industrial sectors[36].

34 Gomulka, *op. cit.* p. 192.
35 Stanislaw Gomulka, in the work cited in footnote 32, stresses the importance of this rate of diffusion of technical innovations. But he lacks any class analysis in which to anchor this. The character of the class coalitions initiating industrialization has long been recognized as central to its subsequent character, and not least to the ideologies within which it was pursued and by which it was legitimated. 'The fusion of aristocratic and business circles in Britain weakened the drive for industrial expansion and technological advance' (Aaronovitch and Smith, *op. cit.* p. 61), whereas in Japan and Germany a similar alliance had the reverse effect. The character of the aristocracies involved, and in particular the stridency of their nationalism and their militarism, were crucial, for in those two countries 'strong nationalist ideologies . . . attached to the idea of economic expansion led to conscious decisions on systems of education and technical training directly geared to manufacturing and trade' (*ibid.* p. 60). On the whole question, see Barrington Moore *Social Origins of Dictatorship and Democracy* (Penguin, Harmondsworth, 1967) T. Skocpol *States and Social Revolutions* Cambridge University Press, Cambridge, 1979 and P. Anderson *Lineages of the Absolutist State* New Left Books, London, 1974.
36 As late as 1975 and 1976 'a study conducted by N.E.D.O . . . suggested that British manufacturing investment was more heavily weighted towards traditional industries such as textiles and iron and steel, whereas West German investment was more concentrated in such growth industries as mechanical engineering and electrical machinery' (Aaronovitch and Smith, *op. cit.* p. 282).

The weakness of this impulse to innovate and restructure both reflected and then reinforced the political weakness of industrial interests within the British ruling class to which I have already referred. The initial coalition between industrial and financial interests that was consolidated after 1870 shared a common commitment to free trade, imperial expansion and a non-interventionist state; and this increasingly unsuitable political programme was shed only slowly and with difficulty in the twentieth century because it continued to suit the needs of the City and because industrial interests were often hesitant to adopt a close relationship with the state that was common among their major European competitors but which was canvassed in Britain most strongly by the rising political voice of organized labour.

In any case, the industrial lobby's strength politically always reflected to some degree the market power of the industries on which it was based; and yet another consequence of Britain's early start was that, in the crucial years between the wars, the ability of industrial interests to offset the political pressure of the City was undermined by the fact that those industrial interests – based as they were in coal, cotton, railways and heavy engineering – were themselves in secular economic decline. Even the industrial interests that were to replace them in leadership by the 1960s – in the second-wave growth industries of cars, chemicals and light engineering – lacked the political weight of the financial sector, because from the beginning they were industries of the second league, dwarfed by their US equivalents on whom they drew for technology and capital and, as such, lacking the world-wide resources that the City remained able to mobilize[37]. Only the oil companies (and the occasional giant firm such as Unilever) stand as long-established exceptions to this; and neither they, nor the multinational monopoly concerns that emerged in British industry after 1960, altered significantly the balance of pressures operating on the state from capital. On the contrary, the interests of the new multinationals were as global as those of the City, and their arrival largely left nationally based industrial capital in the political position it has occupied all century, namely that of junior partner to financial interests that were not directly geared to national economic reconstruction. Indeed, the continuous political weakness of this locally based

37 On the changing relationship between finance capital and sections of industrial capital in Britain, see H. Overbeek, 'Finance Capital and the crisis in Britain' *Capital and Class*, 11, Summer 1980, pp. 99–120.

industrial capital can be judged quite simply by the amazingly late date (1965) and the initiating force (of all things, a Labour Government) that at long last created for industrial capital a single all-embracing spokesman organization, the CBI[38].

I will argue in a later section that this historical weakness – both political and managerial – of industrial capital played a crucial role in the 1950s, in 'missing the opportunity' to exploit the temporary dislocation of other capitalist economies in ways that could have locked British capitalism on to a new growth path. Once missed, that opportunity did not return. By the late 1960s, the competitive weakness of British industrial capital was evident for all to see, most visible in the general fall of profits across the sector as a whole[39]. That did at least prompt a new centralization and concentration of capital, a merger movement of an unprecedented scale that has left British industry as monopolised as ever (the top 100 companies are now responsible for nearly two-thirds of all industrial production). But that merger movement was itself defensive, a reaction to market weakness and to the rise of foreign competitors, and did not provide the institutional base for any dramatic increase in industrial investment or rates of capital or labour productivity. For the cartelization of British industry coincided with the end of the long boom and in the new competitive conditions of the 1970s, when markets had not so much to be created as captured, even the new giants of British industry found themselves too limited in size relative to their competitors, too under-capitalized, too short of internally generated funds, and too deficient in organizational coherence, managerial skills and labour discipline, to compete effectively.

The new industrial structures still reflected in their internal organization, existing technologies, scales of operation, main markets, labour practices and rates of return, the way in which the opportunity of the 1950s had been lost. Take British Leyland as one example. Formed in 1968 in a merger to give a home-based car company the size to compete with the US giants (Fords, Chrysler and General Motors), British Leyland lacked the internal reserves to sustain even a modest investment programme. Moreover, it faced competitors whose existing strength

38 On this, see Longstreth, *op. cit.* p. 187.
39 For evidence, see A. Glyn and B. Sutcliffe, *British Capitalism, Workers and the Profits Squeeze* Penguin, Harmondsworth, 1972, and Aaronovitch and Smith, *op. cit.* pp. 284–295.

enabled them to raise vastly greater sums for their new models than BL could ever hope to do, and it found itself saddled with a product range and widely scattered number of production units that were already outmoded and uncompetitive when compared to the rising power of the Japanese. When the recession after 1973 left the world car industry at least 25 per cent over capacity, British Leyland was bound to be in crisis, the weakest of the giants in an industry in recession, put there by the cumulative failure of an entire national industry over 30 years to restructure its industrial location, capital base and labour practices in line with the dictates of a by now fiercely competitive world market system[40].

What the creation of vast monopolies across the whole of British manufacturing industry after 1960 did was not to facilitate the reindustrialization of the home economy. Rather, it acted to permit the more profitable sections of industrial capital to move abroad, and to reduce their own dependence on (and therefore interest in) the viability of production within Britain itself. In this way, City interests found new and powerful allies within the industrial sector, and the CBI found itself wracked by internal tension between large companies and small. In fact, big or small, industrial capital in Britain is now in serious difficulty. On the world scale, the multinational companies that dominate its growth sectors are themselves caught in a serious crisis of profits that is encouraging them to redistribute their investment away from high-tax, strong-labour-movement economies to more compliant political regimes. Small and medium size businesses increasingly lack the capacity to compete with foreign penetration of the home market that has been precipitated by the same crisis of profits on a world scale; and neither national nor multinational industrial capital possesses the political leverage to pull the Conservative Party under Margaret Thatcher away from monetarist policies of high exchange and interest rates, and restricted levels of home demand. As the recession deepens and factories close at an unprecedented rate, the historic weakness of British industrial capital is rapidly turning into a rout.

VI

This long-established and ever-increasing competitive weak-

40 For more details, see D. Coates *op. cit.* chapter 3.

ness of industrial capital in Britain has been compounded by two other social forces of importance: the general character of the political class to whose leadership it has been subject; and, since the war at least, the defensive strength of the labour movement that it faced. There is no denying 'the fact that the British working class is [now] integral to the fundamental problem of the British economy, the slow rate of growth of productivity'[41]; but nor can it be denied that this problem of worker resistance to capitalist restructuring is a secondary and derivative one, of relatively recent centrality. It is important to get the timing and position right, and to see that 'while early instances of class conflict may be cited for the UK, as for other countries, the relative failure of UK economic performance *predated* the *main* growth in the strength and scale of working class organisation'[42].

The roots of that defensive strength do, however, lie far back, 'in the nature and timing of Britain's industrialisation and its nineteenth century dominance in the international system'[43]. Trade unionism was established early among skilled workers, and Britain's initial industrial monopoly and subsequent period of imperial expansion enabled at least those unions to establish a degree of job control (and traditions of militancy in its defence) that were only slowly challenged by an employing class predisposed to avoid class confrontation by a retreat into the protected markets of an empire. There were challenges. The 1890s saw one and the First World War another; and craft control was under threat from the Great Depression onwards; but there is plenty of evidence too of 'entrepreneurial failure' brought about by the 'constraints which the sharing of control over work with strong unions placed on the possibilities for redivision of labour and the introduction of new technology'[44]. It was this combination of strong craft unionism and imperial expansion that 'postponed the necessity to improve productivity in many of Britain's main industries, including cotton, textiles, and railways' as UK exporters found it to their advantage to avoid conflict with workers over an accelerated remoulding of the structure of produc-

41 D. Elson, 'Discussion: economic trends and crisis' in D. Currie and R. Smith, *op. cit.* pp. 66–7.
42 Currie and Smith, *op. cit.* p. 11 (my emphases).
43 Jessop, *op. cit.* p. 33.
44 A. Kilpatrick and T. Lawson, 'On the nature of industrial decline in the U.K.', *Cambridge Journal of Economics*, 4, 1980, p. 91.

tion, and instead redirected sales to the new or protected markets often with the aid of capital exports'[45].

This industrial power was restricted to certain craft unions until 1945, and was even there eroded by the general defeat of working class militancy in 1926 and the prolonged unemployment of the inter-war years. It was only after 1945 that the balance of class forces generally changed, and unions (and work groups within unions) among even semi-skilled and unskilled workers in the new industries of engineering, vehicle construction and chemicals, established a significant degree of control over many key aspects of the work process. These included, in well-organized factories, 'demarcation, apprenticeships, manning levels, work rates, [and] overtime'[46] and the ability to maintain effective resistance to managerial attempts to reorganize the work process. The strength of such work groups and their stewards was a direct consequence of three major processes at work in late capitalism. It was a feature of industries with the high capital/labour ratios that were characteristic of many of the growth sectors of the post-war boom, where capital could easily be immobilized by the strategic withdrawal of relatively few units of labour. It was a consequence of the lack of fierce competition in the product markets of those industries in the immediate post-war years, and indeed has been a casualty of precisely the intensification of that competition brought on by the world recession. It was predicated on government maintenance of full employment for a whole generation, and on the only restricted availability in Britain of the reserve armies of unskilled labour (of peasants, women and immigrants) available to the West German and Japanese industrial bourgeoisies. Skilled workers in particular were in short supply, and enjoyed industrial power accordingly.

The maintenance of full employment, and the financing of welfare services by the taxation of profits that shifted GNP away from capital and towards labour[47], were the political consequences of the enhanced power of the British labour movement after 1940. It was as a consequence of working class political strength that up to 'the crisis of 1973–74 adherence to a full

45 *Ibid.* p. 98.
46 Jessop, *op. cit.* p. 35.
47 Glyn and Sutcliffe, *op. cit.* p. 43; and Aaronovitch and Smith, *op. cit.* p. 286.
    They give the fall of profits as a percentage of GDP as one of 18 per cent in the
    1950s dropping to 11.5 per cent in the 1970s.

employment regime [was] . . . a major parameter of ruling class policy', reducing that 'class's ability to make use of unemployment and recession as a disciplinary instrument against the working class (and, incidentally, as a renewal mechanism for weeding out backward and inefficient firms)'[48]. As a result, shop floor bargaining on wages kept 'hourly earnings in manufacturing [rising] ahead of output per man hour'[49] well into the 1960s, and meant that 'Britain became the only imperialist power which proved unable to increase the rate of exploitation of its working class significantly during·or after the Second World War'[50]. The contrast here with the experience of Japan and West Germany is striking. The weakness of plant bargaining in those countries during the long boom left their capitalists stronger, and the fact that their labour movements were less extensive in their recruitment, divided internally on religious, political or skill lines as the British TUC was not, and seriously weakened or destroyed by pre-war fascism and post-war employer and state offensives (as again the British labour movement was not), all affected the relative strength of class forces in the various national capitalisms and helped to erode British industrial capital's competitive position. For 'it was the lesser ability and willingness of the average capitalist enterprise in Britain to subordinate the working class to the requirements of rapid growth, whether in introducing technical innovation or in raising and maintaining the intensity of labour with given technical conditions . . . which differentiated British capitalism from its rivals in the post-war period'[51] and whose origins lie in the degree of defensive industrial power achieved by a well-organised and class conscious labour movement in a context of full employment.

The result, of course, in capitalist terms was 'an erosion of the rate of profit and a much slower rate of economic growth and accumulation'[52] in Britain than in other OECD countries. Even successive British governments found that they too lacked the resources to tackle this defensive power directly: both because they lacked any legal means to alter class practices at factory level, and because they found a labour movement that was wil-

48 D. Purdy, *op. cit.* September 1976, p. 274.
49 R. Williams, *The May Day Manifesto* Penguin, Harmondsworth, 1968, p. 107.
50 E. Mandel, *op. cit.* p. 179.
51 D. Purdy, *op. cit.* October 1976, p. 311.
52 E. Mandel, *op. cit.* p. 179.

Socialist strategies

ling in the 1970s to strike against the introduction of such legal changes, and that was unwilling to tolerate prolonged bouts of incomes policy and productivity bargaining that attempted the same erosion of working class power and living standards by a more conciliatory route. Indeed state employees – both manual workers and the increasingly unionized white collar strata – proved particularly intransigent in the face of policies of income restraint that discriminated against them, as governments tried to set a good example to private employers by taking a tough line themselves. They, and a miners' union strengthened in its bargaining by the rising price of oil, effectively destroyed two Labour and one Conservative governments in the decade after 1969, in a process of defensive labour militancy which (1968 apart) had no parallel elsewhere in the advanced capitalist world.

Industrial regeneration in Britain in the 1970s, by either capitalist or socialist routes, was blocked by this balance of class forces in industry, in which 'workers [could] stop management taking certain positive action but [could] not stop them exporting capital; and management [could] stop workers realising money wage increases by passing these on in higher prices, but [could] not get them to increase output from the same machinery and plant'[53]. The significance of the Thatcher Government's monetarism lies precisely here, as a dramatic attempt to break that stalemate in favour of certain sections of capital by creating mass unemployment, falling living standards and tougher labour laws.

VII

Finally, this process of industrial competitive decline was compounded by the particular character of the political leadership offered by successive British governments over a long period. The whole policy thrust of the entire political class (and that, to their shame, has included every Labour government to date) has been to maintain the world role of British imperialism – either as an autonomous power, as with Conservative governments up to 1956, or in a junior relationship with the USA or latterly with Europe (a project so dear to the hearts of the social democratic

53 M. Barratt Brown, 'The record of the 1974–79 Labour Government: the growth and distribution of income and wealth' in K. Coates (ed), *What Went Wrong?* Spokesman, Nottingham, 1979, p. 51.

wing of labourism). Governments of either party have, as a
result, been reluctant to shed a level of military spending and a
scale of military operations reflective of an earlier period of
industrial monopoly and world empire, and have proved disproportionately sympathetic to the political programme of the City
because of the symbolism afforded to this world role by the
possession of a strong currency.

The cost of the defence of sterling in the post-war years has
been a heavy one. It has necessitated high interest rates, to hold
speculative capital in London and to reassure a nervous financial
community, at the cost of discouraging private manufacturing
investment. It has cheapened imports in ways that have eased the
foreign penetration of the domestic market. It has gone along
with a proclivity for free trade in capital and goods, and only
limited state intervention in industrial restructuring, that has
corresponded less and less well to the actual needs of a weakening industrial base. It has left the economy vulnerable to periodic
flights from sterling by nervous foreign holders of a patently
over-valued currency – sterling crises often precipitated by
balance of payments difficulties that have then necessitated cut-
backs in state spending and the deflation of the entire economy,
to the detriment of industrial sectors that rely on buoyant home
markets and on extensive state orders and financial assistance.

The maintenance of a military budget no longer in keeping
with the competitive strength of the civilian economy that has to
sustain it has been equally burdensome. Defence spending in
Britain in the post-war years, though moving from its peak of 11
per cent of GDP at the time of the Korean War to only 5 per cent
in the 1970s, still exceeded that of any OECD country other than
the USA. The cost of that defence spending to the civilian
economy was at times quite direct, taking investment funds
(particularly at the critical time of the Korean War[54]) that might
otherwise have assisted in the restructuring of the civilian
engineering industry. At other times, the effect of high defence

54 The experience of the Korean War was particularly important, for that
rearmament programme 'cost the loss of two billion dollars from the U.K.'s
international reserves, represented the loss of one year's increment in
national output, brought capital formation to a halt [and] led to a standstill or
even a fall in productivity per man'. At a time when the U.K. alone of the main
capitalist powers in Europe 'had the opportunity to take advantage of the
immense post-war reconstruction and replacement needs, the heart of British
manufacturing industry, engineering, was virtually pulled out of the operation' (Aaronovitch and Smith, *op. cit.* p. 70).

spending has been less direct but equally serious, slowing the general rate of accumulation by its unproductive absorption of surplus, and trapping as many as 40 per cent of all research scientists and engineers in research and development programmes geared to military ends. It is noticeable that those industrial bourgeoisies denied the right to sustain a large national army (the Japanese and the West German after 1945) proved to be the most technologically efficient and competitive thereafter, as their engineering sectors were forced to operate entirely in the open markets of civilian production, as their research scientists were obliged to concentrate on civilian projects, and as their salesmen were denied the 'feather-bedding' afforded to military producers by the 'cost plus' basis of so much armament procurement by the state[55].

This pattern of political leadership and stalemated class forces in industry was particularly important in the 1950s, for it was then that West German and Japanese industrial capital established the basis for its subsequent strength and British capital did not. In retrospect, it is relatively easy to see why. 'The necessity for a favourable balance of class forces and for an entrepreneurial class able to take advantage of production and trading opportunities'[56] played into the hands of the German and Japanese ruling groups just as it did not into the British. As militarily defeated and economically weakened classes, under direct US political control until the late 1940s, the West German and Japanese industrial bourgeoisies had fewer established patterns of production, trade and finance on which to fall back. Their political elites had no world role to play that might divert resources from industrial reconstruction into wasteful military expenditure. They each had to reconstitute their war-damaged economies through a rapid expansion of their manufacturing sectors, with its attendant favourable consequences for general labour productivity[57]. They each had large reserves of cheap and non-unionized labour on which to draw (in their urban unemployed, in the Japanese countryside, in Eastern Europe and in

---

55 Of course, not all the spin-offs from military spending are negative. The US space programme, for example, inspired considerable leaps forward in electronics and computerization.
56 Aaronovitch and Smith, *op. cit.* p. 164.
57 This is discussed by N. Kaldor, *Causes of the slow rate of economic growth of the U.K.*, Cambridge University Press, Cambridge, 1966; and by G. B. Stafford, *op. cit.* pp. 28–36.

the poor economies of the Mediterranean). Their labour movements had been destroyed in the 1930s, and the accumulated
profits of the resulting period of intensified labour exploitation
remained to be harnessed for manufacturing reconstruction.
When those labour movements were reconstituted, their moderation was guaranteed, initially by deliberate employer offensives against militants (in Japan) and communists (in West
Germany), and then consolidated by particular institutional
arrangements (the famous company unions and cradle to grave
employment practices of the Japanese *ziabatsu*, and the industrial democracy schemes of the US-designed and highly
centralized West German trade union movement). Since both
countries came to possess a crucial strategic importance to the
USA in the emerging battle lines of the Cold War, so the industrial bourgeoisie in each had no difficulty in attracting large
amounts of US military spending, foreign aid and private corporate capital. As Ron Smith had described the situation:

These factors, together with the 'catching up' process as war torn
economies started to restore output levels, led to generally rapid growth
in manufacturing industry. The dynamic benefits from this . . . meant
sharp gains in productivity. Real wages could also rise quickly, although
the existence of labour reserves meant that this increase generally was
not large enough to threaten the high profitability on which it was based.
Rapid growth in demand was ensured by the heavy demand for capital
goods, the rapid expansion in consumer expenditure consequent upon
large real wage increases, and the general expansion of world trade as
tariff barriers and other obstacles to trade started to fall in the fifties.
Those countries that were initially able to expand rapidly found that the
correspondingly higher growth in productivity acted to sustain this,
avoiding too rapid a depletion of labour reserves and helping to maintain
their competitive position internationally (a factor that assumed particular importance in the sixties, when international competition
intensified). By contrast, initially slow growing economies found
themselves caught in a vicious circle of slow growth, low investment and
low productivity gains.[58]

Britain was one of those slowly growing economies because
there the situation in the early 1950s was so different. British
manufacturers enjoyed a temporary easing of competitive pressures because of the war-time destruction of many of their competitors and because of the heavy demands for manufactured

58 Aaronovitch and Smith, *op. cit.* p. 165.

goods created by the programmes of post-war reconstruction. The under-investment that had characterized British industry between the wars had been compounded by the exigencies of war-time production, and yet the market conditions of the early 1950s made production viable on even the oldest and most exhausted of machinery. Not until the balance of payments crisis of 1961 did it really become generally obvious that the easy market conditions of the immediate post-war years had gone, and could no longer be maintained even by favourable terms of trade with the Third World or the semi-protection afforded by the existence of the Sterling Area.

Then too there was the labour movement, undefeated in Britain since 1926, with its own political party in or on the edge of power, standing as a barrier to any substantial shift in social or public resources away from consumption to investment, or to any major reorganization of methods of production[59]. Only relatively limited supplies of ready available labour stood easily to hand (West Indian and Pakistani immigrants in particular, and women in general); and the legacies of Empire, not least in the 1948 Nationality Act, prevented the use of immigrant labour as guestworkers of the West German kind. The English peasantry had long vanished as a source of cheap labour to fuel an 'economic miracle' that could parallel the Italian and the Japanese ones; and imperial connections still froze British trade into markets that were to grow more slowly than the emerging European community from which the British political elite chose to exclude itself. As we have seen, that political class was still in the 1950s preoccupied with the maintenance of a world role for themselves that their economic base could no longer sustain and, as a result, military adventures (at Suez and in the colonies) continued to drain resources and manpower; and the

59 As Glyn and Harrison put it, 'A number of factors appear to have inhibited mechanisation. Two related ones are the low rate of accumulation and the lack of an aggressive competitive environment. A low rate of investment, geared to maintaining a constant share of a slowly growing market, tends to involve small-scale additions to existing plant. If a productive structure is dominated by old vintages of machine, this tends to inhibit the integration of radically innovative techniques. In contrast, large-scale investment, intended to undercut competitors and increase market shares, tends to involve wholesale incorporation of modern technological developments in 'greenfield' plants built from scratch on new sites. Step-by-step defensive investments involves smaller increases in the technical composition of capital than aggressive 'greenfield' accumulation.' A. Glyn and J. Harrison *The British Economic Disaster*, Pluto Press, London, 1980, pp. 49–50.

exchange rate of sterling (fixed and protected at $2.80) came to diverge more and more from a level appropriate to the actual international position of the economy that it was taken to symbolize. With little market pressure, a profoundly conservative and imperialist political and financial ruling class, and a strongly defensive labour movement, it is hardly surprising that industrial capital in Britain was slow to see the threat posed to it by the rise of West German and Japanese economic power, and that instead 'at least up to the late 1950s, habituation to the protection of Empire and the expectation that this could be perpetuated removed any strong incentive from the average enterprise to overhaul its means and relations of production'[60].

VIII

The missed opportunity of the 1950s was difficult to recapture. A domestic economy weak in investment, low in managerial and innovative skills, and with a strong labour movement, quickly found itself locked into a series of self-sustaining disabilities, a syndrome of economic decline, where low investment bred low profits that in turn attracted even lower investment. The very absence of rapid economic growth in the 1950s removed the possibility of rapid gains in labour productivity, and so left the economy disproportionately vulnerable to inflation, to international competition as that intensified, and to the persistence of low rates of economic growth. That same low rate of growth 'hardened worker resistance. The sluggishness of markets meant that new labour saving techniques generally brought redundancies in their wake'[61] and so encouraged worker opposition to technical change vital to strengthened competitiveness. The absence of that competitiveness precipitated balance of payments deficits that required internal deflation, and increased still further the inability of British industry to offset its weakening position by a sustained growth in demand and the associated exploitation of economies of scale. Instead low investment, low rates of return on capital, and a low productivity of labour produced a manufacturing sector less and less capable of sustaining high levels of government spending and employment without creating inflation; and the inflationary pressures (stronger here

60 D. Purdy, *op. cit.* p. 315.
61 Glyn and Harrison, *op. cit.* p. 52.

Socialist strategies

than elsewhere because of the strength of political support for high welfare spending, and the low productivity of the manufacturing sector that had to sustain it) eroded international competitiveness still more, and intensified class conflict as governments were forced by their own need for economic growth to make a late but quite sustained attack on working class living standards and control over the labour process.

But by then it was too late. The mistake was to have fallen behind. The British economy had already become locked in a 'low growth spiral' by which 'from being a high wage economy at the end of the Second World War [it] progressively became a low wage [but high cost] economy with consequent exacerbation of class stalemate'[62]. Once weak in international competitive terms, that weakness became and remained cumulative, with each deflation making for further decline and each relative expansion in the economy's overseas competitors putting them further ahead[63]. 'The Marxist law of unequal development was never more obvious'[64] than in this. So that when, after 1973, the whole of the capitalist world was in recession and beset by inflation, the degree of restructuring that was then necessary for Britain industrial capital to survive in the intensified competition which the recession called forward was quite literally beyond the grasp of governments seeking to persuade a labour movement to co-operate in the dismantling of its members' hard-won industrial gains. The 'corporatist' road to industrial regeneration beloved of Labour governments since 1964 just could not stand the strains of the restructuring it required[64]; and when that is recognized,

62 Aaronovitch and Smith, *op. cit.* p. 165.
63 'The most important point to note here is that if the economy happens to be in disequilibrium (e.g. in a weak competitive position and with balance of payments difficulties) all these effects *may* work together in a cumulative and circular chain of causation . . . and thereby help to perpetuate the disequilibrium. Such a country, because of the operation of these forces, will tend to have a lower rate of increase of effective demand, and hence a lower rate of investment, and a lower rate of technical progress and growth in productivity. It will thus be in an even weaker competitive position than before, especially as the same forces will be working in the opposite direction to improve the position of its more successful rivals.' (A. Singh 'U.K. industry and the world economy: a case of deindustrialisation?' *Cambridge Journal of Economics*, 1977, p. 119.
64 Barratt Brown, *op. cit.* p. 54.
65 For a discussion of this, see D. Coates, 'Britain in the 1970s: economic crisis and the resurgence of radicalism' in A. Cox (ed), *Politics, Policy and the European Recession*, Macmillan, London, 1982.

the rise of Thatcherite monetarism can then be seen for what it is – the application of the ruling class's other and latest strategy for the restoration of capitalist profits: a forced increase in the rate of labour exploitation through the escalation of unemployment, state repression and tightened industrial discipline. It is the social costs of that particular strategy, and its bankruptcy even as a mechanism of saving national industrial capital at the workers' expense, that makes the forging of a socialist alternative all the more pressing.

It should now be clear why the explanations mentioned earlier need to be revised if an appropriate socialist strategy is to be forged in Britain in the 1980s. The defensive power of the unions has not created, but has only compounded, a competitive weakness whose roots lie elsewhere, and much nearer to the class forces with which monetarists identify. The social costs of their solutions are, in any case, appallingly high, and disastrous even for the industrial interests they claim to represent. State spending is no artifact of electoral politics alone, but has been a crucial strand in the consolidation of 25 years of economic growth by private industry. If inflation and stagnation are now its legacy, these arise from contradictions in the class structures and monopoly institutions of Late Capitalism, and cannot be resolved by a return to a free market economy that had lost its economic rationale for British industrial capital as long ago as 1914. The inadequacy of management and education, the amateurishness of a civil service without direct industrial experience, and the twists and turns of government policy, are not accidental or easily removable phenomena either. They reflect the particular history of the first industrial capitalism, and the character of the political and social elites that have dominated it. That is why the Left is on stronger grounds when calling for the expropriation of that class, the subordination of finance capital to public ownership, and the redistribution of power within industry. But that solution will necessarily meet heavy resistance, and unless it can generate new structures of decision-making to harness the untapped productive potential of a classless society, will degenerate quickly into a 'statism', a bureaucratized state capitalism, in which problems of labour alienation, low productivity and dwindling international competitiveness will continue behind a hollow rhetoric of socialist advance.

The problem that the Left has to face is how to design a political strategy that is capable of shifting class power dramatically downwards whilst coping with the internal economic and social repercussions of a sharp break with the established networks of international capitalist trade and finance, and the established patterns of class privilege in this society. The Left has to do that in a context too, in which the defensive power of its own natural constituency – the labour movement – is itself a vital constituent element in the crisis of British capitalism to which the Left offers socialism as a solution. This means that there is no easy way in which the Left can shift class power away from capital towards 'working people and their families' without at the same time aggravating problems of profit realisation and capital accumulation for an already weakened industrial capitalist class. At the very least, therefore, any socialist alternative that is canvassed as a solution to the failure of that class to sustain employment and wealth-creation in contemporary Britain will have to be more radical than the programme of welfare capitalism that has characterized the Labour Party's understanding of socialism since 1918. Such an alternative is difficult to design, and even more difficult to sell. The Left now faces a constituency which, for quite understandable reasons, (as we will argue at greater length in chapter nine) is generally sceptical of politicians, and which is in any case increasingly exposed to alternative and obfuscating ideologies and programmes. It is to that project, of designing and disseminating a viable socialist alternative, that the rest of the essays in this volume have necessarily to address themselves.

FURTHER READING

Aaronovitch, S. and Smith, S. *The Political Economy of British Capitalism*, McGraw Hill, New York, 1981.

Coates, D. *Labour in Power?* Longman, London, 1980.

Crouch, C. *State and Economy in Contemporary Capitalism*, Croom Helm, London, 1977.

Currie, D. and Smith, R. (eds). *Socialist Economic Review 1981*, Merlin Press, London, 1981.

Glyn, A. and Harrison, J. *The British Economic Disaster*, Pluto Press, London, 1980.

Kilpatrick, A. and Lawson, T. 'On the nature of industrial decline in the U.K.' *Cambridge Journal of Economics*, 4(1) March 1980.

Pollard, S. *The Wasting of the British Economy*, Croom Helm, London, 1982.

Purdy, D. 'British Capitalism since the war' *Marxism Today* 20(9 and 10) 1976.

Singh, A. 'U.K. industry and the world economy: a case of deindustrialisation' *Cambridge Journal of Economics*, 1(2) June 1977.

Stafford, G. B. *The End of Economic Growth?* Martin Robertson, Oxford, 1981.

Chapter three

THE STATE OF CONTEMPORARY
BRITISH POLITICS*

Gordon Johnston

One of the more notable features of the twentieth century British history has been the combination of relentless economic decline and political stability. For many, of course, this simply serves as a smug affirmation of the political institutions themselves or, as it is often expressed in more arcane formulations, a reflection of the common-sense and moderation of the British. For others, these remarkably resilient institutions become archaic structures of political impotence presiding over and largely responsible for a century of national decline. A more considered account would rightly question the presumption of any clear or direct relationship between economic torpidity and the political institutions. It would go on to emphasize that economic decline has been relative rather than absolute, and that the very reality of national decline has been masked by the longevity of imperial withdrawal, the illusion of world status conferred by the 'special relationship' with the USA, and the phenomenal growth of the world economy in the post-war period. But in acknowledging the validity of this, attention also needs to be directed to the particular character of those domestic political settlements that followed victory in two world wars. For it is these settlements and, crucially, the one forged after the Second World War, providing as it did a popular basis for the consensus politics of the 1950s and 1960s, that have been increasingly undermined in the context of the present world recession.

It would be wrong to suggest that all the changes that have taken place in British politics in the last 15 years can be explained solely with reference to the undermining of the post-war consensus or the failure of successive governments to

* I would like to thank David Coates for his helpful comments on an earlier draft of this chapter.

restructure a sagging national economy. Undoubtedly, this provides one essential starting point for any explanation of the conflicts within and between the Labour and Conservative Parties, the emergence of the Social Democratic Party (SDP), the volatility of the electorate in the 1970s and 1980s and, crucially of course, the emergence and consolidation of Thatcherism itself. But to dwell exclusively on the public drama of party politics, and to focus solely on those themes of discontinuity and conflict which their rhetoric at least suggests, is to miss the significance of longer term structural developments. In particular, such an approach misses the significance of the development of the state[1] and fails to appreciate the ways in which the internationalization of capital and the particular structure of 'British' capital have made it increasingly difficult for the state to manage the domestic economy in any serious sense. Finally, to over-emphasize the political discontinuity of the present is to obscure the fact that much of the ideological strength of Thatcherism derives from an assertive celebration of the past. To comprehend the potency of Thatcherism, of that appeal to national pride, market discipline and family life, requires not only that we are clear what the post-war concensus was actually about, but also that we view its breakdown as partial and its legacies as contradictory.

THE POST-WAR SETTLEMENT

As many commentators have remarked, the post-war consensus was based on considerably more than a simple policy coincidence between post-war administrations. It embraced a much broader set of assumptions about the nature of both domestic and foreign policy objectives and a fundamental agreement about the political means of realizing those objectives. Five main features of this settlement can be identified. Firstly, there was a clear attempt to sustain Britain's role as a world power: an attempt which entailed the defence of sterling as an international reserve currency, the maintenance of military forces overseas, the decision to develop and maintain an independent nuclear programme, and a slavish adherence to the dictates of US foreign

1 This will be discussed in detail by R. Bush and G. Johnston in 'The State and British Capitalism', *A Socialist Anatomy of Britain*, Martin Robertson, Oxford, forthcoming, 1985.

policy. A second feature of the post-war settlement was an endorsement of the mixed economy, in which the vast bulk of productive assets remained in private hands and where the publicly owned sector of the economy was subject to market criteria and devoid of any form of worker participation. Thirdly, there was a commitment to maintain and expand the provision of welfare, education and social services. Fourthly, the post-war settlement involved an adherence to Keynesian techniques of demand management for regulating the economy, and the presumption that the implementation of Keynesian techniques could both generate and sustain economic growth and full employment. Finally, that settlement rested on a clear recognition of the right of independent working class organizations to exist, and for their activities to be free of circumscription by legal codes of practice.

Before considering some of the modifications to this settlement which took place in the late 1950s and 1960s, it will be useful to draw some general conclusions about it. In an important sense it marked both a break and an essential continuity in the trajectory of twentieth century politics. The break was forced by that shift in popular opinion which took place during the war and by the very real advances that had been made by the working class. The contingent nature of the resulting commitment to full employment, the welfare state and trade union rights are now all too apparent, as indeed is the contradictory legacy of the welfare state itself. But it is essential that we acknowledge that these were important gains for the working class, and that their defence is and always has been a vital necessity. If the break forced by the working class was important, the continuity suggested most crucially in Britain's attempt to sustain a world role was decisive. It was decisive not only for the implications it had for a whole range of foreign policy decisions: the rabid endorsement of muscular US anti-communism, the persistent ambivalence towards Europe and that history of military fiasco that takes us from Suez to the South Atlantic; but also for the implications that all this had for the domestic economy. For that commitment to sustain a world role involved a high level of overseas military expenditure, while the priority given to the defence of sterling meant that the automatic response to a sterling crisis, invariably signalled by a deficit on the balance of payments, was a deflation of the national economy, giving rise to the notorious 'stop–go' cycle. What all this meant in straightforward terms was that one of the central contradictions of the post-war settlement, and one which became more acute as the 1950s wore on, was that the political commitment to maintain a world role and the policy decisions this entailed blocked any sustainable expansion of the domestic economy.

A growing awareness towards the end of the 1950s that all was not well with the domestic economy prompted what we may usefully regard as phase two of the post-war settlement. A basic consensus emerged and was endorsed by both the Conservative and Labour Parties, and to a lesser extent and for different reasons by the FBI and the TUC, of the need to embark on what is conventionally referred to as a 'modernization' strategy: of the need, that is, for the state to intervene more directly in the economy than was implied by the orthodoxy of demand management. In many respects, this was an explicit recognition of the inappropriate nature of Keynesian techniques for bringing about the sort of structural revitalization that the domestic economy patently required. The range of new policy largely initiated by the Wilson Government of 1964 but anticipated at least in principle by the outgoing Conservative administration was bewildering:

– the attempt to establish a tripartite framework of the state, industry and trade unions to deal with questions of growth, planning and resource allocation, and the setting up of the Prices and Incomes Board to monitor a permanent incomes policy
– the drawing up of a National Plan with declared growth objectives for the domestic economy, but no clear specification as to how they were to be achieved
– the establishment of an Industrial Reorganisation Corporation to promote rationalization and restructuring within British industry and the setting up of two new ministries, the Department of Economic Affairs (DEA) and the Ministry of Technology, whose general brief was to concern themselves with the national economy, while the DEA was also given the more specific task of countering what was regarded as the excessive and damaging influence of Treasury thinking on questions relating to domestic economic policy.

This 'modernization' strategy also involved an increase in the level of public expenditure not simply to finance the initiatives noted above but also to update and expand the education system and the health services essential for Harold Wilson's New Britain.

The thinking behind the 'modernization' strategy was as clear as were the reasons for its failure. To break out of that spiral of industrial backwardness, non-competitiveness and low growth required not only a major re-evaluation of Britain's traditional relationship with the rest of the world, but also a political consensus capable of sustaining those policy decisions that such a re-evaluation would entail, and which the 'modernization' strategy at least implied would be necessary. Yet, as has been well documented, the 'modernization' strategy was blown off course by the government resorting to the very deflationary orthodoxy that it was designed to challenge. From George Brown's short-lived National Plan to the 1970 election, it was balance of payments crises and runs on sterling that dominated Government thinking. The result of all this was that by the end of the 1960s the economy had stagnated, profits declined and the level of taxation increased: an increase moreover which fell heavily on the working class, who were already subject to severe pay restraint and facing in the *In Place of Strife* proposals the beginnings of what was to become a concerted attempt to undermine trade union organization and negotiating rights. The final demise of the 1960s 'modernization' strategy was as spectacular as it was predictable. An increase in the rate of inflation, the collapse of incomes policy and a massive pay explosion were more than enough to persuade the electorate of the need for Harold Wilson to look for new lodgings, leaving behind him a healthy surplus on the balance of payments.

Although the policies of the 1964–70 administrations fell within the parameters of the post-war consensus it is important to note three aspects of that settlement which were to differing degrees questioned during the 1960s. The first, and one already referred to above, was Keynesianism itself. The second concerned the whole question of trade union power – the question whether or not the power of trade unions was responsible for the poor performance of the domestic economy, and if it was, of whether the law could be used to curb that power. Finally, though much less dramatically, the period of 'modernization' raised the question of what was to happen to public expenditure commitments, especially in the areas of education, welfare and social services, in the absence of economic growth. Of course all these questions were to assume a much more dramatic importance in the 1970s and 1980s. But the point to emphasize is that by the end of the 1960s the economic basis for the political consensus that had existed since 1945 was undergoing a process of rapid erosion.

In many respects, the Heath administration of 1970–74 marks an important watershed in post-war British politics. All the assumptions of the post-war settlement were questioned – questioned moreover in the context of the break up of the Bretton Woods international monetary system, the massive increase in world oil prices and the onset of a generalized world recession. The end of the long post-war boom simply served to highlight and exacerbate Britain's accumulated economic problems and made the need to forge some new form of political consensus increasingly urgent for an embittered and resentful capitalist class. But if the Heath years demonstrated this need they also demonstrated just how difficult that task was to be. The notorious 'U' turn, the switch that is from free market policies to intervention in industry and the introduction of a statutory incomes policy, was more than just an ill-conceived gambit in the game of electoral politics. Rather, it reflected a genuine problem of political direction and political support which Heath least of all was able to resolve.

On coming to office, Heath's sense of Churchillian purpose was apparent. 'We were returned to office' he informed the Tory conference at Blackpool 'to change the course of history of this nation – nothing less'. To this end he pursued EEC membership – a belated recognition of Britain's incapacity to sustain a world role – informed industry of the need for it to survive in a 'bracing climate' without the mollycoddling of government, and suffered a spectacular set-back when trade unions and large employers, including some Government departments, refused to implement the Industrial Relations Act. The commitment not to sustain that 'sodden morass of subsidized incompetence' was effectively reversed in 1972 with the rescue of the Upper Clyde shipyards, quickly followed by the Industry Act establishing a new system of development grants and the setting up of an Industrial Development Executive to assist firms. Barber's reflationary budget of 1972 stimulated feverish speculative activity on the property market, and pushed up the rate of inflation; and with the failure to get agreement on a voluntary incomes policy the

Government announced a wages and prices freeze in November 1972 as a first stage in a statutory incomes policy. A general expansion of the world economy in early 1973 combined with the apparent success of the Government's anti-inflationary policies were eagerly seized on as grounds for optimism. But by the end of 1973, the OPEC price rises, and industrial action against Stage III of the incomes policy by the electricity workers and the miners, signalled the failure of Heath's attempt 'to change the course of history'. It was, as subsequent years have demonstrated, history itself which was changing, with the 1974 election results and the emergence of Thatcher as leader of the Tory party providing indications as to what some of those changes were all about.

THE BREAKDOWN OF CONSENSUS?

If the end of the post-war boom and the onset of a generalized world recession served to highlight and exacerbate Britain's accumulated economic problems, it also accelerated the break up of that political consensus between the Labour and Conservative parties that had been so central a feature of post-war British politics. This discussion, as we shall see, needs handling with care. Care is needed not simply because there was an obvious continuity between the economic policies of the Callaghan and Thatcher administrations. Care is also needed because, as the events surrounding the Falkland Islands indicated all too dramatically, *both* parties are fundamentally implicated not only in that persistent ruling class appeal to the 'national interest' but also in that ritual of political mystification expressed in those increasingly assertive appeals to the 'sovereignty of parliament'. All this suggests that the whole issue of the breakdown of consensus and the attempt to construct the basis for a new one involve considerably more than a focus on the political parties themselves, or indeed on those fissures within them. In order to inform and extend this discussion it is worth looking at some of the more general legacies of the break-down of the post-war settlement.

One of the first and most obvious things to note is that the process of disillusionment with the performance of post-war governments had set in well before 1974. The re-emergence of the nationalist movements in Scotland and Wales, and the revitalization of republicanism in Ireland, posed and continue to pose major questions concerning the boundaries of the British state. The inroads that SNP, Plaid Cymru and the Liberals made into the parliamentary fortunes of the Labour and Conservative parties at the two 1974 elections testified to a fundamental discontent with post-war Westminster rule, while in regional terms the election results of 1974 and 1979 confirmed and, indeed, consolidated that long-term trend in which Tory party support has mostly increased in the South of England. The industrial militancy of the late 1960s and early 1970s, and the unrest fermented by Britain's hawkish endorsement of US genocide in Vietnam, also testified to a profound resistance to those spurious appeals to the 'national interest'. Important though this clearly focused disenchantment was, there was another process of disillusionment under way, much more difficult to pin down precisely because it was diffuse and inchoate. It took a number of forms, a generalized hostility or apathy to politics in general and politicians in particular, some of which, especially amongst white working class youth, undoubtedly sustained the murky revival of the fascist right, which along with Powell's populist racism and the increasingly restrictive immigration legislation of the 1960s and 1970s all served in the construction of a convenient scapegoat for Britain's economic malaise. But more than this, that process of disillusionment also suggested that if, as some have argued, Britain had just experienced three decades of social democratic consensus, it had left precious little of a social democratic consciousness behind it.

The evidence for this becomes more apparent from the mid-1970s onwards. For what has characterized the undermining of those very real gains of post-war public service provision has been the very real indifference that many have displayed towards their erosion. In part, of course, one can explain this with reference to that infusion of monetarist and latterly Thatcherite 'common-sense' into the public debate. But an explanation requires more than this. Crucially, it hinges on the very nature of the individual–state relationship itself. For the whole ethic of post-war public service provision has been premised on the assumption of the public as passive recipient, and this has been exacerbated by the very real hostility that certain sections of the public encounter in their dealings with the state. This appears to have provoked an essential ambiguity towards the state itself, an ambiguity which has been exploited most noticeably in the anti-statist rhetoric of Thatcher herself. In exploiting popular resentment towards the state, and in counterposing a malign bureaucratic state with a 'free people', Thatcherism has constructed a powerful rationale for restructuring the state in the interests of the 'people' and, in so doing, has consolidated that association in the popular mind between Labour administrations and the growth of inefficient state bureaucracies. This is just one illustration of a more general phenomena. Although the superficiality of a social democratic consciousness and the failure of social democratic forms of crisis management opened up the potential for an initiative from the Left, it has been the Right which has seized the political and ideological opportunity. Nowhere was this more apparent than in the swing to the Tories of working class and trade union votes at the 1979 election, which was consolidated in June 1983.

If the task of delineating those complex processes of resistance and disillusionment in the wake of the break-down of the postwar settlement remains in many respects still to be done, there were a number of general issues raised by that break-down which can be clarified. Firstly, the breakdown signalled the final demise of Keynesianism as a viable ruling class strategy. It has always been questionable as to how much growth rates of the 1950s and 1960s were a consequence of Keynesian techniques, rather than simply a product of the world boom itself. The essence of the political compromise that Keynesianism signified was that it sustained an essentially non-interventionist position with regard to both capital and labour. But as we have already noted the 'modernization' strategy of the 1960s represented an implicit critique of this view, not least in its commitment to restructure capital and discipline labour by means of corporate forms of representation and intervention. The failure of the Wilson experiment with corporatism, a failure which enjoyed a repeat performance between 1974–76, and the spectacular disaster of Heath's free market initiatives in the early 1970s, suggested that it was not so much the economics of the strategies that were wrong but rather that neither of them commanded sufficiently wide political support. It was, after all, not just trade union leaders but also the head of the CBI who suggested that the 1971 Industrial Relations Act should be scrapped. The reasons for this absence of political support are central for any understanding of subsequent developments. For what this suggests is that the problem for capital was a political one – of a basic impasse at the onset of the recession because of its own weakness in the face of a trade union movement that was strong enough to prevent the sort of job losses, deskilling and speed up that a competitively weak domestic industrial capital required if it was to gain even a semblance of international competitiveness. Of course it was not until the Thatcher Government came to power that any serious attempt was made to shift the balance of class forces decisively. By then, escalating unemployment, declining trade union membership, cuts in capital expenditure programmes, monetarist orthodoxy and a Labour Party increasingly discredited in the eyes of the working class had all contributed to making that task considerably less daunting than it appeared in 1974. However, before we consider the complexities of Thatcherism, it is worth considering some of the general legacies of the breakdown of the post-war settlement for the Labour Party.

THE LABOUR PARTY DILEMMA

That Ladbrokes should have opened a book on Michael Foot's successor as leader of the Labour Party well before the result of the 1983 election was known should surprise no-one. Nor is it remarkable that the opening salvos of the election post-mortem show every indication of reasserting those tensions and divisions within the Party that Foot's leadership was designed to obscure for the purposes of electoral credibility. Before considering the likely trajectory of those divisions and the longer term implications of the 1983 electoral defeat for the Labour Party, it is worth dwelling on the significance of Foot's leadership. Ignore the supposed absence of sartorial style and those seemingly archaic skills of public oratory when faced with the zappy high-tech political cosmetics industry of Saatchi & Saatchi, and focus on the continuity that Foot provides with that revered Labour generation of 1945. It is that very continuity which symbolizes many of the Party's problems. The illustration becomes even more striking when you note the speed with which the Tory Party emancipated itself from the post-war consensus by electing Margaret Thatcher as leader in 1975. This reminds us that the post-war settlement was very much a settlement established by the 1945 Labour Government and consented to by subsequent Conservative administrations. Precisely because of this deep involvement with the construction of the post-war settlement itself, it has been the role and identity of the Labour Party which has been challenged to a much greater extent than that of the Tory Party in the 1970s, and especially since 1979.

This is not, of course, to deny that there are genuine conflicts inside the Conservative Party, but the crucial difference is that the leadership of the party has emancipated itself from the parameters of the post-war consensus, and indeed has made a virtue out of doing so; while the leadership of the Labour Party is still appealing seriously to the Dunkirk spirit. It is the very anachronism of that appeal, and the failure it represents to consider either the lessons of the past or the realities of the present which underpins much of the conflict and division within the Labour Party today. That conflict has taken place in the context of a steadily declining membership, the erosion of the material basis for any sustainable social democratic politics, and falling support at the polls, illustrated dramatically by that 28.2 per cent of the popular vote that the Party secured in the election in June 1983. The nature of the divisions and conflicts within the Labour Party will be discussed in chapter four. Let me focus here on some of the more general questions these divisions pose for the Labour Party in the wake of the 1983 election.

Despite the very real advances of the Labour Left since 1979, their successes over the leadership elections, mandatory reselection and some policy commitments, the party remains remarkably unpopular with the electorate. A preliminary examination of the 1983 result indicates that 22 per cent of 1979 Labour voters switched to the Alliance, with a further 7.5 per cent voting Tory. These figures were offset somewhat by a 9 per cent shift of 1979 Liberals to the Labour Party. Behind these bald statistics it should also be noted that Labour's share of the working class vote continued to decline confirming a long-term trend that has been identified over the last 25 years[2]. But what is the significance of all this? Is it a rout as the media so enthusiastically proclaim, destined to confine the Labour Party to a bit-part in the drama of late twentieth-century politics, or does the next decade provide an opportunity for constructing a viable socialist politics in Britain? If the latter is a real possibility, what role might the Labour Party play in such a scenario? This necessarily brief discussion can be broken down into three broad areas: the

2 See in particular, B. Sarlvik and I. Crewe, *Decade of Dealignment*, Cambridge University Press, Cambridge, 1983.

reasons for the Labour Party's unpopularity with the electorate, the adequacy of Labour Party policy, and the Party's conception of political strategy.

There are clearly many reasons for Labour's unpopularity with the electorate, not least the sustained media campaign against the party and more generally the Labour Party's reluctance to challenge the dominant framework within which politics is discussed, and which the media play so central a role in sustaining. As we shall see in a moment, this particular problem is bound up with discussions about policy and strategy and with the obvious fact that many in the Labour Party are not seriously engaged in questioning this dominant framework in the first place. But the problem is worth isolating from these considerations because the 1983 election campaign provided a dramatic and depressing illustration of the failure of the Labour Party to utilize a political vocabulary capable of penetrating that acrid fog of political mystification that enveloped the country to a greater extent than usual throughout the election campaign. It is no good gleefully exposing endless leaks about future Tory policy unless you can explain their significance in terms other than moralizing accusations of schoolgirl deceit. What is the use of bemoaning the plight of the unemployed and saying 'yes, unemployment is a problem' without pointing out that capitalism has always produced high levels of unemployment in periods of crisis, and very far from being a 'problem', has always regarded unemployment as being part of the solution. If we are talking about capitalism are we not also talking about classes in conflict? If that is what we are talking about, who are these British people whom are told have common interests? One could of course go on. The general point has I hope been made: as long as the Labour Party thinks and talks with a vocabulary that does not challenge the dominant framework within which politics is discussed and 'problems' defined, it cannot expect to be taken seriously as a socialist party. This will involve considerably more than radical resolutions, manifesto commitments, or indeed a more accountable leadership as many on the Labour Left seem to believe, but before discussing these questions it is worth returning to Labour's unpopularity with the electorate.

The Falkland Islands war brought about a remarkable reversal of fortunes for the Conservative Party. It may well have been the case that, if that fiasco has not taken place, the opinion polls would have continued to register as they did at the end of 1981 that Thatcher's administration was the most unpopular since the war. But the problem for the Labour Party was obviously, not that it failed to anticipate the war, though it certainly assisted Thatcher in exploiting it to the full, but rather that it presumed that the economic record of the Government would enable Labour to win any forthcoming election. The problem is not of course a new one. The Labour Party has always displayed an essentially passive attitude towards its increasingly fragmented and shrinking mass base. What is perhaps more surprising is that it has sustained such indifference to the winning of support at a time when the Conservative Government, in spite of its economic record, has actually consolidated its political hegemony. It has done so not just because of the Falklands war but because it has undermined many of those post-war assumptions upon which the ideological appeal of the Labour Party was based: full employment, public sector provision, trade union rights and public ownership. It is this failure of the Labour Party to appreciate the scope and popular appeal of Thatcherism that indicates just how far it has to move in that process of emancipating itself from its own past if it is to convince any future electorate that it represents a viable alternative to the Tory Party. In failing to understand the popularity of Thatcherism, the Labour Party fails to reflect seriously on the reasons for its own unpopularity. For too long the Party has relied on easy scapegoats, from press barons and media hacks to the malevolent whims of leaders, past and present. But beyond these undoubtedly powerful enclaves of conspiracy lives an electorate who are perplexed by the Alternative Economic Strategy, who wonder what it is an alternative to, and who are puzzled by the fact that the Labour Party only seems to exist in newspapers or at election time. These seem to me to be perfectly reasonable things to wonder about.

The debate about the adequacy of the Alternative Economic Strategy is now extensive, so that there is no good reason for repeating the detail of it here. There are, however, two features of that discussion which are central to any serious consideration of the future trajectory of the Labour Party. The first is a need for an unequivocal commitment that the AES is not about the corporate management of late capitalism, and the second is, that such a commitment is impossible outside the discussion of political strategy. Indeed, the latter is of more importance for the simple reason that the Labour Party has never possessed a conception of political strategy other than one which repeats the dull litany of: elect a Labour Government, ensure that the leadership is accountable and that the manifesto is implemented. This is not serious socialist politics. It has no presence in the work-place, it has no input into class and popular struggles that are taking place daily throughout the country, and it has no conception of how the power of capital is to be challenged other than one which relies on a view of the state as some benign instrument for the popular good. In other words, it remains intellectually and physically imprisoned within the world of social democracy, a world which ceased long ago to provide a viable strategy for even a reforming politics. If the Labour Party is to play any serious role in the generation of a socialist politics in Britain in the 1980s, it will have to break decisively with the legacy of its own past. Foot was a symbol of the attempt to sustain that very continuity. The attempt failed as an electoral tactic. Foot has now gone. The questions remains.

GENESIS OF THE POLITICAL CENTRE

Any discussion of the future of the Labour Party prompts the question of the significance of the SDP, officially launched in March 1981, two months after the Labour Party's Wembley Conference on methods of electing its leader. There are very real difficulties in assessing the long-term significance of the SDP. When it emerged it was clearly not just a product of Fleet Street or opportunist Labour politicians seeking to break from those vestiges of class politics that the Labour Party still articulates, but part of that general stuttering re-evaluation of the legacy and future of social democracy. In the context of this re-evaluation and the increasing polarization between the Labour and Conservative Parties, the emergence of a self-avowed centre party was really no surprise, nor indeed was the high level of initial support it received at local and by-elections. Not only was it saying the things that many people would like to believe, but it was doing so at a time when both the main parties were for different reasons decidedly unpopular with the electorate. It is worth remembering too that, since 1959, but more significantly since 1974, the Liberal share of the popular vote has increased substantially, averaging 17 per cent at the general elections since February 1974 (though less than 5 per cent regarded themselves as commited Liberals), prompting not only demands for a change in the electoral system, but suggesting that well before the emergence of the SDP and the subsequent formation of the Alliance there was a basis of support for a centre party in British politics.

Much of the initial attention paid to the SDP–Liberal Alliance focused on whether or not they could receive sufficient support at a general election to sustain a third major grouping in the House of Commons. If they could and no party possessed an overall majority, what would happen then? The Alliance itself was less modest than this, claiming at times that they would form the next government. There was much talk of coalition government, of the conditions under which they might be formed, and whether or not a centre coalition comprising the Alliance, Tory 'wets' and the Right of the Labour Party would emerge. In the short term, at least, the 1983 election suggests that all this was little more than idle speculation. For, although the Alliance secured 25.9 per cent of the popular vote, the largest support for a centre grouping in 60 years, it won only 23 seats (17 Liberal, 6 SDP). In terms of the claims made by the Alliance before the election, the result was clearly a failure, though not an unexpected one given the perversity of the electoral system. In suggesting this, however, it would be unwise to project a future of insignificance for the political centre. Assuming, as is now likely, that the Alliance holds together, given the imbalance of its parliamentary representation, what will be decisive for the fortunes of the centre is the trajectory of the Labour and Conservative Parties and particularly, of course, the Labour Party. So much depends on whether or not the conflicts that have divided that party in recent years are simply the beginnings of a much longer term process of emancipation from the shibboleths of post-war social democracy, or not. If indeed it is this process which is underway, the fortunes not only of socialism but also of the political centre will be advanced. For it would provide the Alliance with an opportunity to consolidate its support. That support at present comprises so sizeable a protest vote that it is premature to talk about the emergence of a coherent and sustainable political centre. With regard to the Tory Party, the size of the new parliamentary majority and the speed with which Thatcher has removed Whitelaw and Pym from her Cabinet suggests that the long-term opportunities for 'wet' MPs are decidedly bleak. It is worth noting too that 13 per cent of 1979 Tory voters switched to the

Alliance. It is perfectly possible, therefore, to anticipate that British politics will witness, in the long term, a consolidation of the political centre, rather than as many have argued, its early demise. Whether or not this will be sufficient to orchestrate some form of national government in the late 1980s, or force through a change in the electoral system inaugurating an epoch of coalition government revolving around the centre, remains to be seen. But what it does signify is that, as popular and class struggles inevitably intensify, that centre appeal to unity and consensus will remain a powerful one.

THATCHERISM

As Stuart Hall has suggested, it has been Thatcherism rather than the SDP which has broken the mould of British politics. It is to an assessment of that complex phenomenon that we must now turn. One of the recurrent problems in Left analyses of Thatcherism is that because the Left does not like it, so many of its commentators either do not take Thatcherism seriously, or if they do, are too quick to dismiss its economic policies as 'irrational' and so bound to fail. Yet, however reassuring such a conclusion might be, it is almost certainly wrong[3]. There are, clearly, a range of levels at which one can discuss Thatcherism. Firstly, we need a clear idea of what its objectives are, and an appreciation of the extent to which the strategy devised to secure those objectives is informed by a sustained and coherent critique of the whole post-war period, including of course the institutions and ideology of social democracy itself. We also need to recognize, and this is perhaps decisive, the ways in which the whole initiative has been translated into an accessible populist 'common-sense' which goes much of the way towards explaining the reasons for its popular appeal; and we need some sense too of what is likely to follow the 1983 election victory.

Earlier in this discussion it was argued that the historic weakness of domestic industrial capital was exacerbated in the post-war period by a commitment to the maintenance of Britain's world role and by the increased strength of organized labour. We also noted the extent to which the growth of the world economy

3 For an important exception, see S. Hall and M. Jacques (eds), *The Politics of Thatcherism*, Lawrence and Wishart in association with Marxism Today, London, 1983.

in the post-war years served to disguise the degree of structural obsolescence that characterized much of the industrial sector of the British economy. With the onset of the world recession, not only was the British economy fully exposed to an international capitalist crisis with all the implications that had for widespread bankruptcy, liquidations, short-time and unemployment, but it also threatened in its very severity to spark off a widespread opposition to capitalism itself. It is in this context that we need to situate Thatcherism, for not only have policies been pursued which have exacerbated the crisis, weakened organized labour and challenged many of the assumptions of the post-war period, but all this has been achieved with minimal levels of opposition and without as yet generating widespread social unrest.

The central objective of Thatcherism is to secure, maintain and guarantee a political and an economic environment which will not only facilitate an improvement in the international competitiveness of British manufacturing industry, but which will also prove attractive to capitalist investment generally. This latter dimension must be viewed in the context of the discussion in an earlier chapter which highlighted the extent to which the internationalization of capital and the diversification of capitalist production by the multinationals to areas of intense labour exploitation has served to expose (and in the case of Britain) exacerbate a growing contradiction between the interests of the national economy and the interests of capital in general. Precisely because of the weakness of the British economy and its unattractiveness to investors, it has proved more vulnerable than most to those very processes of internationalization that the recession has accelerated, and in this it was assisted, of course, by the government's prompt removal of exchange controls in 1979. But it is on the terrain of the 'nation' and with regard to the performance of the domestic economy that governments seek to secure and maintain electoral and political support. Part of the significance of Thatcherism is that it represents a partial attempt to resolve this contradiction between a national economy which is commercially unattractive and capital seeking profitable investment in the world economy, by exposing the national economy to the chill blast of international market forces. The partiality of the attempt needs emphasizing; a sustained application would almost certainly have resulted in the demise of the car, steel and shipbuilding industries, and we have also heard that odd sounding phrase on Tory lips, 'unfair competition' to characterize the exporting zeal of the Japanese and the ruthless exploitation of labour in Taiwan.

The reasons for this apparent lack of total commitment to the moral efficiency of the market economy are important, for they illustrate not only the high risk that is involved in pursuing the strategy in its purest form, but also the extent to which its chances of success are heavily dependent on shifting decisively the balance of class forces inside Britain, and of mobilizing and sustaining a political consensus that will endorse that shift. It is to these ends that we can best view the sustained onslaught that Thatcherism represents towards the whole ethos of the domestic post-war settlement and the consensus politics which it sustained. Of course with regard to the international dimension of that post-war settlement, Thatcherism represents an essential continuity – not least with regard to the US connection. For although that 'special relationship' suffered minor set-backs during the early stages of the Falkland Islands war and over supplies for the Soviet oil pipe-line, it has been firmly reconstituted in the face of the massive resurgence of the European peace movement and opposition to NATO. Yet, despite this international continuity, internally Thatcherism marks a sharp break with the post-war welfare consensus – and in so doing actually consolidates her identification with a US government equally radical in its domestic conservatism.

If, then, the core of the Thatcher strategy hinges on its capacity not simply to shift the balance of class forces but to mobilize and sustain support for the essential legitimacy of that shift and secure a new political consensus around it, it is clear that this requires considerably more than an offensive against the trade union movement and that level of protection and provision afforded in the post-war period by the institutions of the welfare state. These initiatives are of course real enough and are likely to be intensified following the Tories return to office, but it is important to view the ways in which these initiatives have been justified, the method whereby they have been inserted into a very powerful ideological framework which draws on three broad sources for its inspiration. Firstly, on those themes of nationality, the family, the individual, and the choice allegedly afforded by the market itself: all of these are celebrated as universal and necessary components of any free and civilized society. The positive ascription given to these themes is counterposed to those developments in the post-war period which are alleged to have undermined them: trade unionism has not only distorted the operation of the labour market but it also restricts the scope of individual choice; the extension of the role of the state in the economy has interfered with the operation of the market, while its intrusion into the 'private' sphere has undermined the family unit, encouraged the lazy and generated bureaucratic inefficiency. Finally, and perhaps most insiduously, it is argued that the decline of the national economy has rendered Britain vulnerable to import penetration from those more successful national economies and all this has undermined the pride of being British. This argument is quickly collapsed into a racist one which suggests that immigration too has undermined the cultural and social cohesiveness of some essential national identity. But not all the developments in the post-war years are regarded as undermining those core themes of nationality, the family, the individual and market choice, for the third source of this potent ideological cocktail of the New Right is the positive ascription they give to those forces in society which are regarded as essential for preserving what is euphemistically referred to as the 'essentials of freedom'. Central here has, of course, been the emphasis on law and order and discipline. The significance of that endorsement is that, as many have argued, the shift to a more authoritarian state which is indicated by the increased powers and presence of the police and army predated the emergence of Thatcherism. Some have located the years between 1968 and 1972 as a crucial turning point in the 'exhaustion of consent', focusing in particular in the moral backlash to the 1960s, widespread industrial unrest and the insertion of race into the arena of British politics. This is a view which has been largely substantiated by those researchers who have focused on the changing structure, organization, and role of the police force since the mid-1960s[4].

The important question that this brief exploration of the ideological make-up of Thatcherism provokes is why does it appear to work? Of course, the fact that it does work could be disputed. We could concentrate all our attention on the political exploitation of the Falkland Islands war and the reversal of fortunes it represented for the Thatcher Government, but to do so is really to avoid the core of the question. For the fact that the

4 See in particular, S. Hall, C. Critcher, T. Jefferson, J. Clarke, B. Roberts, *Policing The Crisis*, Macmillan, London, 1978; and *State Research Bulletin* No. 19 August–September 1980.

war could be exploited in the blatant way that it undoubtedly was, suggests not that Thatcher mobilized something essentially new, but on the contrary that she mobilized an ideological predisposition which already existed. It is this alarming illustration that the war provided that helps to illuminate the more general reasons for Thatcher's ideological success. If you think back to those core elements of Thatcherism that we identified – the emphasis on nationality and nationalism, the family, individual and market choice – you will appreciate that irrespective of the extent to which they were supposedly undermined in the post-war years this is very far from being the case. At no time did the post-war settlement, or indeed its social democratic twist at the hands of Labour governments, involve a questioning of nationalism, while the character and 'naturalness' of the nuclear family unit has remained a core assumption of all post-war welfare and social policy. Turning to those themes of individual choice and the market, it is clear that the post-war settlement, by endorsing the legitimacy of private sector education and medical services, did not in any serious sense counterpose collective to individual provision; and if you look at the operation of the market, the state, far from undermining its operation, has subsidized it with contracts, investment grants, reallocation incentives and low-cost inputs from the nationalized industries.

The first point to emphasize about the ideological dynamics of Thatcherism is that it revolves around a set of core assumptions, attitudes and values which were not seriously questioned by social democracy itself. The second point is that precisely because of this it has proved comparatively easy to apply arguments concerning the moral efficiency of the market to the public sector without having to combat arguments about social need or the quality and extent of provision. This has been facilitated by the degree to which the services themselves have deteriorated in the course of the recession, and by the level of genuine public frustration which has emerged in the course of dealings with the bureaucratic apparatus of the state. Turning to the ideological initiative against the trade union movement, Thatcherism has largely exploited that build up of resentment to organized labour that we suggested re-emerged significantly in the late 1960s, and has capitalized further on that lowering of morale that the recession and government policies have induced. All this has of course been assisted by conflicts and divisions within the Labour movement iself, the general discrediting of the Labour Party since 1979, and its failure to mobilize a successful popular campaign against Thatcherism.

Even so brief and preliminary an account of the sources of Thatcherism's ideological strength would be incomplete without some recognition of the extent to which the strategy has been translated into a series of apparently self-evident truths for popular consumption. These are familiar and do not require rehearsing here. Their significance lies in the recognition they represent of the need to win popular political support, and of the ability to do so by anchoring that appeal in a range of popular grievances against trade unions, state bureaucracies, the public sector, blacks and immigrants. By doing so, such ideological initiatives do not displace attention from questions of unemployment, but rather block the generalized consolidation of any recognition that unemployment has anything to do with capitalism itself or indeed with the policies of the Government. The accumulated legacy of this, of course, is that those who have suffered most from the onset of a generalized capitalist recession are regarded and frequently regard themselves as being responsible for those very hardships and poverty that capitalism itself has induced.

JUNE 1983: THE END OF THE BEGINNING

What then of the future of Thatcherism? The first point to emphasize about the election result is that the Tories did not secure a 144 seat majority by increasing their share of the popular vote. On the contrary it fell by 1.5 per cent on the 1979 figure. Although 42.4 per cent of those who voted did so for the Conservative Party, this only represents a very modest 30.8 per cent of the total electorate, extremely low by post-war standards. The size of the parliamentary majority was a result of two factors, the constituency boundary changes and the disorganization of the opposition, the fact that the opposition vote was split almost equally between the Alliance and the Labour Party. None of this is likely to be of much significance in the next five years, for the very size of that 144 seat overall majority has a number of important and pretty obvious consequences. It ensures Thatcher's total dominance of the Tory Party, not simply because as we have already seen it has given her the opportunity to purge the Cabinet and Government teams of more 'wets', but also, because what evidence that does exist about the ideological disposition of new Tory MPs suggests that they are preponderantly Thatcherite in their sympathies. These factors, combined with the size of the majority, provide an almost absolute guarantee that all Government legislation will pass through the House of Commons with a minimal amount of opposition or amendment.

If we turn now to the likely initiatives of the Tory Government, it is important to emphasize that the years since 1979 can best be regarded as a period in which the ground-work has been prepared for a much more decisive onslaught against the working class, the welfare state and the public sector. Thatcher's oft-quoted remark that she still needs another ten years is no idle or ill-conceived gesture of public bravado. All the evidence suggests that the Government does possess a fully worked-out strategy for dismantling the welfare state, privatizing large areas of public sector industry and sevices, continuing its attack on trade unions, and tightening the grip of Whitehall on the local authorities. Secretary of Employment Norman Tebbit's Green Paper on trade union reforms, the Serpell Report on the future of British Rail and the leaked documents from the Think Tank, Family Policy Group and numerous Cabinet Committees all contain ample evidence of this. We must locate the likelihood of these initiatives in the context of those that are already well underway. The selling off of 19 ports, British Airways, British Telecom, the subsidiaries of British Rail, British Steel and British Shipbuilders; the early reintroduction of the Police Bill and the attempt to subsidize private capital through Enterprise Zones, Freeports and the cheapening and disciplining of labour power through the Youth Training Scheme. Never in the post-war period have we had such a clear idea of what a future Government would like to do if it was returned to office[5].

5 The leaking of secret documents and speculation as to the detail of future Tory policies was very much a growth industry during the 1983 election campaign. For details of the Think Tank report, see *The Economist* 18–24 September 1982; for Family Policy Group, see *The Guardian* 17 February 1983; for details of National Health Service proposals, see *The Guardian* 31 May 1983 and 1 June 1983. A discussion of the implications of the Serpell Report can be found in *Community Action* No. 61, and an extensive discussion of the detail and implications of privatization can be found in the following: *Public Service Action* Nos 1 and 2, available from SCAT Publications, 27 Clerkenwell Close, London EC1; *Privatisation: Civil Service For Sale*, available from Council of Civil Service Unions, St Andrews House, 40 Broadway, London SW1H 0BT;

Socialist strategies

It would be wrong, however, to assume that any, or indeed all, this will be easy to implement. We have already argued that there will be no effective opposition inside Parliament, but the obstacles the Government could face outside Parliament might well be considerable. Not only can we expect a greater degree of resistance from sections of the Labour Party and the trade union movement contemplating five years of Tory Britain, but the Government will inevitably provoke opposition from within the state itself. It is also arguable that the level of popular public support that the Tories have mobilized thus far cannot be sustained in the absence of any decisive up-turn in the fortunes of the British economy, and this is not something that even a Thatcher Government can easily control, given that economic recovery here will depend far more on developments in the world economy as a whole than on the initiatives of the Government in London.

It was argued earlier that the core of the Thatcher strategy hinged on its capacity not simply to shift the balance of class forces in Britain but to mobilize and sustain support for the essential legitimacy of that shift and to forge a new political consensus around it. Certainly, the balance of class forces has been altered but whether that shift will prove decisive, and whether or not its legitimacy has been secured, is much more open to question. Given that the construction of a new political consensus requires considerably more than an electoral victory (especially one with so large a discrepancy between the popular vote and the parliamentary victory), it is impossible to conclude that Thatcher's victory in June 1983 alone represents a sufficient level of political consent to contain the social and political con-

---

Privatisation & Public Services and *Direct Labour Organisation*, available from GMWU, Thorne House, Ruxley Ridge, Claygate, Esher, Surrey KT10 0TL; *British Telecom: Evidence presented to the Department of Industry*, available from POEU, Greystoke House, 150 Brunswick Road, Ealing, London W5 1AW; *Public or Private: The case against privatisation*, available from Labour Research Department, 78 Blackfriars Road, London SE1. See also, S. Hastings and H. Levie (eds), *Privatisation?*, Spokesman, Nottingham, 1983, and H. Levie, 'Britain Goes to the Sales', *Marxism Today*, April 1983. For an excellent discussion of the Youth Training Scheme, see P. Scofield, E. Preston, E. Jacques, *The Tories' Poisoned Apple*, available from ILP, 49 Top Moor Side, Leeds, LS11 9LW. Finally, for Thatcher as a 'sister' see, *Women Fight The Tories*, available from Rights of Women, 374 Grays Inn Road, London WC1.

flicts that a sustained implementation of Thatcherism would provoke. Even after the Tory victory at the polls the battle for legitimacy will go on and its nature and outcome will turn in the end on the character and impact of the Left's counter-assault. It is to a discussion of how best that can be constituted that the remaining chapters in this volume will now turn.

SOCIALIST STRATEGIES

Chapter four

THE LABOUR PARTY AND THE TRANSITION TO SOCIALISM[1]

Geoff Hodgson

[W]hen you ask people on the Left what vision they have for the future, for socialism; how can you best describe, represent, urge the advantages of socialism on the mass of the people; significant silences occur. Our eyes and minds are so full of the things that surround us, and the desirability of what they tell us, that there is no room for another vision.

Jeremy Seabrook, *What Went Wrong?*

On 9 June 1983 the British Labour Party suffered what is probably the worst electoral defeat in its history. The Party polled 28.3 per cent of the vote – the lowest figure since 1918. Before the First World War the Labour Party never fielded more than 42 candidates in a general election, and on inspection its 1983 performance compares badly with that in the first decade of this century. In terms of popular support, Labour has been hurled back to the Victorian era. It has lost its political hold in much of the South and East of England, its main base being the old, declining industrial areas of the North. Whilst the Conservative victors of the 1983 election would like to reinstate 'Victorian values' throughout British society, they should not be given all the blame for Labour's predicament. Other factors were involved as well.

This defeat raises a number of basic and searching questions. Socialists will ask if the decline of the Labour Party is now irreversible, and if a space has been created for a new socialist party. on the Left of the political spectrum. Others will ask the more fundamental question, whether Labour's decline is associated with the gradual erosion of egalitarian and collectivist

1 I am grateful to David Coates and Gordon Johnston for helpful criticisms of an earlier version of this essay.

values in British culture, and whether this would affect all socialist parties, old, new, and not yet born.

We have indeed reached a turning point in the history of both the Labour Party and socialist politics in Britain. The questions raised are difficult and there are no easy answers. The heady optimism of the 1960s is gone, and we are in austere and threatening times. In this chapter I intend to look again at the past and recent development of the Labour Party to examine its capacity for radical and socialist change in the future.[2] The first part gives a brief account, for background purposes, of the nature and structure of the Labour Party. The second part sketches the development of its political and economic strategy in recent years. The third part assesses the scale of the defeat of the entire Left in the early 1980s, and the final part makes some suggestions for Labour and socialist strategy in the future.

I THE NATURE OF THE LABOUR PARTY

For over two hundred years, mainland Britain has experienced no major social upheaval on the scale of a revolution or civil war. Unlike France, Italy and Germany, Britain did not experience fascism or foreign occupation. It emerged from the Second World War with its social structure modified but intact. In addition, Britain was the first country to industrialize, and to thus create a mass urban working class. This development took place within a society which retained many of its quasi-feudal institutions. Consequently, British society today is elitist and relatively ossified, despite the real social and economic changes since the Industrial Revolution. There is little experience of a fracture or breakdown of society, or of mass mobilization leading to radical change. Hierarchy and gradualism are the hallmarks of our history. It is impossible to understand the nature of the Labour Party and trade unions in Britain without reference to these facts.

In 1900 the British trade unions came together, with the support of the Independent Labour Party, to form the Labour Representation Committee (LRC). The object was to get working class and trade union representation in Parliament, as a defensive response to attacks on the trade unions in the 1890s. The object of the LRC was not to transform society, but to

2 See my earlier attempt to do this: *Labour at the Crossroads*, Martin Robertson, Oxford, 1982.

defend the organized labour movement from an attack mounted by the employing class. The LRC was renamed the Labour Party in 1906. At that time it had no individual membership: it was simply a federation of affiliated bodies, mainly trade unions. The 1914–18 War brought about a major change in working class militancy and attitudes. As a consequence the Labour Party adopted individual membership in 1918, and adopted socialist aims for the first time. These were expressed in the famous Clause Four of the Party Constitution which remains, with very slight modification, to this day:

To secure for the workers by hand or by brain the full fruits of their industry and the most equitable distribution thereof that may be possible upon the basis of the common ownership of the means of production, distribution and exchange, and the best obtainable system of popular administration and control of each industry or service.

Another important statement published in 1918, entitled *Labour and the New Social Order*, further classified the socialist aims of the Party:

We of the Labour Party ... must ensure that what is presently to be built up is a new social order, based ... on a deliberately planned cooperation in production and distribution . . . not on enforced domination over subject nations, subject races, subject colonies, subject classes or subject sex, but in industry, as well as in government, on that equal freedom, that general consciousness of consent, and that widest participation in power which is characteristic of democracy.

1918 was really the birth of the Labour Party in its modern form. Whilst creating individual membership, affiliated membership was retained, and the 'block vote' formula was not removed, giving *both* forms of membership voting representation at its annual conference[3]. Whilst the individual members staffed the party machine, the trade unions held the majority of votes at conference, and thus could have the major say in determining policy. Thus Labour is very much a working class or trade union party. It was formed and moulded by the trade union movement, in contrast to many other countries where the trade unions were formed by the socialist or communist parties. The party has overwhelming support amongst the leaders and activists of the trade unions and this remains, despite the erosion of support for

3 See L. Minkin, 'Politics of the Block Vote', in *New Socialist*, No. 1, September–October 1981.

Socialist strategies

Labour at elections amongst the more passive trade union members[4]. Since the formation of the Labour Party, the trade union movement has turned to it as an instrument to win elections and obtain support in the legislature. The goals have often been limited and defensive, but the instrument of change still has deep roots in the working class movement. Attacks on the trade union movement by the Conservative Government in the 1980s inevitably renew a desire to re-elect a Labour Government which, above all other parties, would repeal the anti-trade union legislation again as it did in 1974. This link between working class organization and militancy and the consequent desire for a Labour administration is a fact of life of British politics[5].

Given the long stability of the British social and political system, however, renewed support for the labour movement is expressed primarily in electoral and parliamentarian terms. The Labour Party tends to function as the electoral machine for the trade union movement, thus spawning a number of Labour Members of Parliament which then function with a degree of autonomy. Social and political change is seen as the prerogative of Parliament, and not of the organized working class. The ingrained hierarchy of British society becomes reflected as a hierarchy of status and prerogative within the Labour Party itself. All eyes are focused on Parliament as the agent of social change.

In fact, however, the Labour Party annual conference is technically sovereign in determining the policy of the Party as a whole, not the Parliamentary Labour Party nor the (Shadow) Labour Cabinet. Critics of the Labour Party often forget this. Sometimes Labour Party and Labour government policies have been diametrically opposed. For example the 1968 Labour Party conference passed a resolution condemning the Labour Government's support for United States action in the Vietnam War. Yet Perry Anderson, for example, describes the record of the 'Labour Party . . . on Vietnam . . . [as] beneath contempt'[6]. More recently,

4 In the 1983 general election as few as 39 per cent of all voting trade unionists voted Labour, compared with 53 per cent in 1979 (*The Guardian*, 13 June 1983).
5 This is well argued in K. Coates, 'Socialists and the Labour Party', *Socialist Register 1973*; reprinted in K. Coates, *Beyond Wage Slavery*, Spokesman, Nottingham, 1977.
6 P. Anderson, *Arguments Within English Marxism*, New Left Books, London, 1980, p. 123. This statement marrs an otherwise excellent and stimulating book.

94

the Labour Party opposed the policies of pay restraint and public expenditure cuts under the 1974–79 Labour Government. By becoming a member of the Labour Party it is wrong to presume that one necessarily gives financial or moral support to the actions of any Labour government. In the past, especially in recent years, Labour governments have been criticized by Labour Party conferences for their actions when they violate official party policy.

This difference between the official policy decisions of the Labour Party conference, and the various stances of Labour governments and Labour Shadow Cabinets, has created periodic conflict within the Labour Party since its formation. This conflict results, in part, from the fact that the Labour Party is less elitist and stage-managed than the other main political parties, and dissident voices are given greater means of expression. Since 1973 the Campaign for Labour Party Democracy has been instrumental in reforming the structure of the Labour Party, helping to introduce mandatory reselection of MPs, and the election of the parliamentary leader and deputy by an electoral college[7]. There has, thus, been an attempt to bring the Parliamentary Labour Party more into line with the Labour Party outside parliament and the Labour Party conference.

The structure of the Labour Party ensures that the trade unions are decisive in informing and influencing policy. This happens formally through Labour Party conference and informally elsewhere. There are both vices and virtues in these arrangements. The main virtue is that the Labour Party keeps its roots in the organized working class. The main vice is that the Labour Party reproduces many of the defects of the trade unions and their leaderships. The narrow, defensive character of British trade unionism permeates the Labour Party, especially in its failure to promote a detailed and realistic vision of a future socialist society, despite the socialist resolutions of 1918 and thereafter. The routine of local and parliamentary elections, combined with the routinist and inflexible habits of much of the trade union movement, imposes and inertia on the Labour Party which is difficult to transcend.

In my view it is the 'trade union' structure of the Labour Party

7 See D. Kogan and M. Kogan, *The Battle for the Labour Party*, Fontana, Glasgow, 1982. For a detailed study of the structure of the Labour Party see L. Minkin's classic, *The Labour Party Conference*, Manchester University Press, Manchester, 1980.

Socialist strategies

and its ingrained electoralist routine which are the most important factors in explaining its character. This contradicts the majority of analyses of the Labour Party elsewhere. These analyses, from Right and Left, tend to concentrate on ideological factors to the exclusion of structures, institutions and routine. Thus, for example, Ralph Miliband saw the failure of the 1964–70 Labour Government to implement radical policies as being 'above all' due to their 'ideological dispositions' (failing to mention the decidedly less radical 'ideological dispositions' of the majority of the electorate at that time)[8]. Just as the Parliamentarian Right of the Labour Party places too much stress on the efficacy of ideas, argument and oratory in changing the world, the Far Left condemn the same party for harbouring 'reformist ideas'. Whilst incorrect ideologies and theories (including 'reformism') are indeed a political problem, it is wrong to place sole emphasis on these to the exclusion of the organizational structures and routines which enable such ideas to take hold. The character of the Labour Party is moulded not simply by its ideas but also by its structures, its practices, British institutions and over two centuries of history.

For example, the past influence of Fabian and gradualist ideas within the Labour Party has a great deal to do with the lack of rapid change in the British social and political system. The general over-emphasis on Parliament as the agency for social transformation stems in part from the uninterrupted supremacy of the British Parliament since 1688. The failure to promote a clear vision of the socialist future is related to the defensive (and often conservative with a small 'c') character of British trade unionism. The rise of technocratic and corporatist-style politics within the Labour Party since the Second World War (associated with the names of Hugh Gaitskell, Anthony Crosland and Harold Wilson) has a great deal to do with the growth of a caste of local and national government planners within the party as it gained many footholds in administration and government after 1940 and 1945[9]. It would be wrong to see all these ideological tendencies as 'things in themselves'. They are based in social reality.

Changing the Labour Party involves changing the character of British trade unionism, the practices of the party, and much

8 R. Miliband, *Parliamentary Socialism*, 2nd edn., Merlin Press, London, 1973, p. 360.
9 See P. Addison, *The Road to 1945*, Jonathan Cape, London, 1975.

else besides. The fact that considerable change is possible is illustrated in the next section, where the development of political and economic policy is considered. It is evident that change has come about not simply from the top, but also through changing relations and contradictions within the labour movement as a whole.

II THE DEVELOPMENT OF POLITICAL AND ECONOMIC STRATEGY

Before the Second World War there was little to commend either the Left or the Right of the Labour Party in terms of strategic sophistication in political and economic matters. The Right of the party, led from 1922 to 1931 by James Ramsay MacDonald, believed in a gradual and mechanical evolution from capitalism to socialism. Thus, in the crisis of the late 1920s and early 1930s they rejected Keynesian measures of economic intervention as doomed and misguided interferences with the 'laws' of the economic system. The Left reacted to MacDonald's betrayal of the party in 1931 not by embracing interventionist policies but by exclaiming the slogan 'Socialism Now!'. Neither Left nor Right had a realistic strategy to cure unemployment or to begin the socialist transformation[10].

The policies of the first post-war Labour Government (1945–51) involved the adoption of Keynesian methods and economic management to the ends of full employment and economic growth. Extensive state planning, however, was rejected. In addition, the Labour Government did little to promote industrial democracy in the basic industries it had nationalized, or elsewhere. Its approach was elitist rather than participatory, paternalistic rather than democratic. The rise of the 'revisionism' of Gaitskell and Crosland in the 1950s was an extension of the tradition of the preceding Labour government, with the significant modification that the verbal goal of traditional socialism was explicitly abandoned[11].

From 1945 to the election of the second post-war Labour Government in 1945, Labour maintained a high level of support throughout the population, even during the 13 years of Tory

10 See B. Pimlott, *Labour and the Left in the 1930s*, Cambridge University Press, Cambridge, 1977, for a modern account of the Labour Party politics of this period.
11 C. A. R. Crossland, *The Future of Socialism*, Jonathan Cape, London, 1956.

97

rule. Its lowest share of the vote was 43.8 per cent in 1959, compared with 47.8 per cent in 1945 and the highest figure of 48.8 per cent in 1951. This mass support was largely due to the shared experience of the Second World War, in which a collectivist and egalitarian ethos prevailed, and in which a section of the establishment was discredited by its previous policy of appeasement of the Nazi regime. Furthermore, the wartime coalition government of 1940–45 had made significant concessions to Labour Party policy by laying the foundations of the post-war welfare state. The strength of these collectivist ideas was illustrated in the resistance of the block votes of the trade unions in the Labour Party conferences of 1959 and 1960 to Gaitskell's attempt to amend Clause Four of the Constitution. He and Crosland proposed that the Labour Party should, instead, be committed to the 'mixed economy'. Despite the right-wing control of most of the large trade unions, the so-called 'revisionists' were outvoted.

The second post-war Labour Government was elected in 1964 with no clear manifesto commitment to radical change. It was simply entrusted, by the party and trade unions, with getting on with the job. Events in 1966–67 changed all that. Shortly after Labour's general election victory of 1966, the National Union of Seamen staged an important strike. The bitter and unsympathetic reaction of the Labour Government dented the confidence of many trade unionists that their parliamentary leaders supported the general aspirations of the trade union movement. This six-week strike was followed by a heavy run on the pound. The government reacted with traditional conservative measures – cutting public expenditure and imposing a wages freeze. The so-called National Plan (a diluted version of French 'indicative planning') was abandoned in 1966.

These events were decisive. On the economic front the long-term decline of British capitalism was dramatically accelerated. As Robert Bacon and Walter Eltis put it: 'In retrospect this was the decisive turning-point after which the structure of the United Kingdom economy deteriorated almost without interruption'[12]. The decline has not been interrupted since their book was published.

After 1966, automatic trust by the trade union movement in

12 R. Bacon and W. Eltis, *Britain's Economic Problem: Too Few Producers*, Macmillan, London, 1976, p. 51. Use of this quotation does not imply support for the Bacon–Eltis thesis.

the actions and policies of a Labour government was shattered. At the same time, there was an increase in trade union recruitment. From 1948 to 1966, the percentage of the employed workforce in trade unions declined from 49 to 44 per cent. It 1967 it increased, and by 1969 it had reached 46 per cent. In 1970 the figure was 50 per cent, and the recruiting momentum kept up during the 1970s. Also, strike activity increased after 1967. From 1964 to 1967 the number of working days lost annually through strikes was between two and three million. In 1968 it leapt to 4.7 million and in 1969 it was 6.8 million. The average annual figure for the 1970s was 10.8 million.

These developments helped the position of the Left within the trade unions. The Transport and General Workers' Union had began to move Left in the late 1950s. The Amalgamated Engineering Union elected a Left president in Hugh Scanlon in 1967. From that date the leaderships of several major unions moved to the Left. This process continued until 1975 when the Left of the Labour Party was defeated in the referendum on the European Economic Community. For nine years after 1966 the balance of forces within the Labour movement tilted gradually in the Left's favour.

At the same time, however, before the public was fully aware of the growing power of the Left, popular support for the Labour Government snapped. By June 1968, public opinion polls showed support for the government as low as 26 per cent[13]. This was then the lowest indicated support for the Labour Party for any time in the entire post-war period. Labour's electoral support was severely damaged well before the Left of the Party scored its major victories and moved into the public eye.

The international events of 1968, and to some extent 1969, also had a significant effect on the Labour Party. It is from this period that Tony Benn has traced his move to the Left[14]. The influence of organizations such as the Institute for Workers' Control began to be felt. Stuart Holland and others drew from the European experiments in planning and worker participation which had been given a great impetus after 1968[15]. The failure

13 The figure quoted is from Gallup Poll Ltd.
14 T. Benn, *Speeches*, Spokesman, Nottingham, 1974, p. 11.
15 See G. D. Garson, 'Recent Developments in Workers' Participation in Europe', in J. Vanek (ed.), *Self-Management*, Penguin, London, 1975; S. Holland, *The Socialist Challenge*, Quartet, London, 1975; M. Carnoy and D. Shearer, *Economic Democracy*, Sharpe, New York, 1980.

of Labour's paternalistic and exclusively parliamentarian approach in 1964–70, combined with the re-emergence of a more grassroots oriented politics in Europe as a whole, made an indelible mark on the thinking of a number of members of the Labour Left.

In 1969 Labour Prime Minister Harold Wilson attempted a counter-attack with the proposals to limit trade union action in the White Paper *In Place of Strife*. It met with the opposition of the TUC, the National Executive Committee of the Labour Party, and 53 Labour MPs. The proposal was dropped, and a loose alliance between the trade unions and the Labour Left was thus cemented.

At the 1970 Annual Labour Party Conference, for the first time since the 1930s, the Left gained a majority on the National Executive Committee. It set itself the task of developing a socialist economic strategy for the next Labour government. The Labour Party conference of 1973 carried proposals which have been regarded since as the basis of the 'Alternative Economic Strategy'. The key elements of this strategy are as follows[16].

(1) Extension of public ownership to at least 25 of the largest manufacturing firms.
(2) A strong and well-financed National Enterprise Board as an instrument of national planning.
(3) Provision for compulsory Planning Agreements to force firms to act in line with government policy and the wishes of workers within the firm.
(4) A general extension of industrial democracy, according to a formula to be worked our by the trade unions.
(5) Price controls, with accents on food and public transport, and rents restraint.
(6) An effective wealth tax.

The 1973 proposals did not include import controls (these were adopted at the 1976 Labour Party conference), nor an incomes policy (this was accepted in 1975 but rejected in 1978). None of the measures were put into full operation during the 1974–79 Labour Government, as they were opposed by the leadership of the Parliamentary Labour Party at the time.

However, *Labour's Programme 1973* is a landmark in the

16 *Labour's Programme 1973*, Labour Party, London, 1973.

development of socialist economic strategy. In it there is a clear recognition that Keynesian policies of demand management (whilst being superior to monetarism and *laissez-faire*) are no longer sufficient to ensure economic growth and maintain full employment. The record of post-war Labour administrations in terms of creating greater equality of wealth and power was also found wanting. The problem, the *Programme* makes clear, is compounded by the fact that the power of monopolies and multi-national firms has grown to unprecedented heights. In addition to adjustments to aggregate demand along Keynesian lines, the *Programme* proposed to 'act *directly* at the level of the giant firm itself'[17].

Hence *Labour's Programme 1973* is a true 'supply side' strategy which was developed before the new 'supply side economics' of the Right became fashionable. The latter is not really about the 'supply side' of the economy at all. It is more about tax-cuts and 'incentives', based on no clear evidence to presume their success[18]. The 'supply side' economics of the New Right is Conservative market economics in a new guise. In contrast, the ideas in Labour's programme present a real 'supply side' solution for low productivity and industrial inefficiency.

Another important feature of the 1973 strategy was its conscious emphasis on mobilization and democratic accountability. Implicit in the document is the idea that radical change cannot come from Parliament alone. In addition to an extension of industrial democracy the *Programme* proposes, for example, committees in the community to gather price information and monitor price rises.

After the election of the third post-war Labour Government, in February 1974, there was strong pressure from the Left in the trade unions and the party for a radical course of action. The Government had been elected on a wave of trade union militancy, including opposition to the previous Conservative Government's Industrial Relations Act and the miners' strike of 1974. The trade unions played an important extra-parliamentary role in bringing down the 1970–74 Conservative Government. Subsequently the trade unions played a greater political part in the 1974–79 Labour administration.

Whilst it is arguable that the political consciousness of the

17 *Ibid.* p. 13.
18 S. Weintraub, 'Keynesian demand Serendipity in Supply-Side Economics', *Journal of Post Keynesian Economics*, Winter 1982–82.

trade union movement advanced to some extent in the early 1970s, the trade unions did not, however, effectively defend the 1973 strategy of the Labour Party when it was under attack from the Labour Right in 1975. Wilson took the opportunity of the defeat of the Left in the 1975 referendum on the Common Market. He asked Benn to stand down as Secretary of State for Industry. Despite earlier gestures of support for Benn from key trade union leaders, the big battalions did not mobilize in his support: he was forced to resign. If the trade unions had acted in his defence things would have been different. However, the trade unions were not strongly committed to the radical elements in Labour's industrial and economic strategy. Since the election of the Labour Government in 1974 the hated Industrial Relations Act had been repealed, and there had been significant reforms in trade union and employment law. The trade union leaders did not wish to risk a confrontation with the government, and a return to Tory rule, thus endangering those reforms. The primarily defensive character of the British trade union movement was unchanged, despite the developments since 1966.

This defeat allowed Wilson to move quickly and impose an incomes policy for the first time under the 1974–79 government. Opposition to this policy was muted by the fact that it was of a relatively egalitarian nature: an increase of £6 per week for all employees. Unable to fight a concerted and effective battle against this policy, the Left was further isolated, particularly from a large section of the trade union base. The trade union movement which had played a significant part in the radicalization of the Labour Party no longer provided the muscle for further reform. As a result, Left politics were caught in a logjam lasting over three years. The defeat of June 1975 was critical. An immense opportunity for radical socialist change was lost.

After the defeat of the Left in 1975, and until the election of Thatcher in 1979, there is little but a wearying tale of a weak and right-wing social democratic government. It failed to tackle the underlying problems of the British economy and, in the end, in the 'winter of discontent' in 1978–79 was rebuffed by the very trade union movement to which it owed its existence. In the future it is likely that the government of 1974–79 will be remembered for its abandonment of both radical socialism and Keynesianism, and its introduction of monetarism. In 1976, for example, the government cut public expenditure at the behest of the International Monetary Fund. In a famous statement to the

1976 Labour Party conference, soon after he had replaced Wilson as Prime Minister, James Callaghan embraced monetarism and implicitly repudiated Keynesianism:

We used to think that you could spend your way out of a recession, and increase employment by cutting taxes and boosting government spending. I tell you in all candour that that option no longer exists, and that in so far as it ever did exist, it only worked on each occasion since the war by injecting a bigger dose of inflation into the economy, followed by a higher level of unemployment as the next step.[19]

This speech has been repeatedly and proudly quoted by Milton Friedman and other monetarists ever since. The acceptance of monctarism and public expenditure cuts by the Labour leadership contradicted the social democratic policies of the old Crosland wing of the party. Crosland realised this, caved in under the pressure, and died a few weeks after voting for the IMF cuts. Amongst those supporting cuts in public expenditure from within the Labour Cabinet were Shirley Williams, David Owen and Roy Jenkins – three future leaders of the breakaway Social Democratic Party. Ironically, the era of post-war Keynesian social democracy had, in fact, come to an end.

From 1975 to 1979 the Labour Government produced little legislation of radical importance. The only major exception was the Bullock Report of 1977 which proposed a scheme for greater industrial democracy. This was too radical and upsetting for many trade unionists, accustomed to narrow collective bargaining without responsibility[20]. In addition, the Confederation of British Industry mounted a hysterical campaign against the Report and the subsequent White Paper. The Labour Government rapidly retreated under fire from both the employers and several trade union leaders. The legislation was abandoned.

Meanwhile, many activists in the Labour Party were angered by the policies of their government. Radical economic policies had been rejected, public expenditure had been cut, unemployment had increased, and a restrictive incomes policy had been imposed from 1976. The Left began to campaign for changes in

19 *Report of the Seventyfifth Annual Conference of the Labour Party, Blackpool 1976*, Labour Party, London, p. 188.
20 For a defence of the Bullock Report and a critique of some trade union attitudes see P. Q. Hirst, 'On Struggle in the Enterprise', in M. Prior (ed.), *The Popular and the Political: Essays on Socialism in the 1980s*, Routledge and Kegan Paul, London, 1981.

the structure of the party. Led by the Campaign for Labour Party Democracy, and with support from a section of the trade union movement, mandatory reselection of MPs was almost carried at the 1978 Party conference. After the election defeat of 1979, the party membership continued moving to the Left, and mandatory reselection was carried at the 1979 party conference. In January 1981 an electoral college (consisting of 40 per cent of delegates from the trade unions, 30 per cent from the Parliamentary Labour Party, and 30 per cent from the individual membership in the constituencies) was set up to elect the leader and deputy leader. This was arguably the most important change in the party constitution since 1918.

Another result of the 1974–79 period was a further large increase in trade union recruitment. Although the level of strikes went down in 1975–78, trade union membership shot upwards continuously from 1973. In that year, the percentage of employed workers in trade unions was 50.5 per cent. It increased every year thereafter until it reached an unprecedented peak of 58.2 per cent in 1979[21].

The explanation must be along the following lines. The 1974–79 Labour government, having already strong institutional links with the trade unions, was born in a situation of pronounced class conflict, being nudged into power with the assistance of a miners' strike. The government, partly as a consequence, brought in strong pro-trade union legislation, such as the Employment Protection Act and the Health and Safety at Work Act. This legislation both legitimated and reinforced trade union organization. The irony of 1974–79 is that the Government largely contributed to the strength of the very movement which would help to lead to its own defeat: first by trade union refusal to accept rigid pay restraint in 1978, and second by the strikes of the subsequent winter. A government which lives by trade union power can also die by trade union power.

In short, the crisis of the British economy led to the abandonment of social democratic and Keynesian policies by the Labour Government. In turn, the problems of this government were compounded by the continuing adherence of the Labour Party conference and the Trades Union Congress to the Alternative Economic Strategy, and the growing strength and dissatisfaction

---

21 Department of Employment figures calculated as a percentage of all persons in employment excluding the armed forces and the self-employed.

of the trade unions themselves. In 1979, an era in Labour Party politics was ended: the Labour Party will never be quite the same again.

III FOUR YEARS FOR THE LOCUST

Monetarist policies had their supreme victory in Britain with the election of the Thatcher Government in May 1979. More zealous attempts were now made to cut public expenditure. The government set about reducing trade union power through restrictive legislation. One by one, pieces of the public sector were privatized. The consequences of these policies were disastrous[22]. Bankruptcies reached record levels. Unemployment rose by two million. Manufacturing output slumped by one-sixth. Productivity showed no substantial overall improvement even after the bottom of the recession had been reached. Britain entered a slump of proportions unprecedented since the 1930s.

Contrary to the expectations of many on the Far Left, however, there was no shift towards socialist ideas amongst the bulk of the British population[23]. Neither did the widespread riots in the cities in the summer of 1981 lead to anything approaching a revolution. The long-awaited 'crisis of capitalism' had come, but the socialist movement, both inside and outside the Labour Party, was at its weakest for decades in terms of popular support. The shift of public opinion to the Right which had progressed since 1975 was not reversed by the crisis. On the contrary, it moved on relentlessly, and not yet to its finale.

The Parliamentary Labour Party elected Michael Foot as leader of the Labour Party in November 1980 in a dramatic victory over Denis Healey. At the next Labour Party conference the electoral college came into force. The contest, for deputy

---

22 For a popular analysis of the record of the 1979–83 Thatcher Government see D. Keys (ed.), *Thatcher's Britain: A Guide to the Ruins*, Pluto Press, 1983. See also my 'Thatcherism: The Miracle That Never Happened', in E. J. Nell (ed.), *Free Market Conservatism*, George Allen and Unwin, London, (forthcoming).

23 Ted Grant, leader of the Militant Tendency within the Labour Party, was quoted in *New Society*, 10 January 1980, as saying that at the next general election 'Labour will sweep in. There will be a mass radicalisation. When the swing comes, the Tory Party will be absolutely shattered, and reduced to the commuter belt and rural areas.'

leader, was between Healey and Benn, with John Silkin as third runner. On the final ballot Benn won the support of 81 per cent of the delegate votes from the Constituency Labour Parties, 39 per cent of the trade union block vote, and 34 per cent of the Parliamentary Labour Party. Healey narrowly won the contest.

During 1981 support for the Labour Party slumped badly in the opinion polls. At the time the Conservative Party was low in public esteem, but the launch of the new Social Democratic Party in March 1981 began to dent Labour support (and, at the time, that for the Tories as well). Labour's allegiance fell to well below 40 per cent of electorate, according to public opinion polls, and it was not to recover from this depression for at least two years. This disastrous collapse in popular support occurred well before the Falklands War in the Spring of 1982. Things began to go badly wrong before Thatcher's imperialist adventure. What was the cause?

It has to be pointed out, first of all, that Labour support has always slumped badly during post-war periods of Conservative government. In the thirteen years of Tory rule from 1951 to 1964, Labour support as a percentage of the poll fell by 4.7 percentage points. In the period of the Tory Government from 1970–74, Labour support fell by 5.9 percentage points. It fell by 8.6 percentage points from 1979 to 1983. In contrast, Labour has tended to hold on to its support while in office. Labour support actually increased by 1.0 per cent from 1945 to 1951. It fell slightly by 1.1 per cent from 1964 to 1970, and by 0.2 per cent from February 1974 to 1979. Thus the slump in support from 1979 to 1983 is a more disastrous repetition of those in 1951–64 and 1970–74.

These facts have to be borne in mind when we search for an explanation of Labour's decline. Despite the manifest inadequacies of post-war Labour governments it is not their 'betrayal of socialism' that has led to their defeat. In all cases, Labour has been removed from office because of the temporary shift of the Liberal vote to the Conservatives. When in government, Labour's support has been much more resilient than when in opposition.

This, in turn, should not lead us to presume that Labour's generally poor showing when in opposition is primarily due to 'internal feuds' or poor tactics in the parliamentary arena. These problems have been apparent in times of government as well. I would suggest that the underlying process explaining Labour's decline when in opposition is the way in which the prevailing values and practices of our conservative culture[24] become legitimated, and Labour's more radical ideology is eroded by its absence at the level of government. When in office, Labour's approach and ideology is, to *some* extent, rendered legitimate and persuasive in popular culture. It is a feature of parliamentary democracy that the complexion of government has a recurrent influence in society as a whole.

Given this argument, and other things being equal, a fall in Labour's support from 1979–84 of roughly five percentage points would have not been unusual. However, the fall was much greater than that, and the circumstances were not equal to 1951–64 and 1970–74 periods. Under the Thatcher Government Britain experienced mass unemployment unprecedented since the 1930s, the greatest industrial decline since the early 1920s, and urban riots on a scale not seen on this island for over a century. In these circumstances, why did Labour fail so badly?

A number of possible factors were involved and it is impossible to compare their weight and importance. The strident and recriminatory style of the deputy leadership contest and its unsympathetic coverage in the popular press must explain much of the additional fall in popular support during 1981. The jingoism of the Falklands War in 1982 was a decisive factor. The mistakes and deficiencies of Michael Foot as leader (particularly the fiasco over Peter Tatchell and the bungled organizational attempt to expel *Militant* organizers) have also to be mentioned.

24 See E. Preston, *Labour in Crisis*, ILP, Leeds, 1982, for an important and persuasive statement of the necessity to recognize the prevalence of a conservative culture in Britain. This pamphlet is an important antidote to the politics of *Militant* and much of the Far Left inside and outside the Labour Party. However, what is lacking is any investigation of the social, historical and institutional basis of this conservative culture and, thereby, any explanation of the real changes in culture and ideology which have occurred. Consequently, the pamphlet lacks any realistic strategy as to how a radical counter-culture can be assembled other than to 'take the socialist message back to the working class'. This is important, but a conservative culture cannot be undermined simply by presenting an alternative set of ideas, however attractive and coherent those ideas may appear to be. Ideas have to be rooted in practical reality and present social institutions. For part of an explanation of Labour's secular decline since 1951 see J. Seabrook, *What Went Wrong?*, Gollancz, London, 1978. Seabrook's explanation has possible flaws, but it is an impressive attempt to root the decline in social practice and popular experience.

At the end, an uninspiring 1983 election campaign probably lost Labour a couple of percentage points at the polls. It would be wrong, however, to allocate blame on a personal basis, or seek further recriminations[25]. Labour lacked style, it lacked money, it lacked unity and it lacked vision.

It is important to point out that the biggest loss of the Labour vote in the 1979–83 period was to the Liberals and Social Democrats. The Alliance gained many more voters from the Labour Party than it did from the Conservatives[26]. This contrasts with the performance in many by-elections in the 1979–81 period[27]. The launch of the Social Democratic Party and the rise of the Alliance robbed Labour of much of its support but failed to displace the Tory Government.

This change in political support was in part an expression of the break-up of that loose combination of social groupings and classes which had sustained the Labour Party in the 1940s, 1950s and 1960s[28]. The fracturing of this combination in the period from 1979 to 1983 was dramatic. The party lost one-third of its 1979 support amongst the professional and managerial class, one-quarter of its 1979 support amongst the skilled manual workers, and one-fifth of its 1979 support amongst the unskilled and semi-skilled[29].

Another important trend, present since the 1950s but exacerbated in 1979–83, was the greater decline of the Labour vote in the South and East of England. Other than in London, Labour in 1983 held very few seats south of a line from the Severn Estuary to the Wash. Labour no longer has broad support, in either geographical or class terms. Allegiance to it is concentrated in the North and West of Britain, amongst sections of the manual working class and the unemployed. It can claim little else.

Given the scale of this rout it is deception and no solace to argue, as did Tony Benn, that Labour's support in 1983 represented over eight million votes for 'an openly socialist policy'

25 Note the unhelpful and Pavlovian response in *Tribune*, 10 June, 1983, where Labour's defeat was blamed on four 'guilty men' in the Labour Party.
26 See the analysis by I. Crewe in *The Guardian*, 13 June 1983.
27 See B. Pimlott, 'Alliance Takeover?', *New Socialist*, No. 3, January–February 1982.
28 See G. Stedman Jones, 'March into History?' *New Socialist*, No. 3, January–February 1982.
29 I. Crewe, *op cit.*

for 'the first time since 1945'[30]. It is true that Labour fought the election on a radical manifesto, probably *more* radical than 1945, but this does not mean that many people voted Labour for that reason. As Peter Kellner pointed out shortly afterwards, according to an extensive opinion poll held during the 1983 election campaign, only 53 per cent of *Labour supporters* wanted to take Britain out of the Common Market, only 54 per cent wanted to cancel the decision to buy the Trident missile system, only 48 per cent believed in borrowing money to finance economic expansion, and only 39 per cent wanted to reduce the power of the House of Lords[31]. This does not mean that a less radical manifesto would have won more votes. What it does indicate, however, is that less than half of those who voted Labour in 1983 were socialist by any minimal criterion. Labour's support in 1983 was largely residual and habitual, rather than the result of a renewed socialist crusade.

For any socialist there is little solace from the results of recent general elections. Labour's defeat and decline is associated with a general shift to the Right which has affected all socialist organizations. It has not created a space within which other Left groupings can prosper. The Communist Party, for example, did very badly in 1983 as it did in every general election in the recent past. Its vote per candidate fell to less than 1 per cent of the poll. The performances of the Revolutionary Communist Party and the Workers' Revolutionary Party were even worse. The Ecology Party put up over 100 candidates, but its best single poll was little over a thousand votes. The swing to the Right in British politics affects all socialist and radical parties: there is no comfort for those who would wish to see the rise of a new socialist party.

Indeed, contrary to the views of many socialists outside the party who have suggested that it is beyond the pale, the very radicalism of Labour's election manifesto in 1983, including unilateral nuclear disarmament, an expansionary economic strategy and the abolition of the House of Lords, suggests that the Labour Party *can* be converted to socialist policies. Even after the isolation and defeat of Tony Benn and his supporters on the National Executive Committee, and the subsequent expulsion of five leading supporters of *Militant*, the Party produced a manifesto which strongly reflected the Left-ward shift of the

30 *The Guardian*, 20 June 1983.
31 *New Statesman*, 24 June 1983.

conference since the 1970s. More than any preceding manifesto, the 1983 document was an assembly of Left policies adopted by successive Party conferences. It satisfied the aims of the Campaign for Labour Party Democracy far more generously than ever before.

In short, Labour's rout in June 1983 was a defeat for socialist politics and for all socialists. From whatever standpoint and perspective, the task of building a broad and effective socialist movement is more difficult than it has been for a long time.

IV THE PATH TO RENEWAL

The construction of socialism is not possible without the active support of the majority of the adult population. The mere reiteration of this truth alongside the scale of recent defeats show how far the Left has to go. In some ways the position of the Left in 1983 has similarity to that in 1931. Previous to both these elections, a section of the Labour Party had broken away in an attempt to constitute a centre force in British politics. Unemployment levels in the early 1980s are similar to those in the 1930s[32]. From its defeat of 1931 to the general election of 1935 the Labour Party managed to increase its share of the popular vote by 7.3 percentage points. However, it was unable to form a government on its own terms until 1945, when as a result of the radicalizing experience of the Second World War it was catapulted into power with a large majority in Parliament.

Labour cannot rely on the repeat of a similar radicalizing experience in the 1980s or 1990s. Another world war would result in the extermination of democracy and much, if not all, of mankind. There is another important difference between the 1930s and the 1980s. The Left was able to make gains before the Second World War partly because of the growing threat of fascism on the Continent. Mussolini came to power in Italy in 1922 and Hitler in Germany in 1933. Both dictators dismantled democratic institutions and broke up the trade unions and opposition parties. Thus, in Britain, the Left was seen as the principal antagonist of, and countervailing force to, insurgent fascism. Furthermore, whilst facts about Stalin's regime in the Soviet

32 See J. Tomlinson, 'Unemployment and Policy in the 1930s and the 1980s', *Three Banks Review*, September 1982.

Union were sparsely reported or believed in the West, the Soviet state was seen as the major international bulwark against the fascist advance. The Left could then form bonds with liberals and democrats, and there was fertile ground for the spread of socialist (and communist) ideas. The situation is very different today. The Soviet Bloc, rather than fascism, is widely regarded as the main threat to democracy. The post-war experience of state paternalism in the West has created suspicion and disquiet about the growth of the state. Socialism is increasingly identified with statism, bureaucracy, and constraints on individual choice and freedom. The standard of 'liberty' has been grasped by the Right. This, of course, is not the true picture, but what is perceived by perhaps the majority of the British population. Unlike the 1930s, the Left is no longer identified as the champion of democracy and freedom.

An important consequence of this state of affairs is that the intelligentsia is moving to the Right rather than the Left. In contrast, in the 1930s, a large number of influential intellectuals moved from being anti-fascists to proselytes of socialism. As it has been shown above, the move to the Right in British politics in the 1980s is more pronounced amongst the professional classes than it is even amongst the manual workers. The Left is losing the battle of ideas, at the same time as its support is being eroded in the working class.

Another reason why recovery for the Labour Party in the 1980s will be more difficult than it was in the 1930s is that the 1983 election places the SDP–Liberal Alliance as close rival for second place in British politics. In contrast, after 1931 Labour was clearly the second party, and any desire to remove the Conservatives from office was likely to be reflected in an increased vote for Labour. In the 1980s Labour will be in close competition with the Alliance for defecting Tory votes.

Given these facts, there is little doubt that the Left in Britain faces a long haul. There are no easy solutions or quick routes to success. The primary objective is to recapture mass support for socialist ideas. Given the relationship of forces between rival organizations on the British Left, there is no alternative focus other than the Labour Party at the present time. Labour's institutional and historical links with the trade union movement put it in a position which no other party can rival.

The politicians of the long haul could choose three words as their maxim: defence, democracy and definition. As the alliterative appeal exceeds immediate clarity, for the remainder of this essay I shall elaborate.

1. *Defence*. I refer not to Trident and Polaris but to the fact that the long struggle for renewal must employ a primarily defensive strategy for some time to come. But there are different sorts of defensive strategy[33]. Elsewhere in this chapter I have criticized the defensive attitudes of many trade unionists. This kind of defensiveness involves conserving things which have to be changed, such as outdated technology, trade union bureaucracy and lack of democracy, and the prerogatives of management in capitalist industry[34]. In contrast, a positive and radical defensive strategy involves a thoughtful selection of the ground that is most important to defend. This must be chosen with a view to providing a basis from which it may be possible to begin further advance in the future. There must also be an attempt to prioritize those issues of greater value and under ominous threat. Defence has to be strategically conceived, rather than a Pavlovian or semi-conscious reflex action.

The next few years of Thatcher Government will mean growing authoritarianism and intolerance in industry, government and society. Police powers will grow and many of our civil liberties will be eroded, as the Police Bill portends. The National Health Service is being deliberately undermined, despite claims to the contrary. Much of state education is under threat. The powers of democratic local government are to be further undermined or actually removed. There are dangerous proposals to limit the powers and rights of trade unions. The logic of these proposals is a 'free economy and strong state'[35] in which a well-armed, nuclear, state machine rules (with the assistance of authoritarian industrialists and chief constables) over a fragmented society and a collapsing market economy.

33 The more intelligent Far Left thinkers realize the importance of defensive formulations. See G. Munis and J. P. Cannon, *What Policy for Revolutionists – Marxism or Ultra-Leftism?* Merit, New York, 1969.
34 For an example of fruitful defensiveness from a Left position see A. Scargill's critique of workers' control in *A Debate on Workers' Control*, Institute for Workers' Control Pamphlet No. 64, Nottingham, 1978. Note also the response by A. Wise in the same publication.
35 For two valuable discussions of New Right thinking see A. Gamble, 'The Free Economy and the Strong State', *Socialist Register 1979*, Merlin Press, London; and C. Mouffe, 'Democracy and the New Right', *Politics and Power 4*, Routledge and Kegan Paul, London, 1981.

A fruitful strategy for defence should concentrate on attempting to obtain the *widest possible* support for the defence of the welfare state, state education, civil liberties, local government, and trade unions. It should highlight the underlying themes of the Right's attack as being general authoritarianism, individual selfishness, and a strong central state. By mobilizing around these issues it may be possible to win support for a democratic, decentralized and co-operative form of socialism in the future.

2. *Democracy*. The essence of socialism, as the Labour Party document *Labour and the New Social Order* made clear in 1918, is the widest possible democracy in the economy and society, as well as in the policy[36]. It means the widest possible democratic and co-operative control over our industry, our environment and our government. By accenting these issues in present and difficult times it becomes possible to change the terms of debate between Right and Left. At the moment, socialism is identified in the minds of the majority of the population as state bureaucracy, inefficient nationalization, and public housing landlordism. The terms of debate have to be changed so that socialism is seen more as being a wider democracy and positive and free involvement in decisions that affect people's lives.

It has to be shown in practice that the attacks from the New Right will not result in wider freedom, decentralization and autonomy as many of their advocates and supporters believe. Their logic is to undermine democracy, to centralize government and erode freedom. Realizing the force and consequence of these attacks should lead us to choose our weapons and tactics with care. The old artillery of corporatist social democracy, and the undemocratic cart-horse cavalry of much of the old trade union movement, should not, to say the least, be deployed as the main strength of our defence and future counter-attack.

To fight effectively on the ground of democracy means, at the same time, putting our own house in order. It is indefensible that every Labour Party member should not have a vote on crucial questions such as the selection of the Prospective Parliamentary Candidate or the election of the national party leader. It is indefensible that trade unions should not elect their leaders, or determine their party or other affiliations other than through the periodic vote of their membership. The fact that the Right makes

36 See my forthcoming book *The Democratic Economy* (Pelican, London, 1984).

these points does not mean that they are incorrect. Neither does the greater lack of democracy in the Tory Party or the industrial board room make its insufficiency in the labour movement any less serious, or give us an excuse why it should be ignored. Knee-jerk reactions to Right-wing policies will not do.

3. *Definition.* The New Right has a clear vision of the society it desires to create. It is an allegedly 'free' and 'self-reliant' society based on private ownership and the market. Despite the unfeasibility of this vision in practice, it has attracted many people[37]. It has meant that the Conservative Party now in the minds of voters seems to stand for a new future (despite Thatcher's policies being a return to the Victorian past) and the Left appears to stand for old and failed policies (despite it being the standard bearer for a future socialist society).

The failure of the Left to assert a clear and attractive alternative vision is its own fault. Where is there a book, pamphlet or article which clearly, and with contemporary relevance, explains to the uninitiated the features and workings of a socialist society of the future? There are very few such publications. Futhermore, when attempts are made to sketch a feasible form of socialism, many problems arise and a number of the formulas of the traditional Left are found wanting[38]. No movement will be able to capture widespread support for the radical transformation of society unless it has a clearly worked-out vision of where it is going. A feasible socialism has to be defined.

The future of the entire Left, not just the Labour Party, is tied up with these issues. For Labour to become the principal architect of a humane and democratic, future socialist society, it has now to provide a lead. Its failure, if it occurs, will not in all likelihood lead to the emergence of a more viable force of the Far Left, because, for them, defensive strategy, internal democracy, and socialist definition are also lacking. Their alternative strategy for the socialist transformation has failed as well[39]. The entire socialist movement is in crisis, and clear thinking and careful action are the order of the day.

37 See S. Hall, 'Whistling in the Void', *New Socialist*, No. 11, May–June 1983.
38 See A. Nove, *The Economics of Feasible Socialism*, George Allen and Unwin, London, 1983; S. Moore, *Marx on the Choice Between Socialism and Communism*, Harvard University Press, Cambridge Mass., 1980; and K. I. Vaughn, 'Economic Calculation Under Socialism: The Austrian Contribution', *Economic Inquiry*, October 1980.

FURTHER READING

T. Benn, *Arguments for Socialism* (Penguin, Harmondsworth, 1980).

T. Benn, *Arguments for Democracy* (Cape, London, 1981).

M. Carnoy and D. Shearer, *Economic Democracy* (Sharpe, New York, 1980).

D. Coates, *The Labour Party and the Struggle for Socialism*, (Cambridge University Press, Cambridge, 1975).

D. Coates, *Labour in Power?* (Longmans, Harlow, 1980).

K. Coates, *Beyond Wage Slavery* (Spokesman, Nottingham, 1977).

K. Coates (ed), *What Went Wrong?* (Spokesman, Nottingham, 1979).

F. Cripps *et al. Manifesto* Pan Books, London, 1981.

M. Hatfield, *The House the Left Built* (Gollancz, London, 1978).

G. Hodgson, *Socialism and Parliamentary Democracy* (Spokesman, Nottingham, 1977).

G. Hodgson, *Labour at the Crossroads* (Martin Robertson, Oxford, 1981).

S. Holland, *The Socialist Challenge* (Quartet, Nottingham, 1975).

D. Howell, *British Social Democracy* (Croom Helm, London, 1977).

R. Miliband, *Parliamentary Socialism* (Merlin Press, London, 1973).

L. Minkin, *The Labour Party Conference* (Manchester University Press, Manchester, 1980).

L. Panitch, *Social Democracy and Industrial Militancy* (Cambridge University Press, Cambridge, 1976).

M. Sloman, *Socialising Public Ownership* (Macmillan, London, 1978).

39 For a related debate on political strategy see D. Coates, 'Labourism and the Transition to Socialism', *New Left Review*, No. 129, September–October 1981; T. Ali and Q. Hoare, 'Socialists and the Crisis of Labourism', *New Left Review*, No. 132, March–April 1982; G. Hodgson, 'On the Political Economy of the Socialist Transformation', *New Left Review*, No. 133, May–June 1982; D. Coates, 'Space and Agency in the Transition to Socialism', *New Left Review*, No. 135, September–October 1982.

Chapter five

EUROCOMMUNISM AND *THE BRITISH ROAD TO SOCIALISM*

Sarah Benton

During the span of the twentieth century, and the lifetime of today's adults, communism has emerged as a force both majestic and monstrous. The majesty has lain in the boldness of its vision and the grandeur of its ambitions: nothing less than the holding of all property in common and the liberation of human effort from the corrupting constraints of scarcity. It has been a hymn of the poor as well as of poets and intellectuals; it has formed the boundary of the ambitions of the rich and powerful. But communism has also been a practice of governments and parties. Here the horror lies not so much in the failure of communist parties to provide the same measure of political freedom as does the Western world, as in the ugly rupture between the common vision of communism and the practice of communist parties. In other words, the policies of the Government of the Soviet Union would have caused socialists far less distress if it had not claimed to be building communism. It cannot be forgiven for having appropriated a universal inspiration.

Inevitably, as myth endures as a language of politics, communism has been the God and Devil and, for the more sophisticated, the God that Failed. In that belief, Richard Crossman reassured a generation that joining a communist party is essentially a religious conversion. Having garnered the second thoughts of his selected ex-communist intellectuals, he says of them:

They saw it at first from a long way off – just as their predecessors 130 years ago saw the French Revolution – as a vision of the Kingdom of God on Earth; and, like Wordsworth and Shelley, they dedicated their talents to working for its coming. They were not discouraged by the rebuffs of the professional revolutionaries or by the jeers of their opponents, until each discovered the gap between his own vision of God and the reality of the Communist State – and the conflict of conscience reached breaking point.[1]

Communists have always irritably rebutted such religious analogies just as they have rejected the post-Victorian orthodoxy which attributed political deviance to psychological flaws. Both attributions denied rational choice. Yet by the end of the 1970s, when the British Communist Party had split into three unstable and irreconcilable tendencies, Eurocommunists often reached for religious analogy to explain the 'psycho-politics' of the hard-line communist. Party tenets had become a dogma drawn from a bowdlerized rendering of Marx, Engels and Lenin. The Revolution was as real in imagination and as unlikely in reality as the Day of Judgment when the capitalists would be condemned for ever and the elect of true communists would inherit the earth on behalf of the meek. If the fatal flaw of the analogy was that it contained no God, then at least there were prophets who had been sanctified.

It can be argued that the ancient myths, human needs and aspirations that go to create religion must inevitably reappear in modern political form, and that communism would have better pleased the people had it, in recognizing this, had more to say about death, pain, loss, love, sex, joy. Even the great political moralities have been starved into threadbare polemic by many post-war parties, accompanied by a boom in fundamentalist religions in the West and Third World and traditional Christianities in Eastern Europe. For some people, the break between Eurocommunism and orthodox communism lay precisely in the hope that the former could fashion itself around ethical ideas. Thus:

It is possible to win people to communism on the basis of the ethical ideal, without having to lead them on to accept and even make a virtue of the necessities of hatred and dehumanization that accompany violent revolution – particularly in its historical form of Leninism.[2]

---

1 Richard Crossman, in the introduction to *The God that Failed*, which he edited (Harper and Row, London, 1950). Crossman's analogy with Wordsworth and Shelley seems rather perverse. Wordsworth was nineteen when the French Revolution broke out in 1789 and Shelley was not yet born. Both wrote of its failure to usher in a new world.
2 David Fernbach, "Eurocommunism and the ethical idea", in Mike Prior (ed), *The Popular and the Political*, Routledge and Kegan Paul, London, 1981.

For others, more pragmatic in their inspiration, Euro-communism was the first realistic attempt to understand what sort of power was exercised in a modern capitalist state and thus what sort of strategy socialists should have. Eurocommunism also became the banner behind which battles for independence from Moscow and the old guard of the past could be fought by more conventional party leaders.

Although the Communist Party of Great Britain (CPGB) is one of the communist parties in a capitalist country which have been described as Eurocommunist, its leaders have always rejected the label. This arises partly from their habitual conservatism, partly from their recognition that escaping the jaws of Moscow to find oneself in the mouth of Rome or Madrid would not seem much of an improvement. Instead they argued that the origins of the party's 1977 programme were to be found in the CPGB's own history, owing much to tradition and little to new and foreign ideas[3]. As a method of both appeasing the Stalinists and holding the Eurocommunists in check, it was not very successful; only the leadership of a party has any inherent interest in asserting it never changes. However, the studied neutrality of the British party leadership (who will never use the word 'Stalinist' either) also ensured that the last decade of British communist politics has never been able to free itself from the battle to win that central ground of the party. Thus the divisions within the CPGB which became entrenched in the latter half of the 1970s were the conflicts which both produced Britain's version of Eurocommunism and almost ensured it was stillborn.

Various individuals have come forward to claim they first used the word 'Eurocommunism'; the award seems to go to the Yugoslav journalist F. Barbieri who used it in an article in the Italian paper, *Il Giornale Nuove* in June 1975. It was intended to be an apolitical word because he could not decide whether the contemporary developments of Western communist parties were merely modern style or marked a fundamental break with the past. The new tone was especially noticeable in the communist parties of France, Spain and Italy – and Japan, the first party to replace the label Marxist–Leninist with 'scientific socialist.' In a succession of speeches, documents and official resolutions between 1975 and 1978, these communist parties asserted their right to determine their own 'path to socialism' which suggested

3 See, for instance, Gordon McLennan's introduction to *Reformism and Revolution* by John Gollan, Communist Party, London, 1978.

amongst other things, that criticism from the Communist Party of the Soviet Union (CPSU) of another party's domestic politics would not be welcome and that no communist party was obliged to focus its foreign policy on the defence of the Soviet Union. They asserted that they would, like any other political party, compete openly in the electoral market for popular support and would only exercise power, on the basis of a published programme, if elected to do so. They would, therefore, by working openly, co-operate with other organizations and movements with whom they had some common interest. The existing state institutions would not have to be destroyed instantly, for not only were those institutions to some extent a product of popular demands (like comprehensive 'free' education and health services); but the conflict within those institutions between serving capitalism and satisfying popular need laid them open to change from within.

As well as these statements about political practice (many of which were in operation anyway) the parties shared a new analytic ground. They agreed that because of the nature of the modern state and class structure, the bourgeoisie ruled as much by the consent of the people as through coercion; that the working class on its own, through the assertion of a narrow economic interest, could not take power from the bourgeois state; that revolution – still the desired goal – could not be a single act or seizure of power in capitalist countries but could only be a process of uneven change. All this amounted to a third way between administrative social democracy and insurrectionary violence[4].

Such published changes in direction were not really all that different. After all, the absolute domination of all communist parties by Moscow had lasted a relatively short time, from around 1929 when Stalin had defeated his major critics and the Comintern enunciated the doctrine of 'social fascism'[5] to the

4 There are now countless books defining the common ground of Eurocommunism. They include Santiago Carrillo, *Eurocommunism and the State*, Lawrence and Wishart, London, 1977; Fernando Claudin, *Eurocommunism and Socialism*, New Left Books, London, 1978; Richard Kindersley (ed), *In search of Eurocommunism* Macmillan, London, 1981; and Carl Boggs and David Plotke (eds), *The Politics of Eurocommunism* Macmillan, London, 1980.

5 Social democrats were labelled social fascists, and communists were instructed to regard them as enemies, not allies, until the seventh congress of the Comintern in 1935.

dissolution of the Comintern in 1943. Five years later, Yugoslavia had already defected and the USSR was building its 'empire' of East European States as a far more secure defence than the West's communist parties. The differences in the programmes of the European communist parties can often only be detected by code-breakers, adept in the communist terminology. What Eurocommunism did challenge, however, was a set of practices which had become entrenched under Stalinism, and which were based on the absolute defence of the Soviet Union in public and on a system of internal party control that was designed to perpetuate the power of the party leadership. Thus, Eurocommunism was not an attempted break with Bolshevism – which had died before Trotsky had as a model of party practice in Western Europe – but with a far more recent past of actually experienced Stalinist orthodoxy.

To Trotskyists, however, Eurocommunism was merely an evolution of Stalinism: it was not revolutionary for it took as its task the saving of capitalism from its self-inflicted wounds. Its governmental practice could only mean the elaboration of a labyrinthine bureaucracy. It was unnecessarily cowed by fear of provoking war because, in Ernest Mandel's words, it failed to take up the 'secret weapon' of the slogan *'For the Socialist United States of Europe! For a socialist development plan for Europe and the Third World!'*[6]. Its fatal flaw was 'its lack of understanding of the *structural character of bourgeois relations of domination*, which cannot be abolished gradually"[7]. As for social democrats, Eurocommunism was yet another devious ploy to fool people into voting for communists as normal people, a 'latter-day Trojan horse' which, once allowed into the secure environs of democracy's walled city would leap out to inflict 'dictatorship and totalitarianism' on the unsophisticated inhabitants[8]. Not only could no party sever so abruptly its lifeline to its own past, but one look at each party's internal structures would show that communists could not possibly find their way in so foreign a city as democracy.

The disbelief of outsiders, distressing to those communists who longed to come in from the cold and gratifying to those whose identity depended on being a threat, was not surprising. If

6 Ernest Mandel, *From Stalinism to Eurocommunism* New Left Books, London, 1978. (Italics are Mandel's.)
7 *Ibid.* (Italics are Mandel's.)
8 David Owen, *Human Rights* Jonathan Cape, London, 1978.

a Western communist party were ever to win an election there was no guarantee that it would abide by the unwritten rules of Western governments, even if it stuck to the constitutional ones. In the countries where Eurocommunist parties were serious contenders for governmental power, right-wing governments had been more or less continuously in control since the war. The popular pressure for radical changes in the duty and style of government was enormous, the machinery for containing the representatives of that popular pressure, not yet tested. In France, for instance, the government-controlled broadcasting services commanded far less popular support for those in Britain and no national newspaper commanded the mass readerships of Britain's popular dailies. The British state, with its obsessively secret inner core, seemed a model of public probity and flexibility compared with the corruption and inefficiency that seemed to paralyse the workings of the Italian state. In Spain, no democratic election had been held since the Popular Front victory of February 1936.

Thus, the communist parties in those countries were aware of how vulnerable their societies were to the 'crisis of capitalism' that had developed at the end of the 1960s. The brutality of the military overthrow of Chile's Marxist government in 1973 had crystallized the fears of communist parties about causing destabilization. Indeed, Giorgio Napolitano, a leading member of the Italian Communist Party (PCI), spoke of their fear that 'narrow' economic pressures from the working class could 'contribute to making the crisis more gangrenous, which can even lead to phenomena such as the disintegration and dissolution of society. This is a real danger'[9]. An analogous problem faced the British Labour Government of the 1970s, though its leaders were less articulate about it, and their response was far less political. They were seen as the captives of a labour movement driven by narrow economic interests: Eurocommunism would therefore be far worse. Because it was far more political and had a disciplined party structure, its leadership would not be accountable to the imperatives and rules of a capitalist state's inner circles. Because of its historic connections to Moscow, however strained now, communist parties could not be expected to accept the imperatives and assumptions of Western military alliances.

The scepticism of the non-Trotskyist Left about Euro-

9 The interview of Giorgio Napolitano by Eric Hobsbawn, *The Italian Road to Socialism* Journeyman Press, London, 1977.

communism similarly focused on these two distinguishing marks of communist parties, their internal organization and their allegiance to at least an international communist movement, if not to the CPSU's politbureau itself. While a number of English Marxists were giving a cautious welcome in the late 1970s to the upsurge of open discussion in communist parties and the sorts of progammatic ideas they were coming up with, they balked at the same hurdles. If communists were to be trusted as creative and honourable allies, they must jump right out of Moscow's pocket and cut any last connecting threads, must reform their own internal organization and must both acknowledge and reject openly what their own Stalinist heritage has been[10].

None of the communist parties had, by the mid-1970s, chosen to give itself a thorough overhaul. Only the leaders of the Spanish Communist Party talked openly of Stalinism – Manuel Azcarate, its international secretary, stated unselfconsciously for instance: 'We believe we are eliminating the remnants of Stalinism'[11]. Had it not been for the lead given by reputable intellectuals in the mass communist parties, it is likely that the CPGB would have carried on trudging down its British Road, staggering under the weight of the terrible old man of Stalinist loyalty. It would have become, at best, an irritating eccentricity of British political life.

But it was the brother parties, more independent and confident, which made the first parricidal thrusts at Soviet paternalism, and here lies one of the paradoxes of Eurocommunism. In defending a reformed communist strategy against the magnet of Soviet orthodoxy, each party had had to insist on the importance of choosing its unique national path. Yet the energy, and in some cases courage, for reform came in part from the common experience of all communist parties. They had all accepted Moscow's leadership, all sanctioned the so-called 'crimes against socialist democracy'. Now they all asserted the paramouncy of individual national conditions, and in so doing gave each other the ideas and a confidence to reform that could never have come from any national support alone.

10 See, for example, E. P. Thompson, *The Poverty of Theory* Merlin Press, London, 1978; and Ralph Miliband 'Constitutionalism and revolution: notes on Eurocommunism' in R. Miliband and J. Saville (eds), *The Socialist Register 1978* Merlin Press, London, 1978.
11 Manuel Azcarate in R. Kindersley, *op. cit.*

In 1951, the CPGB had produced its own national programme, the first British Road to Socialism. Invigorated by its growth during the war as a patriotic party, when an allegiance to the USSR enhanced its role, the party leadership was probably more anxious to prove its independence because General Secretary Harry Pollitt had been forced to resign when he would not accept the first Comintern line that the war was a reactionary clash between imperialist powers. (He was quietly rehabilitated after the USSR was forced into war in June 1941, turning the conflict into a decisive battle between fascism and communism.) From the first the CPGB both saw the British labour movement as unique and having the 'leading role' to play in ushering in socialism, and believed that this could only be done with the support of sympathetic interests outside the organized working class. It acknowledged the importance of parliamentary power but believed the capitalist state would have to be replaced by a socialist one. It saw the support for anti-colonial movements and ending of British imperial domination as crucial and was utterly orthodox on foreign policy and the moral and political superiority of the USSR.

The programme was both a genuine attempt to create a native working class challenge for power and a break with British syndicalism; it was a modest assertion of a communist party's right to decide for itself what its strategy should be and it used many of the phrases and ideas that were emerging with the 'building of the People's Democracies' in Eastern Europe. Now, over 30 years later, when the first question asked about the British Communist Party is 'Why was it so Stalinist and pro-Soviet?', several points are worth remembering. The first is that the CPGB had its own reasons for being dogmatic and sectarian – characteristics that are common to small, embattled parties convinced they must be the vanguard. Secondly, there was no coherent alternative source of ideas about political strategies and the Soviet Union. The Communist Party was the dominant influence on Left intellectuals, and whatever unease other socialists expressed, communist parties in most countries sustained their hegemony over socialist theoretical thought until 1956: 'An adolescent in a Glasgow slum worships . . . Al Capone. A *New Statesman* reader worships Stalin'[12], wrote George Orwell in 1944.

12 George Orwell, 'Raffles and Miss Blandish' reprinted in G. Orwell *Decline of the English Murder and Other Essays* Penguin, Harmondsworth, 1965.

Socialist strategies

The war time adulation of the Soviet Union as the ally which had saved the perfidious West passed without a breathing space into the Cold War. With that, a political Manicheanism, the absolute division of the world into good and evil, settled less like an iron curtain than an iron strait-jacket round the world. 'Yes, it is no longer possible to talk of "the world", wrote Willie Gallacher, transient Communist MP in 1949. 'Today it is necessary to talk of two worlds'[13]. For many even vaguely left-wing people, in the early 1950s, poverty, decay, war, race riots, television and chewing gum came from the USA and capitalism. From the USSR and socialism came peace, progress, the equality of women and the Bolshoi ballet. It was quite possible for communists both to say, with disingenuous honesty, that they did not know about the mass repression in the USSR and to recognize that they could not afford to know. The great denial induced a form of political schizophrenia in many communists. The images of politics had to be formed from a language and a set of principles that became increasingly separate from those used by 'ordinary' people. The images had to become an impregnable fortress against any 'common sense' criteria used to judge what was right or wrong, real or unreal. If the facts of popular discontent of Eastern Europe could not be disputed, the causes had to be found in the machinations of counter-revolutionary agents. This corruption of language so that it could no longer express what communists saw and heard around them, was international. In the small parties it was as much the need to conceal from party cadres how limited, if worthwhile, their efforts must be, that created some of the worst euphemisms – rather than merely any mechanically adopted duty to echo an international language. (The humble coffee morning with non-communists becomes the cadre's 'mass work' in Jessica Mitford's merciless satire on US communist jargon)[14]. A journalist in Poland, describing the summer strikes of 1980, noted:

Along the length of the coast, yet another battle was being fought out – about the purity and clarity of our Polish tongue, about restoring to words their precise and explicit meaning, about washing out the

13 William Gallagher, *The Case for Communism*, Penguin, Harmondsworth, 1949.
14 Jessica Mitford, *A Fine Old Conflict*, Michael Joseph, London, 1977.

platitudes and drivel that sully it, about freeing it from the corrupting effects of constant insinuation.[15]

Such a divorce between beliefs and critical faculties has seemed almost mad to later commentators. 'No lie about the United States was too grotesque, no flattery of the Soviet Union too sickening for the infinite credulity of the French communist' wrote Neil McInnes, of the PCF in the 1950s[16]. But although the Manicheanism appeared to be a product of the Cold War, the Cold War itself was necessary to sustain the Manicheanism. That is, the creation of the 'other world' which could not be judged by faculties impaired by bourgeois notions became indispensible to most party leaderships. It was their greatest protection against members testing their efforts and party pronouncements against a wider political reality. In other words, communist leaders had their own reasons for sustaining Willie Gallacher's two worlds.

Kruschev's secret speech to the Twentieth Congress of the CPSU in 1956 was, therefore, shattering. He revealed that the substance of many of the rumours and 'capitalist' accusations was true: that under Stalin one of the greatest processes of mass repression in history had taken place. Hundreds of thousands of people had died, millions were sent to labour camps. He did not give any figures, and to this day the CPSU has issued none. But the fact of the mass repression – and the years of categorical official denial – were enough. Representatives of the CPGB were not invited to the secret session and were never officially shown a copy of the speech. The speech has still not been published in the USSR. Kruschev made his speech in February. At the CPGB's national congress in April delegates passed a resolution deploring the failure of the Central Committee of the CPSU to make any public statement about it. In June, still no statement forthcoming, the political committee of the CPGB published its own statement, saying:

All Communists, in common with all democratic and progressive people, are deeply shocked by the injustices and crimes which, during

15 Ryszard Kapuscinski in *Kultura* 14.9.1980, translated in *Comment* 25.10.1980.
16 Neil McInnes, 'From Comintern to Polycentrism' in Paolo Fileo Della Torre *et al.* (eds) *Eurocommunism, myth of realitty* Penguin, Harmondsworth, 1979.

the period under review, violated the essential principles of socialist democracy and legality and dishonoured the noble cause of Communism.[17]

The immediate effect of Kruschev's speech was not liberating for other communists. (It was said that Harry Pollitt never recovered from the shock which caused his premature death three years later.) It did not offer an analysis of how Stalinism had developed, nor a strategy for transforming the Soviet state that had evolved with it. It did, however, offer the first bridge between a humanist politics and a Stalinist corruption of politics.

In less than nine months, that unreformed state had sanctioned the invasion of Hungary and the forcible suppression of the rebellion against Communist Party rule there. The door that had been opened for Marxist intellectuals to start enquiring into what a democratic socialist state might be was peremptorily and brutally slammed shut again. Over a third of all Communist Party members in Britain left the party during the following year. The CPGB did not regain its hegemony amongst Marxist intellectuals, nor did it exercise a clear influence amongst them for another 20 years.

The traumatic events of 1956 brought an epoch of European communism to an end. In Britain, the Marxist intellectuals who could now liberate socialist thinking were dispersed. Some tasted the forbidden fruit of Trotskyism but it remained disappointingly small and dry. Some became work-place socialists, whether in universities or factories, too isolated to offer any effective challenge to the mainstream thought of the labour movement or Labour Party. Quite a few stayed in the Communist Party but, lacking in confidence and purpose, could not form a coherent alternative to the party leadership. Some, including E. P. Thompson, took the journal *The Reasoner* they had produced within the Communist Party and turned it into the *New Reasoner*. The journal became *New Left Review* under their management in 1960 and then, in 1962, *New Left Review*, (NLR) under new management which has broadly retained control of the journal to this day.

17 *In L'URSS et Nous*, Editions Sociales, 1978; French communists A. Adler, F. Cohen, M. Decaillot, C. Frioux and L. Robell estimated that ten million people had died as a direct result of the repression and that one-fifth of all CPSU members were arrested. An extract from this book and CPGB statements were published in *Comment* 25.11.1978.

From this group came a distinctive interpretation of the fraility of socialism in Britain and a consequent cultivation of the proper Marxist intellectuals on the other side of the channel. England's bourgeoisie had never had to revolt, but rather had deferentially wormed their way into power. One consequence was that its intellectuals had never had to embrace theory and another, argues Tom Nairn in one essay, was that the Labour Party had become accepted as a permanent and inevitable feature of bourgeois society:

a kind of monument about which it was pointless, if not impious to ask too searching questions. Something of the mindless complacency of British bourgeois society was in this way transmitted to British socialism.[18]

The ex-communist historians salvaged English socialist traditions more tenderly, perhaps better prepared to cherish a native politics because of the distorted internationalism of a world communist movement perhaps because of those years in a party with a working class amongst whom patriotism has been inextricable from class culture. The impatient new young editors of NLR had little time for this root-finding because, as one of them said later:

For us, the central historical fact which such enterprises always seemed designed to burke or minimize was the failure of British society to generate any mass socialist movement or significant revolutionary party in the 20th century – alone among major nations in Europe.[19]

Being despised is no invitation to take part in a debate, and the empirical, labourist, economist, philistine leaders of the British working class stayed out of it. Without the discipline of such a debate, and indeed finding little of theoretical interest in the society in which they lived, much of the content of NLR passed far over the heads of that very 'stratum' of society who provide the day-to-day political leadership – the Labour Party and communist activists, the thinking trade unionists and state employees. Nor did they take up what 1956 had made epochal – the character of Stalinism, and popular support for communism.

18 Tom Nairn, 'The nature of the Labour Party' in P. Anderson and R. Blackburn, (eds) *Towards Socialism* New Left Review, London, 1965.
19 Perry Anderson, *Arguments within English Marxism*, New Left Books, London, 1980.

In these silences, some of which have been described by Donald Sassoon[20], the Croslands and Crossmans were left free to develop their notions that communism can only appeal to religious bigots and socialism can be forked down the power structure of Britain with a firm but gentle, bureaucratic hand. The Communist Party was left free to organize its struggles to gain higher wages, lower rents, lasting peace, trade union positions and more party cadres. Nobody, apart from the still tiny group of Trotskyists and remaining dissidents in the CPGB, had any interest in sinking its teeth into Stalin's corpse to make sure it was really dead or to find out how it had grown to such larger-than-life proportions in the first place.

Thus it was that the next shock which propelled the CPGB into a period of change again came from Eastern Europe. The Prague Spring, the Action Programme for reformed socialism launched by the Czechoslovak Communist Party, did indeed appear to presage a new era of communism after the frozen, if unavoidable, winter of Stalinism. It was officially and apprehensively welcomed by the CPGB, some of whose members were sceptical about what Dubcek had the power to change, others of whom saw the all-powerful hand of bourgeois decadence in any talk about freedom or human faces. It is a measure of how much the CPGB still felt its own political options were pinioned in the Soviet bloc that the Prague Spring should have brought this apprehensive relief. When Russian tanks rumbled into Prague the following August, such crude violation of another country's freedom was, at the least, unforgivable. The CPGB Political Committee condemned the 'intervention – the strongest words they would allow themselves – more clearly and sharply than many communist parties. A sizeable proportion of the membership rebelled.

Some of the leadership never got over their terror that their decision to condemn publicly an action by the Soviet Union might have been overturned by the members – a loss of authority for which they had no precedent. Many of the members never got over their rage that their milksop leaders, made flaccid by their diet of western liberalism, should have betrayed the cause of 'international proletarian solidarity', the guardian of true socialism against all corrupters of the faith. If political

20 Donald Sassoon, 'The silences of New Left Review' in *Politics and Power 3* Routledge and Kegan Paul, London, 1981.

tendencies begin at one time, this was the moment when the CPGB began its inexorable drift into three factions: the hard-liners (known as Stalinists or tankies because of their support for the use of tanks to suppress opposition); the centrists, which usually comprised the leadership and all loyalists; and the reformers, regarded as the right wing by the hardliners and as Eurocommunists by the mid-1970s.

Sandwiched between these two events in Czechoslovakia was one whose impact was more diffuse: the May–June uprising in France, initially of students in Paris and later supported by mass strikes and demonstrations. It was almost the first time in the West that young, white, middle class people were seen being assaulted in the streets by paramilitary police. The brutality of the state was shocking, unexpected and not understood. If this was the Revolution, it was all wrong – but apart from de Gaulle, not many thought it was. Certainly the French Communist Party did not. Their absence as radical leaders at the moment of crisis became for a generation of students the decisive absence of communist policies. More, it was the decisive conservatism and caution of a bureaucratic party that lacked the vigour and creativ-ity to spark off its own challenge to the establishment but was too 'vanguardist' to support anyone else's. Unlike the impact of the Chilean coup in September 1973, the Paris uprising created amongst the young Left no fear that pushing the state into crisis could cause a harsh and punitive repression.

The 'era' of 1968 lasted ten years, from the onset of deepening economic and social crisis which could still be managed without jeopardizing social democracy, to the point when it could no longer. In this time the state expanded enormously in its func-tions, its overall role, and through all the many employees needed to carry out those functions. Many of the familiar mechanisms for regulating social relations were disappearing or falling into disarray. Capitalists were fleeing from the manufacturing employer/employee relationship in Britain, find-ing it too unprofitable and unmanageable within the restrictions it carried in comparison with banking, insurance, property, oil shares or Korean assembly lines. Traditional divisions of labour, one of the chief determinants of the economic order, were being eroded. The working class comprised more women in offices than men who had served an industrial apprenticeship. Swathes of the economy depended on employing people who hardly earned a 'living wage' – immigrants and black people, women in part-time jobs, farm labourers and tourist 'servants' in the depressed rural areas. In the inner cities, many of these underpaid, unorganized or unemployed people were forming an underclass – invisible and with no political voice. At the same time, the pressure from those who were organized for higher wages seemed impossible to contain. It was the age of inflation and, in lieu of anything else, of a mass consumer democracy. It was also a decade in which no group of politicians were able to provide any political leadership. No single section of any class seemed hegemonic in the sense that it could express its interests as universally beneficial, around which society could be organized accordingly.

Into the fissures flowed the state, propping up lame ducks, paying benefits to the needy, providing a new stratum of professional social managers from a hugely expanded sector of state higher education, and 'health care' for those who could not cope any longer. It was an expansion both of ad hoc measures to deal with impending crisis and of conflicts within the state. For example, more and more people had to look to the state to provide the aid and money that private organizations like the family or trade union could not offer. Each new need had to be met with a special sort of benefit – Family Income Supplement, rent rebate, rate rebate, home improvement grant, to add to maternity benefit, widow's benefit, means-tested student grant, invalid allowance, disability benefit, mobility allowance, old age pension, child benefit, unemployment benefit, supplementary benefit. Simpler by far to have streamlined the whole thing to ensure that no-one's income fell below a certain level or that no-one was penalized through physical disability. But this would have been revolutionary, for it would have declared social equality to be the guiding principle of the state. Thus, sorting out the complex of conflicting demands was in itself a major source of new jobs within the state.

Orthodox class war between the private manufacturing employer and organized labour only sporadically surfaced in the 1970s. There was nothing to resemble, for instance, the great 1922 engineering lock-out over the 'managerial functions' of private engineering employers, or the resounding clashes between miners and the great landowning interests. In every dispute of significance the state was implicated, whether as paymaster (miners and health workers) or law maker (abortion and race relations) or mediator (Grunwick). The large manufacturers appeared prepared to abandon the field and the rebellion finally came from those whom state aid did not benefit and whose social authority and status were most undermined by it. Belligerent small business owners, the self-employed, the one-time craft workers of Birmingham and Bedford, found in the Conservative Party, under its new leadership, the petty bourgeois moral lead they were looking for. It was in the truest sense reactionary, a vindictive rejection of the social change the decade had brought, a desire for an earlier world in which no state, or trade unions, could deprive them of the limited powers which commercial wheeling and dealing could give them. Their election of a Conservative government in 1979 mercilessly exposed the political panic and loss of ideas of the Labour Party leaders.

Eurocommunism as a trend in Britain had grown in this short-lived era between 1968 and 1979. Internally, it was a reaction against Stalinism and Moscow's domination, the product of power struggles within communist parties; externally an attempt to understand, take part in and ultimately direct the popular response to the crisis in state capitalism. Those characteristics were common to all the Eurocommunist parties, though none had been faced by reaction on the scale of British politics where the political flaccidity of social democratic parties, the absence of any clear class political hegemony, and the staving off of social crisis through state managerial and financial intervention was most acute. In Britain in particular, with its tradition of mass movements, Eurocommunism drew its inspiration from feminism, from anti-racism and student policies, from those trade union actions which challenged divisions of labour or held out the vision of self-management. Its fundamental flaw in Britain was that as a strategy for change it depended on a mass involvement in political action, with disparate campaigns and organizations made into a coherent opposition by the Communist Party. Yet Communist Party membership continued to decline throughout the period and, perhaps more importantly, its propaganda organ, the *Morning Star* had moved from selling several copies for every member in the 1950s to less than one copy for every member by 1979.

This was not the problem in the heartlands of Eurocommunism – whose differences from each other became increasingly marked in the 1980s. But despite all the emphasis on unique national roads to socialism, what was common to all the parties seemed more important than what differentiated them (the rejection of the leading role of the CPSU and the embracing of many of the political practices of 'bourgeois democracy'.) Significantly, the crucial few years of change in Britain, 1975–9, were officially ushered in by a lengthy article on Socialist Democracy by ex-General Secretary John Gollan, published in *Marxism Today* in January 1976. The heart of the article was an attack on the denial of law and democracy in the Soviet Union under Stalin, and it argued that socialism and democracy within the rule of law must be indivisible. It was significant that this should be the first major piece of work that John Gollan chose to write in his retirement, and that he was unable to initiate the discussion while still general secretary. Besides this, an analysis of what exactly were the national conditions of Britain seemed far less important. (Significantly too the succeeding general secretary saw the article as having settled the party's account with Stalinism.) It also gave early warning of how the sides would be drawn in the next year's contest over the British Road to Socialism (BRS), the CPGB's programme that was due for revision in 1977. For these crucial few years, the leadership allowed the Eurocommunists to set the pace and allied with them, to prevent a successful Stalinist reaction.

The decision to revise the CPGB programme had been made by the 1975 Congress – the sovereign meeting of delegates held every two years. New versions of the BRS had been approved by the Congresses of 1957 and 1967. A commission of eight members plus John Gollan as secretary was appointed. Of the eight, three were clearly within the Eurocommunist camp, and a further three were 'reforming' full-timers. They produced their draft early in 1977 and public discussion on it began in March – the most prolonged period of official policy debate in the party's history. Episodes from the discussion – branch meetings, Commission deliberations, Congress debates – were filmed by the Roger Graef/Charles Stewart team for the Granada TV 'Decision' series. The readiness of the party leadership to let some of its most private discussions be televized appeared to be irrefutable evidence of their commitment to open political debate. The televizing of the discussion seemed to bestow on the party's decision-making processes the qualities of modernity, popularity and national importance which belonged to the medium of television.

At the beginning, the reformers were poised to argue against

the new draft as a whole. Too many of the new streams of
thought, such as feminism or the critique of narrow trade union
consciousness, received only a formal acknowledgement in the
draft. But it soon became clear that the most vehement opposition was being nurtured by the other camp. On 30 April
Comment, the party's fortnightly journal and main discussion
forum, published a letter from the Surrey District Committee
calling for the rejection of the new draft. More and more known
hard-liners followed their lead. Ironically, many of the objections made by Stalinists could have been voiced by their bitter
foes, the Trotskyists. The draft, said Surrey District Committee,
'panders to liberal prejudices' to such an extent that it could only
turn the Communist Party into 'a left social democratic party
with a left social democratic programme.' It was 'too short on
coercion and too free with liberalism.' On paper at least the
Surrey road to socialism was very straightfoward: the working
class, through its vanguard the Communist Party, would, when a
revolutionary situation was created by the 'interplay of deepening capitalist economic and political crisis', 'take state power
unto itself to crush the resistance of the displaced exploiters'. It
would *then* 'win to its side the majority of the people for the
creative task of building a socialist Britain' during which it
would be naive to guarantee the right of 'parties hostile to
socialism' to operate freely. Nor could trade unions be independent from the state because they are 'key mass organizations
which help the working class to operate state power'[21]. In fact,
despite the echo of some of the phrases, the Surrey position
shared only a sectarian style with the Trotskyist tradition, but
owed a great deal to the example of the People's Democracies of
the East.

An alternative programme was produced by hardliner Charlie
Doyle, husband of the *Morning Star* women's page editor Mikki
Doyle, and for this he was censored. (By rule, all discussion had
to take place within the fortnightly journal *Comment* or the
Morning Star, maximum 900 words.) It became clear that the
reformers were going to form an alliance with the leadership to
push the programme through. Rumours of secret meetings and
plots against hardliners began to dart around the party. In July, a
section of the party, led by Surrey District Committee Secretary
Sid French, broke away to form the New Communist Party. At

21 *Comment* 30.4.1977.

first, this seemed as though it might be the great split, threatened since 1968. In the end it was estimated that less than 1000 members joined the NCP out of a party of over 25000. More reassuringly for the leadership, they were concentrated in the smaller, non-industrial districts where the labour movement could remain a sort of ectoplasm conjured up, for lack of any manifestation of the real thing, with such incantations as 'vanguard role', 'dictatorship of the proletariat' and 'overthrow of capitalism.' The smallness of the split meant that many more hardliners stayed in the party than left, but many were left in a state of sullen resistance rather than active combat.

The split was surrounded by some of the most successful events organized by the CPGB during the 1970s, and each of them was a product of the new thinking. At Easter 1977 a Communist University of Feminism was organized at Bristol University. It attracted more people than the organisers had hoped for, many of them outside the Communist Party, and stated that communism and feminism could form a fruitful alliance. In June, a People's Jubilee was held at Alexandra Palace in North London. It was a lively alternative to the Queen's Jubilee, then in full spate, and was the first public expression of the belief in forming an 'alternative culture'. It teased out of the mass support for the Queen a popular enthusiasm for creative, community celebrations and allowed the Left to feel something other than a stern and isolated disapproval at the people's misguided pleasures. The organizers hoped for an attendance of 8,000. Over 11,000 turned up, once again thrusting the Communist Party into the mainline news. In the summer, the annual Communist University of London attracted its peak full-time attendance (gleaning what turned out to be the end of the generation of radical students), its courses and speakers heavily weighted in favour of Eurocommunist interests. All these successes appeared as a testament to the vigour of a reformed communism and the proper role of a communist party. The party would set things up, but the activities would be non-sectarian, would suggest how life could be changed for the better now, and would be celebratory and creative. The activities would thus make sense to ordinary people who would not feel they had to enter a strange sect with its own secret rites, setting them apart from the rest of society, to be a communist. The success of these events, especially the People's Jubilee, was of considerable importance for the conflict over the draft of the British Road to Socialism. The sight of the Communist Party taking popular, and news-catching initiatives probably convinced more of the uncertain members that the reformers were on the right lines than many a bitter argument over whether, after the revolution, there would a dictatorship of the proletariat or a multiplicity of political parties. In place of the split persona of the 1950s, today's communist could allow her interest in television or reggae or sex to elide with her commitment to changing the world. That, anyway, was the hope, and it had a liberating effect. Whether or not a small party can push through radical changes in inauspicious times as well as in optimistic ones without a puritanical single-mindedness, is a different matter.

This was the mood of many communists leading up to the 1977 Congress. This was the argument of the programme they discussed from 12–15 November:

- Britain is in a deep economic, political and social crisis due to the crisis of capitalism;
- reforms won by democratic struggle after the Second World War are being lost;
- as evidence of this we see the special oppression of women and blacks as well as the attacks on trade unions;
- the environment is being damaged, culture is commercialized, human relationships are distorted;
- the government has reacted by increased authoritarianism;
- the answer is far-reaching democratic change leading to the replacement of capitalism by socialism.

After a section describing the 'contradictions' of capitalism' the programme then introduced the first new idea: that the power of the ruling class 'relies primarily on the fact that millions of people believe that the capitalist system is the natural way to organize society'[22]. Rises in the standard of living are visible – and attributed to the virtues of the system. The leaders of the Labour Party have always failed to challenge the system and thus the growth in trade union organization has 'not been matched by a growth in social consciousness'.

This section of the programme was one of the most controversial. For the hardliners it was acceptable to blame right-wing

22 All further quotations are from the *British Road to Socialism*, Communist Party, London, 1978, unless otherwise stated.

Labour leaders – but to suggest that there was any measure of voluntary consent to, or approval of, 'the system' by 'ordinary people' was a lily-livered get-out. Capitalism first brainwashed, then forced people into obedience. They lost their argument, though perhaps if they had looked further into, for instance, repression in Northern Ireland, black people's relationship with the state or those actual areas of murky capitalist intrigue they might have got further. But the hardliners relied on dogma, not analysis.

From the other side, feminists would have liked the family and sexism identified more explicitly as forces for social control. But the programme, being the product of compromise, settled with rejecting the notion that there is a monolithic ruling class which rules only through conspiracy and coercion. Rather, it said, the ruling class and its allies 'relies mainly on achieving a social consensus and class collaboration through its ideological control and influence, its allies and the effect of right-wing ideas in the labour movement'. The State appears in this section as a conglomerate of institutions, mainly of the coercive sort, and it is an odd thing in a programme which was seen as embodying some of the key ideas of the Italian communist, Antonio Gramsci, that throughout the programme little was said to clarify the form and function of the State during this particular crisis of the British economy. This is particularly so as the notion of capitalist rule in the programme is a derivative of Gramsci's notion of hegemony – meaning, roughly, the particular form of order at any time which directs the activities and ideas of society. His notion of hegemony is inseparable from a notion of the form and functions of the state.

Because of the suggestion in the programme that capitalist 'hegemony' (though it does not use that word) was largely an *ideological* power, it therefore followed that the working class had to 'overcome capitalist ideas and build alliances also in the fields of politics, ideology and culture.' The pursuit of economic aims, though necessary, could not constitute the wider challenge for power that would initiate changes towards socialism. The criticism, of narrow economic demands was not a new idea in the Communist Party. Ever since its final break with syndicalism during the Second World War and the influence of setting up the People's Democracies afterwards, the Communist Party had always seen the state, and not the point of production, as the crucial repository of political power. From the 1950s, however, communist influence in the labour movement had become increasingly synonymous with holding office in trade unions. It had also become dependent on the tacit tolerance of the top officials in many of the left-wing unions. Communists were, after all, hard working officers, reliable at carrying out many of the boring and necessary jobs of union organization. Electorally, they could be useful supporters, as long as one knew when to shut the door on them.

In return for their acceptance within the union movement, communists did not challenge the status quo within that movement too vigorously. The reliance on 'winning positions' within the existing structure meant communists did not lead any moves for the reform of the structure. Thus it was often the Right who first voiced criticisms of union democracy or anachronistic union machinery, the communists who regarded new trade union forms, like combine committees, with suspicion. In addition, the profound hostility during the 1960s and early 1970s between communists and the quasi-syndicalism of Trotskyist groups meant few unions had a united Left movement on anything, let alone union reform.

At the 1977 Congress, the division between Eurocommunists and more orthodox communists on trade union policy was debated in an amendment of 'economism' – the focus on economic demands to the exclusion of more far-reaching political challenges. The Eurocommunists lost this argument, in part because they were divided amongst themselves, in part because the party's Industrial Department felt its role, strategy and integrity were being impugned. The development of the Industrial Department as the party's leading, and most self-sufficient regiment, had made it peculiarly resistant to change. The conflict had been pushed to a head by a number of the party's economists and feminists. It had begun with a material disagreement over the government's social contract and incomes policy of 1976. The social contract had been quickly and absolutely condemned by the then industrial organizer Bert Ramelson as a 'con trick'[23]. The dissident position, articulated most forcefully by economists Mike Prior and Dave Purdy, was that trade union success in pushing up wages was one cause of inflation, and that a 'socialist incomes policy' was a necessary starting point for

23 Bert Ramelson, *Social Contract or con trick?* Communist Party, London, 1976.

both dealing with inflation and launching a working class bid for hegemony. From this disagreement, Purdy and Prior elaborated their position into a lengthy alternative to the draft programme which, like Charlie Doyle's, was ruled out of order as a discussion document. They later turned their argument into a book on how the 'politics of hegemony' could be created, taking as their starting point the current paradoxical situation

where the richness and diversity of the left has outrun the political concepts that we possess to handle their co-ordination, mutual support and unification around common political objectives.[24]

Many other party reformers baulked at going so far with them; they thought Purdy and Prior overestimated how far state agencies could be used as agencies for socialism, underestimated the potency of ritual conflict between unions and employers and feared that, in an open clash, the party's working class members would be led by the Industrial Department into an entrenched hard-line position. The dispute became one of the most rancorous in the party. Within three years, most of those who most strongly supported Purdy and Prior's position had left the party, including the two proponents themselves.

A pragmatic strategy for socialist trade union action depended of course on knowing who was who on each side of the class divide and this – the definition of class – became one of the most complex theoretical debates of the programme. In one theory, the working class were all those who 'sold their labour power', and this definition was, with qualifications, accepted in the BRS. Yet it caused much unease, for could the state-salaried manager of a DHSS office really be in the same class as a Liverpool docker, and wasn't the chap who 'typed' the newspapers in the compositors' room somehow more working class than the woman who typed the letters in the carpeted office upstairs?

The debate was more international than the question of incomes policy, and a packed conference on class structure, organized by the Communist Party's sociology group in November 1976, had drawn heavily on European thinkers[25]. In the end, no-one agreed on whether, as Nicos Poulantzas

24 M. Prior and D. Purdy, *Out of the ghetto* Spokesman Books, Nottingham, 1979.
25 The conference papers were published as Alan Hunt (ed), *Class and Class Structure* Lawrence and Wishart, London, 1977.

proposed, there was a distinct petty bourgeois class with its own *political* interest to defend; or whether, following Santiago Carrillo's position, it was enough just to refer to 'intermediate strata' whose support could and must be won by any socialist party. There was disagreement over what measures should be used to determine class relationships, and feminists further complicated the question by asking whether or not sex might be as important an organizing principle for political and social structures as class. The Political Economy of Women group, an offshoot of a socialist feminist conference, had pioneered analysis of the 'domestic economy' – all those services carried out unpaid by women in the home and largely ignored by traditional economists. What were the links between this domestic economy and capitalism's public face? Could one be that the much vaunted militancy of the organized craft workers – the vanguard of the working class – was in effect a sectarian battle for their own status, the very strength of which had sent employers scurrying off to employ, in preference, ranks of married women whose domestic commitments would ensure that they would never demand control over the work process? Did not the raison d'etre of individual trade unions lie precisely in such divisions with a consequent vested interest in keeping women in their place?

No consensus amongst the debators emerged in time to lobby for a more coherent analysis of class to be incorporated into the BRS; the programme was left to assert a theoretical position that all those who sold their labour power were the working class, and it negotiated a political problem by asserting that those in the 'traditional' working class of mining, engineering and transport, were necessarily the political leaders of that class. The programme also reasserted that 'the basic force for change in our society is the class struggle between workers and capitalists'. But here, in a much more explicit move away from earlier programmes, it went on to list the political movements that were thriving in the mid-1970s as examples of struggles against the way 'capitalism not only exploits people at work, it impinges on every aspect of their lives'. At the time, the anti-racist movement (led by the Anti-Nazi League), the women's movement and the movement for Scottish nationalism, were all particularly vigorous.

Earlier programmes had recognized a form of 'progressive' politics outside class struggle, but had always subordinated them to direct class confrontation and seen them as being essentially ideological. Different ideological concerns could therefore be merged in what had been the key CPGB strategy – the 'anti-monopoly alliance'. For, however differently people expressed their dislike of the status quo, they were objectively united by a common material oppression – monopoly capitalism. This notion had evolved from the 1957 programme where the alliance was between the working class and those 'sections of the population' which also 'want peace and social and economic progress'[26]. This definition according to desire was not very discriminating; even Tory big business owners might be supposed to want peace and social and economic progress. It was a paper populism, spurred on both by the Communist Party's commitment to electoral activity and the model of the People's Democracies. By the 1967 programme, state monopoly capitalism was identified far more sharply as the cause of all social ills. From this there followed the paper strategy that all those whose interests were not directly served by state monopoly capitalism were, objectively speaking, against it even though only a handful of monopolists and communists might be aware of this truth. Nonetheless, the strategy expected shopkeepers, farmers and owners of small businesses to follow the vanguard of the working class into the final confrontation with capitalism.

Missing from this strategy, was the notion of *material* conflicts within society other than a polarized class conflict. Missing also was any explanation of why, for instance, small shopkeepers failed to perceive the objective truth of their situation. Finally, what was also missing was any actionable strategy for change before the vanguard of the working class launched its assault on state monopoly capitalism. The great test of the anti-monopoly alliance had been the campaign around the 1975 referendum on the EEC. (Only in the 1980s have some communists argued that in fact the best defence against multinationals is a strong EEC. At the time, the Communist Party was wholly opposed to staying a member.) Theoretically, the anti-monopoly alliance worked, for Enoch Powell popped up as, objectively speaking, an ally of the Communist Party. But such an historical compromise would have been going too far.

The new strategy proposed in the 1977 CPGB programme was christened the 'broad democratic alliance'. It was different partly

26 *British Road to Socialism*, Communist Party, London, 1958.

because it recognized that the political movements of the 1970s –
what it called 'new social forces – were a product of material
conflicts within society on the basis of race, age, region, etc.
Thus, each of these movements would, quite properly, fight
against their oppression in their own way, rather than submerg-
ing their particular goals into a general class conflict. However,
the programme argued:

It is clear . . . that if these movements and their struggles proceed in
isolation from each other, they can do no more than challenge the
position of the ruling class on a series of different issues, and not its
overall domination. If they are isolated from the labour movement, not
only will they themselves suffer from the lack of its support, but the
working class will be unable to fulfil its role of the leading force in
society. The labour movements needs alliances with these other democratic movements because, in supporting their aims and aspirations it
becomes increasingly aware that class oppression, and the struggle
against it, extend far beyond the work place and embrace strata beyond
the working class. Such alliances are needed to bring the political
weight of the overwhelming majority of the population to bear on the
minority ruling class.

What connected all these movements was less the objective
reality of monopoly capitalism than the subjective desire for
more democracy – in the rather vague sense of any particular
group of people having control over some major determinant of
their lives. No conflict between the powers of a centralised state
needed to protect socialism against capitalist interests, and a
decentralised democracy, was acknowledged anywhere in the
programme.

The aspiration for democratic control created the possibility of
'revolution as a process', perhaps the most controversial idea in
the programme. It did not mean that a government gradually
makes more and more changes until it ends up with socialism. It
meant that the Revolution could be brought about neither by a
single act – a coup d'etat – nor by a series of swift successive
measures vesting control of the means of production in either the
state or the workers employed in the factories. It assumed, like
the PCI, that economic and social collapse will produce not
socialism but barbarism. Thus, significant shifts in power must
be achieved during periods of popular political action. In the
process of forcefully asserting their will, the challengers would
have to evolve their own ideas and forms for running things more

democratically. The fact that the ruling class and state are not a monolith would mean that they could not reassert bourgeois domination if the working class manoeuvred itself into enough state power. In fact, the sort of changes envisaged in the programme which would make it possible for the 'working class and its allies' to win state power are largely governmental reforms – industrial democracy, abolition of the House of Lords, the repeal of racist legislation, devolution, the implementation of the alternative economic strategy – and administrative reforms – making the civil service, police and army more 'democratic' and accountable. The programme presupposed the election of a Labour Government 'of a new type' to usher in any process of change, and therefore saw the first political task of the masses as being the changing of the Labour Party.

For the hardliners all this was reformist waffle. Again, however, the hardliners fell back on thin evocations of the Russian Revolution, and being in no position to explain how a revolutionary situation in which the working class could seize the state would come about, lost the whole argument. (It is significant that, since 1980, the Stalinists have been most keen to burrow in the Labour Party behind Militant.) Caught by the need, therefore, to defend the BRS draft against a return to Stalinist methods of organizing, the Eurocommunists had no coherent plan for what should lie between discrete grass roots demands and programmes of sweeping governmental change. One train of thought began with a form of social contract in which trade unions would exchange incomes policy for a set of social demands which they could enforce in the work-place as well as in society at large. The bargain would be with the government, not with employers, thus giving trade unions direct access to (though not control over) state power. From that position, trade unions should have the freedom to negotiate away some of their own sectionalism, as well as to promote their own objectives within the work-place; thus they would be asserting their own alternative view of management rather than merely asserting an alternative to how much they should receive from management and when.

A second train of thought saw the quasi-state bodies that were blossoming in the 'unhegemonic' growth of State administration as ripe sites for 'democratization'. Because the public had some sort of access to them, because bodies like the Manpower Services Commission seemed to be benevolent rather than repressive state bodies, they were vulnerable to being changed by their customers. This view underestimated the powerlessness of the clients and, with hindsight, clearly underestimated what would happen to the independence of these bodies if a class government did assert 'hegemony'.

Running through many of the ideas on how to begin transforming society was the theme of the 'prefigurative society', meaning making changes now that will prefigure the form of society you would like to live in. Its simplest image, if most intractable practice, was that of the commune of adults and children, pooling money and sharing housework equally. Like all Eurocommunist strategies, it resisted the idea that before there can be any fundamental social change the revolutionary party must have state power. It had – and still has – all the attraction of direct action and a deeply moral purpose. Feminist confidence in women's ability to pour energy into changing their relationships was still high. Because they had created methods of organizing which both 'changed the consciousness' of those involved and demanded material changes, the potential for upending oppressive hierarchies seemed enormous. As a strategy, it demanded that women sustained an energetic and angry optimism; paradoxically, it also implied that putting feminist methods into practice would always take priority over any other business – for while a non-hierarchical women's movement can, once in action, pursue demands of general concern, a political action structured along hierarchical and sexist lines is unlikely to voluntarily dissolve its own ranks.

Although the BRS hinted at some of these methods of change, as well as the constitutional and governmental policies, they were only hints. Its finished version was substantially a Eurocommunist document in its emphasis on a broad democratic alliance beginning to make political changes now, with those changes serving to push working class organizations into a leading political and moral position without causing a catastrophic reaction or economic collapse. It was hoped that the programme was watertight against Stalinist scuttling, but in less than two years a number of holes in its own argument had opened up.

The programme assumed that massive industrial growth, injected into the economy, could propel the British economy out of the world recession. It assumed that the Labour Party would stay in one piece to make the injection; that, flushed with the public successes of the mid 1970s and a more attractive programme, the Communist Party would be larger and more purposeful; that the state would continue its role of mediating and managing economic crisis, its internal conflicts becoming more apparent under the strain. None of these things came to pass in the expected form.

Almost the last act of the 1977 Congress had been to vote for a new Commission on Inner Party Democracy, to reform the internal organization of the party in line with the role sketched out in the BRS. The process was a flop, pleasing nobody. The reforming zeal of the Eurocommunists had dissipated, not least because a growing number of them felt the strategy of the new programme gave the decisive role to a mass party, so they joined the Labour Party. Others were dispirited by the sameness of party life; many branches continued to flutter and limp through the same round of monotonous activities, the annual card issue, selling stamps, organizing bazaars, standing in public places on Friday night to sell a paper that commanded less and less confidence in the members themselves. Communist election results were particularly depressing, for whereas the Communist Party had once picked up many of the protest votes (as well as being bigger and more influential itself) in most electoral contests there were now several parties competing for the Far Left/ eccentric vote. From an average of 1,950 votes per communist candidate in 1951, the number had dropped at successive elections to 444 in 1979. By the 1979 Congress, the centre section of the leadership had decided it was time to retreat, to 'heal the wounds' opened up by the conflict over the *British Road to Socialism* and reaffirm the homogeneity of the party. Six members of the Commission on IPD put forward what they carefully called Alternative Proposals to the main report aimed at lessening the power of the Political Committee and the full time officials, abolishing the 'recommended list' of candidates for delegates to elect the Executive Committee, and allowing more freedom for members of similar political tendencies to plan together. Their effective proposals were strongly opposed by the leadership and were rejected by delegates. Although the Political Committee became less powerful anyway, no other clear political leadership emerged to replace them; bureaucratic intertia settled deep into many party offices. By 1980, membership had fallen below 20,000, a loss of 10,000 members in a decade and the lowest figure since the war.

The Communist Party perhaps should accept some responsibility for the huge loss of confidence and purpose in the trade union movement, since it claimed responsibility for optimistic militancy. Apart from the failure to understand how anachronistic much trade union structure and style had become, the one attempt to revive an engineering shop stewards' movement in 1979 received little concerted national support. The *British Road to Socialism*, in one of its most meaningful silences, had had virtually nothing to say on those matters.

Ironically, the recent historic split in the Labour Party came close to the expectations of the BRS. A socialist breakthrough in the Labour Party had always been predicated on a loss of dominance by the right-wing. But it assumed that this would be a result of vociferous mass rejection of right-wing ideas. Instead, a splintered and sectarian Left faced with, at the time, a buoyant right-wing defection to the SDP offered little hope of a renewed socialist leadership. The influence of Eurocommunism on some Labour Party members certainly became apparent, both because of the interest in French and Italian Eurocommunism and the developing role of the Communist Party journal *Marxism Today* as the most persuasive theoretical journal on the Left. In both *Labour and Mass Politics* by Peter Hain, and the establishment of *New Socialist*, the initiating work of British communist reformers is easily detected. This success hints at what role in establishing socialist hegemony the Communist Party could play; but at the moment *Marxism Today* is one of several heads possessed by the Communist Party, and though it may be the most alert, it lacks a body.

The winter of discontent of 1978–79, the watershed of modern British politics, found the Communist Party quite unprepared. Yet, if anything, the events clustered round this time were the unpredicted vindication of the half-sketched theses on the state and trade unions in the BRS. The clash between workers in the state National Health Service and the Labour Government over control of public spending and incomes policy was a rupture that took place within the state. Had the same number of employees of a private company determined to strike for higher wages, it is more than likely that some sort of resolution could have been found. Employers would have had more room for manoeuvre, the workers a lesser claim, the public no stake in the outcome. But the health dispute involved too many contradictory relationships for that: between 'independent' trade unions and government;

between state servants and the state as employer; between public servants and their clients; between an official incomes policy sold as being fairer to the low paid and the low paid demanding that fairness meant higher wages for them: and between a government that was supposed to use state powers in the interests of the working class but that wanted to enforce rigid control over public spending as its last instrument of economic control. In one sense, these various conflicts were over what the state was, and what its functions would be, and were productive of a possible internal rupture within the state – of the kind that, according to Nicos Poulantzas, could lead to the transformation of the state itself.

But for such a Eurocommunist strategy to succeed such internal conflicts had to be co-ordinated both with a national political leadership and with 'a struggle outside the institutions and apparatuses [of the State], giving rise to a whole series of instruments, means of co-ordination, organs of popular power at the base, structures of direct democracy at the base'[27]. There was no such political leadership, for the strike produces the final political paralysis of the Labour Party. There was also a total absence of any co-ordination between the immediate challenge to incomes policy by the health workers and any larger struggle about public spending, the hierarchy of control within the health service or the quality of service provided by state institutions. It could be argued that the crisis of 1978–79 did indeed lead to a transformation of the state. What it did not do was to transform it in a democratic, Eurocommunist direction. Instead and on the contrary, as a consequence of that historic dispute, significant sections of the bourgeisie decided that the state, in its form as a representative democracy, could not cope with the employer/employee relationship. The lesson they took from the winter of discontent was that this relationship needed to be returned to private control through 'hiving off' manual labour to private enterprise. In this way, the potential of union-organized state employees using their power to democratize the state would be (and now is being) destroyed by the replacement of their single, publicly accountable employer with a number of separate, unaccountable private employers free of national public pay settlements.

27 Nicos Poulantzas interviewed by Henri Weber in 'The state and the transition to socialism' *International* Vol. 4(1) 1977.

It could also be argued that the failure of the working class protagonists in the winter of discontent to decisively alter the balance of power is the failure of British trade unionism. Trade unions on their own cannot win political confrontations, even if they seem to walk off with the economic spoils of war. But, ironically, it has only been the Communist Party and a few trade union leaders gripped by brotherhood machismo who have allotted to trade unions the role of *the* vanguard of the working class. Had the health service strikes created new 'organs of popular power at the base', or a system of support groups from health service consumers, and from the women's and black groups who identified with the low paid women and black health service workers (and who, for their own reasons challenged the government's control over pay as its means to control the welfare state service), then the rupture could well have been about political hegemony. But the Communist Party, guardian of the notion of such a broad democratic alliance, is too weak and too divided to provide that form of leadership, and the Labour Party, potential inheritor of that role, has been the first victim of the crisis in the nature of state power.

This is not the obituary of either Eurocommunism as a tendency or of the CPGB; both contain vigorous elements. But both need to scale their sights to what they might realistically achieve, and both need to be more humble in the face of those movements which do succeed in channeling the popular imagination against Conservative dominance. While right-wing Tories have 'broken the mould' so too has the women's movement, especially on peace and ecology. The most optimistic role for Eurocommunism in Britain would be as a small but disproportionately influential group which could facilitate links, in ideas and organisations, between radical groups and movements. The problem is, the CPGB would have to eschew all sectarianism for this to succeed; and, if it did not put its own survival first, would the CPGB survive?

Chapter six

THE BALLOT, THE MUSTER AND THE AGE: SOCIALISM AND REVOLUTION IN THE WEST

David Bailey

I

Among those who are still in favour of a socialist society, the question of how to overturn the existing social order is a controversial one. The means used by the Bolsheviks in Russia or by the communists in China seem disagreeable and dangerous. Many people see in them the root of the evils that have since discredited the socialist cause. Indeed, are such methods really needed in the West, where socialists can and do acquire power without bloodshed, and where laws are made by elected parliaments? Could not the peoples of the Western democracies vanquish capitalism without risking their lives in revolutions or entrusting their liberties to revolutionary governments?[1]

Most European socialists adhere to that school of thought. Democratically elected governments with parliamentary majorities will do away with capitalism peacefully and palatably. Such work is necessarily slow. Knowing that property and privilege are prone to industrial sabotage and political violence, leaders like Francois Mitterand and Tony Benn try to avoid extreme or menacing policies which may provoke reaction into closing up the constitutional avenues of change. Several terms in office are therefore required. Some reckless souls believe that democratic traditions are now so strong in the West that one or two turns in office may suffice, but to most the peaceful road to socialism is a labour of decades and of generations. Here is a

---

1 This has been the opinion of international social democracy ever since the Russian Revolution, but the Western communist parties have recently adopted it too. See Santiago Carrillo, *'Eurocommunism' and the State*, Lawrence and Wishart, London, 1977, and Fernando Claudin, *Eurocommunism and Socialism*, New Left Books, London, 1978.

gradualist strategy, and its air of sobriety and caution is inevitably seductive[2].

The tiny but no longer dwindling band of revolutionary
socialists, on the other hand, hold that the true locus of political
power will always lie outside parliament, in the civil service, the
police, the army, the magistracy and other branches of the state.
These bodies, ostensibly public, are run by people who, either by
birth, connection or conviction, invariably fight on behalf of
private property. Those who try to bring about complete public
ownership inevitably bring about a violent collision, which no
parliamentary majority can avoid. Nor will the reactionaries be
entirely lacking in popular support. Many working class people
will oppose collectivism, either from patriotism or religious conviction, or out of fear and self-interest. Even though the socialist
movement may try to spread the work of transition over many
decades, the opposition, sensing the danger of stealth, sooner or
later turns to violence and dictatorship. We saw that recently in
Chile, and in Germany fifty years ago; Germany and Chile were
of course democracies of some standing. Besides, for as long as
capitalism continues, shall we not have wars, slumps and other
calamities by which the trophies of patience are undone? Do not
events again and again take the gradualists by surprise? Are they
not repeatedly confronted with the need to take more vigorous
measures in order to save themselves from the stadium and
humanity from disaster?

The revolutionaries believe that the only effective approach is
to slay the monster by a single blow: do the deed in a single
generation by means of one continuous administration. This
involves taking a series of exceptional measures to break the
propertied classes, disarm their supporters, and bring the full
fruits of collectivism to the people as rapidly as possible.
Revolutionary politicians would, for example, abandon piece-
meal nationalization and take over all major companies, perhaps
by a single Act or Decree. Rather than buy company assets – a
costly and therefore lengthy process – they would confiscate the
larger enterprises, paying minimum compensation where they
must and no compensation wherever they can. Managers and
ex-owners will not be left in charge of the factories, there to
practice sabotage, but either be driven off or be compelled to

---

2 It is hard to find out how long Eurocommunists think it would take to
overturn capitalism by peaceful means.

work under the strict supervision of workers' committees. The policy of the revolutionaries towards the press and the rights of oppositionists is harder to establish, but they are unanimous on the need to transfer military command from officers to privates, and from the soldiers to the workers' militia. Hostile civil servants will be purged. Public servants will nowhere be paid at rates higher than those for skilled labour. Working people will be drawn into political and economic administration at all levels. To transact the business of the revolution there would be an assembly of delegates elected from a network of local workers' councils (soviets), through which the wishes of millions could be expressed directly and the work of the revolution conducted expeditiously. Here is a new type of state, reputedly more democratic than a parliamentary one, and of course having little in common with a Stalinist regime. Living standards would quickly be raised. Abroad, the revolution would be spread by example and exhortation. And at last, whatever the dangers and discomforts of the revolution, a new epoch of social transformation would begin, leading eventually to a free and prosperous socialist society embracing the globe.

Revolution: social or political?

Governments willing to alter the entire structure of society generally emerge only from tremendous convulsions like the Russian or French Revolutions. Great upheavals of this kind consist of a chain of unusual and dramatic events, often spread over several years. The lower classes begin by forming a notion of a new society free of inequality and injustice. They grow increasingly resentful of property and privilege. Then, usually some slump, war or other emergency convinces them that the hour has come to put the policies of revolutionaries into operation. Gigantic demonstrations take to the streets. A thousand loquacious assemblies voice their execrations and proclamations. The peasant burns the manor house and divides his lord's estate. The worker takes over the factory, the mill and the mine. Governments are turned out or coups nipped in the bud by great popular uprisings, from which step forth the men and women who form revolutionary governments and table historic legislation. Insurrections generally deal a blow to all reactionary institutions, public and private, and deliver power and property directly into the hands of the people, a victory that heightens popular ambition the more. There may be civil wars, and sometimes wars of national liberation.

Now if at length there appears a government willing to transfer *once and for all* the governance and property of the nation from one class to another, a *social* revolution is said to have occurred. In the French Revolution, the peasant and the merchant acquired the title deeds to the lands of the clergy and the aristocracy; political power likewise passed to the middle classes. In the Russian Revolution, the factories were declared communal property and the farmer won for a time the right to his land; political power passed to the workers, farmers and intellectuals who thronged the soviet assemblies or took up posts in the Red Army and the new administration. These were social revolutions, one leading to a capitalist society, the other a collectivist. But if the new government is content simply to reverse this or that policy or correct this or that abuse, then property and power will not change hands permanently, the people will return to their accustomed places, and history will record that a *political* not a social revolution has taken place. Political revolutions often bring great benefits to the people, but they do not have the momentous consequences of a social overturn.

Contrary to widespread opinion on the Left, almost every twentieth century European country has been struck by upheavals displaying all the classic phenomena of revolution, including property seizures, soviets and armed uprisings. Even where the changes wrought by these convulsions stopped short of social revolution, they altered significantly the course of our history. Indeed, these revolutionary movements, which we shall refer to by the main uprisings that marked their course, form an impressive chronicle.

Amid the hostilities of the First World War, working class risings brought down a number of the beligerent governments, including those of Russia, Austria, Hungary, Germany, and subject territories like Poland and Finland. The Bolshevik uprising of October 1917 took Russia out of the war. The insurrection in Bulgaria in September and in Germany in November 1918 ended the Great War altogether, the first by causing a fatal breach in the south-eastern front of the Central Powers, the second by overthrowing the Kaiser himself and securing the armistice of 11 November[3]. It is often forgotten that the carnage

3 J. Rothschild, *The Communist Party of Bulgaria, Origins and Developments 1883–1936*, New York, 1959, p. 82. For the role of the German insurrection

of the Great War ended only when revolutionists toppled those intent upon further slaughter.

In the 1920s and 1930s there were a number of risings seeking the removal of regimes that had failed to avert unemployment (which in those days meant starvation), or that were sheltering the fascist movements which the slump had engendered. There was a strong revolutionary mood in Germany during the years of Hitler's rise to power, but the socialists and communists did not pool their political resources or mobilize their extensive militias to seize power themselves. In 1934, Austrian socialists tried to overthrow an administration suspected of Nazi sympathies, but were defeated in a brief but bloody civil war in the streets of Vienna[4]. There were several unsuccessful risings in Spain during the 1930s, including the short-lived Asturian Commune of 1934[5]. In July 1936, however, when Franco set out from Morocco to instal a right-wing military dictatorship in Madrid, the whole Spanish working class rose and arrested the civilian and military authorities that had either declared for Franco or were about to do so: in those early days of the Spanish Civil War, Franco might have been beaten[6].

A third, more successful wave of revolt took place in the Europe of the 1940s. Its most glorious achievement was the contribution it made to the liberation of Europe from Nazi occupation. The armies of the Grand Alliance, most notably of Russia, finally destroyed Hitler in 1945, but the capital of France, the cities of northern Italy, and the entire territory of Greece and

---

in forestalling the plot to continue the war, see R. M. Watt, *The Kings Depart, the German Revolution and the Treaty of Versailles 1918–19*, Penguin, Harmondsworth, 1973, pp. 173, 185, 193.

4 E. Fischer, *An Opposing Man*, Allen Lane, London, 1974, ch. 14.

5 A. Paz, *Durruti, The People Armed*, Spokesman Books, Nottingham, 1976, pp. 117–19, 147–50; for the Asturian Commune see S. Payne, *The Spanish Revolution*, Weidenfeld and Nicholson, London, 1970, ch. 7.

6 The standard historians are H. Thomas, *The Spanish Civil War*, Penguin, Harmondsworth, 1965; P. Broue and E. Temime, *The Revolution & The Civil War in Spain*, the MIT Press, Cambridge Mass, 1972; B. Bolloten, *The Spanish Revolution*, University of North Carolina, North Carolina, 1979; F. Morrow, *Revolution & Counter-Revolution in Spain*, Pathfinder, New York, 1974. A detailed description of the rising is in A. Landis, *Spain, The Unfinished Revolution*, International Publishers, New York, 1975, pp. 101–74, and in Broue and Temime, *op cit*, ch. 4. For the exceptionally favourable military situation in the early days see G. Hills, *The Defence of Madrid*, Vantage, London, 1976, p. 51.

Yugoslavia, were not freed without great national revolts, the culmination of several years of guerrilla warfare by workers in the uniform of the partisan. The French Resistance fielded three-quarters of a million fighters and liberated Paris and other cities by the insurrection of August 1944. The Italian Resistance liberated northern Italy from Mussolini and the Germans by the brave rebellion of April 1945, and Greece and Yugoslavia were liberated in the autumn of 1944 by illustrious national risings in which scarcely a foreign soldier took part[7].

Finally, to come to our own day, the revolution that gripped Portugal, when in September 1974 and March 1975 armed risings of socialists and communists foiled General Spinola, besides leading to land reform and the nationalization of Portuguese monopolies, confirmed the decolonization of Portugal's African territories, and cleansed the country of fascism[8].

No one can reasonably maintain that there has been a dearth of revolution in twentieth-century Europe. Yet only in Russia and in Yugoslavia did revolution transform the social system. We must not forget to count those regimes that were intent upon socialism but fell to military misadventure before completing their mission – the Socialist Republic of Finland, broken in the winter of 1917 by German and Swedish troops, or the Hungarian Soviet Republic of 1919 which collapsed after a Rumanian invasion[9] – but it remains an undeniable fact that despite tearing

7 The best discussion of the role of the Resistance movements is contained in Fernando Claudin's *The Communist Movement, From Comintern to Cominform*, Penguin, Harmondsworth, 1975, chs 5, 6, & 7. A vivid reconstruction of the Paris uprising is given by L. Collins and D. Lapierre in *Is Paris Burning?*, Penguin, London, 1965. Also F. Knight, *The French Resistance*, Lawrence and Wishart, London, 1975. The Italian uprising is described in Claudin pp. 360–1. For the Greek and Yugoslav partisans see D. Kousoulas, *Revolution & Defeat, The Story of the Greek Communist Party*, Oxford University Press, Oxford, 1965, D. Eudes, *The Kapetanios*, New Left Books, 1972, and P. Auty, *Tito*, Penguin, London, 1970.
8 P. Mailer, *Portugal: The Impossible Revolution?*, Solidarity, London, 1977; The Sunday Times Insight Team, *Insight on Portugal*, Andre Deutsch, London, 1975; R. Robinson, *Contemporary Portugal: A History*, London, 1979; T. Cliff, *Portugal At The Crossroads*, International Socialism special issue, September 1975.
9 C. Jay Smith, 'Soviet Russia and The Red Revolution of 1918 in Finland' in T. T. Hammond (ed), *The Anatomy of Communist Takeovers*, Yale University Press, Yale, 1975. For the Hungarian Soviet Republic, see H. Gruber (ed), *International Communism in the Era of Lenin*, Anchor, New York, 1972, pp. 117–52, A. Janos and W. Slottman, *Revolution in Perspective, Essays in the Hungarian Soviet Republic of 1919*, California Press, California, 1971.

down hated regimes, stopping wars, liberating countries from foreign oppressors, and otherwise changing the ways of nations, only a handful of revolutions opened a path to socialism. Why?

The subjective factor

Many writers have claimed that a majority of the workers, especially in countries with democratic political traditions and institutions, never wanted to take that path. This is not true. Revolutionary movements of the most ambitious kind have from time to time appeared against every sort of political background – under the old autocracies of Central and Eastern Europe, in countries with long democratic and semi-democratic traditions such as France and Germany, under the republic in Spain or fascism in Italy.

In the German Revolution of 1918, the insurrection of 4–9 November created in Berlin a government composed wholly of socialists and accountable to a system of workers and soldiers councils formed during the rising. The ministers of the new German Socialist Republic – for so it was called – were mandated not only to sign the armistice but to socialize Germany industry and to draw up a constitution embodying the powers of the councils, into whose hands civilian and military administration had effectively passed. From the city halls of Germany, the councils, led by Independent and 'Majority' Socialists (USPD and SPD), ran the factories – not simply in order to demilitarize production and forestall Hindenburg's plan to renew the war, but to lay the foundations for the permanent socialization of Germany which everyone thought would follow[10]. This regime, although led by ministers who later became infamous, men like Ebert and Scheidemann, was widely mistaken at the time for Bolshevism. One historian writes that on the morrow of the November Revolution, 'All classes knew or thought they knew

10 S. Haffner, *Failure of a Revolution, Germany 1918–19*, Library Press, New York, 1972; R. Coper, *Failure of a Revolution*, Cambridge University Press, Cambridge, 1955; R. M. Watt, *op cit.*; A. J. Ryder, *The German Revolution 1918–19*, Cambridge University Press, California, 1922; and R. Lutz, *The German Revolution: 1918–19*, Stanford, California, 1922. For the terms of the mandate see Coper pp. 93–103, Lutz, p. 80, and Haffner, pp. 99–100. For the powers of the councils, C. Burdick and R. Lutz, *The Political Institutions of the German Revolution 1918–19*, New York, 1966, and personal testimony is in T. Sender, *Autobiography of a Rebel*, New York, 1939, and A. Grezinski, *Inside Germany*, London, 1939.

that they could not resist the councils. They resigned themselves to, or else welcomed, the fact that Germany was to be socialist'[11]. Another: 'Theoretically, this conference [of the Berlin Workers & Soldiers Councils, 10 November], established the dictatorship of the proletariat'[12].

The Spanish working class was in a similar mood in 1936. Between one-third and one-half of Spanish labour had for two decades followed the *Confederación Nacional del Trabajo* (CNT), a trade union whose official policy was to establish libertarian communism by armed revolution[13]. By 1933, its main rival, the Socialist Party, had come to be dominated by the far Left, whose most famous leader, Largo Caballero, known as the 'Spanish Lenin', was by 1934 openly demanding a 'dictatorship of the proletariat'[14]. The electoral victory of the Popular Front in February 1936 was followed by months of bellicose oratory, property seizures and distributions of arms, a time that one historian has compared to the eve of the Russian October[15]. It was precisely to prevent an October in Spain that Franco rose in July. At the outbreak of the Civil War large parts of Republican Spain were engulfed by a social revolution: factories and land were seized by committees of the trade unions and left-wing parties, many of whom were eager to socialize production as well as to defeat Franco; even the tiniest businesses were sometimes taken over[16].

Nor were the Resistance movements of the 1940s concerned solely with national liberation. After 1941, they were led, almost everywhere, by the communists, still supported in those days as parties of social transformation. Capitalism had brought fascism, slump and war. When the Germans conquered, the politicians had fled or turned collaborator; in Greece and Yugoslavia the remnant of the old armed forces fought the communists as well as the Nazis. Against Hitler, socialist Russia fought almost alone. European communism was at the height of its popularity, and millions of workers were under arms. The

11 Coper, *op cit.* p. 99.
12 Lutz, *op cit.* p. 80.
13 A. Paz, *op cit.* p. 68.
14 S. Payne, *op cit.* p. 172.
15 F. Claudin, *op cit.* pp. 214–24.
16 For conditions after the rising: Bolloten, *op cit.* pp. 62–94, Broue and Temine, chs 5 & 6, and eye-witness accounts in F. Borkenau, *The Spanish Cockpit*, Ann Arbor, Michigan, 1976, and George Orwell, *Homage to Catalonia*, Penguin, Harmondsworth, 1962.

socialist potential of these movements was proven after liberation: witness the years of turmoil in post-war Italy; the ferocity of
the Greek Civil War, which lasted until 1949; and above all, the
brilliantly successful socialist revolution in Yugoslavia[17]. Nor
can there be much doubt that the later events in Portugal could
have had a different outcome: parties professing socialism collectively won the largest voting percentage ever polled in a European general election.

The leadership factor

These revolutions failed to reach their higher objectives, not
because the people rejected the revolutionary road, but because
their leaders decided not to take it, a decision creating confusion
leading to disaster. Those whose business it was to form governments, and in whom millions trusted, acted in a quite extraordinary way at the critical moment. For rather than taking office and
introducing socialist measures – for which they had striven and
clamoured all their lives – they joined coalition governments
with bourgeois politicians whose policies and personalities they
had for years reviled.

The Russian Mensheviks and Social Revolutionaries started a
remarkably consistent trend when they formed coalitions with
the Duma liberals in 1917; the liberals by themselves were
without significant support. In Germany, the SPD ditched their
militant partners, the Independents, and formed a coalition with
the bourgeois parties. Largo Caballero joined hands with the
Republicans under President Azana. At the liberation, the
French Communists entered a similar coalition under de
Gaulle, the Italians under Marshal Badoglio, and the Greeks
under the king. In Portugal, socialists and communists formed
six provisional governments with open supporters of capital like
General Costa Gomes. Such governments may have been able to
take radical, even socialist measures – the 8-hour day decrees
by Ebert, or the Portuguese nationalizations – but they were
unlikely to introduce socialism.

Many writers ask how it was that if their followers were so
radical in purpose, the leaders dared to commit such apostasy.
But it must be remembered however that the leaders seldom
declared *openly* that they intended to deny the revolution a
socialist outcome. On the contrary, they everywhere suggested

17 Claudin, *op cit.* pp. 434–53.

that coalition was a tactic designed to make the victory of socialism more certain. Immediately after the Russian February Revolution, the Mensheviks argued that a socialist rather than a 'national' government would provoke the Kaiser to launch an irresistible German offensive, leading to civil war and a monarchist restoration – better to wait until Germany was defeated. In any case, they suggested, the Duma liberals were merely puppets of the Petrograd Soviet and could be dismissed at any time[18]. In 1918, the German socialists argued that in order to secure help for a starving country, the German Socialist Republic should legitimize itself in the eyes of the Entente by holding general elections, which the socialists would win anyhow[19]. They did not demand a capitalist reconstruction or denounce the work of the councils; Ebert's slogan was 'Socialization is on the march'[20]. In Spain, few declared that Spain should be anything other than a socialist country once Franco was beaten. The republicans were being kept in power only to 'camouflage' the social overturn so as not to deter Britain and France from joining in the war against Hitler and Mussolini, and to induce Stalin to send arms[21]. At Liberation, French and Italian communist leaders stated that it would be safe to form a properly socialist administration only when Allied troops had

18 For this theme in Menshevik and Social Revolutionary agitation see W. Roobol, Tseretelli, *A Democrat in the Russian Revolution*, The Hague 1976, pp. 82–92. That the soviets were indeed the masters of the situation in February and thereafter is accepted by most historians of the Russian Revolution. That the proletariat wanted a soviet and not a liberal government in February is argued by L. Trotsky, *The History of the Russian Revolution*, Gollancz, London, 1965, pp. 187, 202, 236, 301, and by Lenin: 'It goes without saying that the Soviet could and should have taken over state power in full (in February) *Selected Works, Volume 2,* Progress Publishers, Moscow, 1970, p. 213.
19 Coper, *op cit.* pp. 128–9.
20 Sender, *op cit.* p. 130.
21 Caballero said in 1937: 'When I assumed this post I renounced nothing . . . But in view of the danger that confronts our country . . . I felt it my duty to assume the responsibilities that naturally devolve upon me because of my office by laying aside for a short time the immediate aspirations inherent in the ideology I have always defended', Bolloten, *op cit.* p. 154. Claudin writes: 'For Largo Caballero and his supporters, alliance with the Republicans signified a sort of *ruse de guerre* in order to adapt to the international conditions in which the Spanish revolution had to take place, while preserving its proletarian purity', *op cit.* p. 228. Appeals to the unfavourability of the international situation, especially the power of US imperialism, are commonly made in justification of coalition during revolutions in Third World countries, e.g. in Nicaragua since the 1979 Revolution.

passed on into Germany and the danger of a reversal of alliances against Russia was over[22]. Portuguese leaders pointed to the need to mollify the armed forces and avoid a Franco-backed rebellion in the north; but they were nevertheless building 'workers power' and a 'socialist Portugal'.

The debacle

These policies led to disaster. To begin with, delay did not produce the benefits claimed for it: the Russian liberals continued with the war; the German socialists lost their election; Spain got neither British intervention nor decent Soviet guns; the Resistance leaders were soon expelled from office; and the Portuguese spent so long courting the generals that the northern peasantry got little land and stayed with the Right. Then, as these distressing facts became known, the workers tried to cajole their leaders back on course. But as some gave this up more quickly than others, the working class movement became divided at a most perilous time. One faction accused its rivals of betraying the cause by too much caution, another by too much haste. Some formed new parties, some stuck with the old. Confusion! It is among these rapids that so many revolutions came to grief. When the communists disarmed the Resistance with promises, rebellion petered out in France, and a 'second revolution' in Italy in 1948 proved abortive. The Greek communists renewed the struggle in less favourable circumstances and were defeated. In the Portuguese Revolution an attempt by dissident communists and far leftists to re-establish the 4th Provisional Government (the most radical of five), led to an armed rising in November 1975 which ended in fiasco. In the Spanish Revolution, the Catalan Left decided in 1937 that social revolution and war with France must go hand in hand after all: an armed clash broke out in May between the Left and communist-led troops in Barcelona. The Left was defeated, and the victory of Franco was made virtually inevitable[23].

In view of the importance of the German Revolution in current strategic debate, the story of its outcome should be more widely known. The Berlin workers lost patience with Ebert

22 Claudin, *op cit.* pp. 434–52.
23 Claudin, *op cit.* pp. 229–34, Broue and Temime, *op cit.* pp. 278–89. Bolloten, *op cit.* is a comprehensive study of the policies of the socialists and communists in 1936–7.

almost immediately after the victory of November 1918. In the first week of January of the following year, almost the entire Berlin work-force took to the streets, urging the Independents to take power from Ebert. The uprising was later misnamed Spartacus Week (to minimize its importance)[24]. Ebert crushed the rising with the aid of monarchist troops (Freikorps), of whose existence Germany had only just learned. This, together with a succession of other events including the murder of the famous revolutionaries Rosa Luxemburg and Karl Leibknecht, the disappointing election results a fortnight later, and the policies of the first new coalition, caused consternation to spread throughout the German working class movement. Between January and April 1919 there was in almost every German city an uprising designed to overthrow Ebert, defend the sovereignty of the councils against the claims of the new parliament at Weimar, defeat the Freikorps and save the socialist cause from disaster. SPD supporters joined in these revolts. As many as 20,000 rebels were killed. Writers who claim that socialist revolution – or revolution of any kind – had little support in Germany owing to its comparatively democratic history, invariably ignore these events. Alas, the Independent Socialists were unable to coordinate the numerous risings, partly because they were suspected by some workers of having started the 'fratricide' by the January rebellion. In the Russian Revolution the Bolsheviks had not made the mistake of a too early revolt during a similar turn of events in July 1917, and it is upon the decisions of a day that the course of history often depend. By the follies of the Right and the blunders of the Left the greatest opportunity to bring socialism to Germany was lost[25].

24 E. Waldman, *The Spartacist Uprising*, Milwaukee, 1958. It was not the tiny Sparticists who organized Spartacus Week but the much larger forces of the Independents. They also led the numerous armed risings in the provinces in the following months. An excellent study of the Independents is D. Morgan, *The Socialist Left and the German Revolution*, Stanford (?), pp. 223–40.
25 A history of the Civil War remains to be written, but details can be found in Watt, *op cit.* pp. 283–80; E. Waldman, *op cit.*; Haffner, *op cit.*, ch. 12; and Morgan, *op cit.* pp. 223–40. A false picture is contained in Geoff Hodgson's *Socialism and Parliamentary Democracy*, Spokesman, Nottingham, 1977: he writes that the German workers 'rejected insurrection' and wanted only a 'liberal parliamentary republic' (pp. 41–2). Hodgson confuses the revolutionary forces with the tiny Sparticists, wrongly assumes that the decisions of the December Congress of Councils to hold early general elections means that the workers rejected the councils, and ignores the civil war altogether. This is poor scholarship.

The predicament of the leaders

To the leadership of the labour movement, to hesitation, faulty vision and lack of probity, must be attributed a large part of the blame for these historic tragedies. Leaders are of course pushed along by their followers, but to the leaders falls the final power to sway the judgement of millions and determine the outcome of events. Especially blameworthy in the log of poor captainship is the role of the more conservative leader, and in a revolution conservatism is concentrated at the head of the movement.

Why was there this display of conservatism in the midst of upheaval? It is superfluous here to argue that trade union and party officials, enjoying material advantages over workers, are a generally moderate group: it is not always true[26]. The pressures upon the leaders in the maelstrom of a revolution should be sufficiently apparent. They know that they will be singled out by the counter-revolution for special retribution, and it would be surprising if fear of personal safety did not affect their conduct. Nor are the risks of civil war and foreign invasion, should the revolution take a socialist turn, entirely imaginary: the fate of Russia remains a terrible warning to all. Thus it was that some felt justified in breaking the headlong rush of their followers, deceiving them, and even shooting them down. Let us not say they acted from base motives. Did they act wisely? For they did not save their supporters from the worst. The miscarriage of the German Revolution led to the victory of Nazism and ultimately to the Second World War. Nor is it clear that the communist Resistance leaders of the 1940s have spared the Soviet Union new and even more horrendous assaults. But this is to take the long view of things. It is hard to take the long view in the panic of the hour. A social revolution is a more daring and in the immediate term more costly thing to accomplish than those political overturns which happen from time to time and in which even the moderate participate. The failure of so many revolutions to fulfil their potential is therefore unsurprising. That revolution has seldom created a durable socialist regime will lead some socialists to reject it as part of their strategic calculations. But parliamentary democracy has created none.

26 E. Mandel, *On Bureaucracy*, IMG Publications, London.

Revolution and parliamentary democracy

This is not to say that parliamentary democracy is antithetical to revolution. The idea that the two never mix is as much responsible for poor strategic thinking as it is for the distortion of the historical record (the claim that revolutions have not broken out in democracies). Fabian and peaceful roads to socialism presuppose stable parliamentary institutions, but it does not follow that the revolutionary will do away with parliamentary institutions or have no use for them. Salvador Allende thought that a parliamentary majority gave him immunity against a coup. He paid for that illusion with his life. But if in 1972 or 1973 he had mustered his followers to crush the conspirators, he might have triumphed. There would have been an armed rising of the people similar to the one that greeted Franco or Spinola, but the Chilean socialist revolution would not have been unconstitutional or non-parliamentary. Engels envisaged this scenario when in 1895 he advised German socialists to win power at the polls, forcing the bourgeoisie to 'shoot first'. All the moral and technical advantages of legitimacy and governmental power would then be with the socialists during the armed conflict, the need for which Engels never denied. Democracy might make the victory more certain[27].

Lenin's advice that socialists should work in parliament only in order to show why it 'deserves to be done away with'[28] is still influential. But it is not at all certain that every revolution will need to do away with parliament. Tito won approval in the general election of 1945 for a government established by force in October 1944. Indeed, Lenin himself, even after seizing power in the October uprising, was eager that the Bolsheviks and Left social-revolutionaries should win a majority in the general elections to the Constituent Assembly – and they probably would have done so if the electoral lists had not been out of date and if Lenin's advice to postpone the elections by just a few weeks had been heeded[29]. He was alert to the substantial advantages of

27 F. Engels, Introduction to Karl Marx's *The Class Struggles in France 1848 to 1850*, Progress Publishers, Moscow, 1952.
28 V. I. Lenin, 'Left-Wing Communism – An Infantile Disorder' in *Selected Works*, Volume 3, Moscow, 1971, p. 381.
29 V. I. Lenin, 'Theses on the Constituent Assembly' in *Selected Works*, Vol 2,

having the Constituent Assembly, a house elected by the votes of the whole nation, act as a second chamber to the Soviet of Workers & Peasants Deputies, an assembly elected by the revolutionary classes alone. This bicameral arrangement was called a 'combined' form of state[30].

In a democracy there seems to be no reason in principle why a social revolution should not begin and end with a majority in parliament. Of course, some revolutions begin in opposition to the will of an elected parliament. After all, historic events often burst upon a country in mid-term. If a government embroils the country in an unjust war, conducts a just war badly, embarks upon a cruel fiscal policy, or otherwise outrages the people, then the people may feel that the government and its parliament no longer represent the wishes of a majority of the nation and may feel compelled to overthrow it without waiting for the next elections to come round. A government installed by an uprising may be unconstitutional. But surely no genuinely popular revolution can or should fail to register the support of the majority of the people in a general election by the time it has run its course?

A unique period?

Revolutions are ubiquitous because they are engendered not by this or that kind of political institution[31] but by changes in the material circumstances of the nation, usually by wars, slumps, famines and other abrupt and catastrophic happenings, which afflict democracies and dictatorships alike[32]. It is at such times

---

op cit. pp. 506–9. Lenin's views are supported by the researches of O. H. Radky, *The Sickle Under the Hammer*, Columbia University Press, New York, 1963, p. 281 ff. and *The Election to the Russian Constituent Assembly of 1917*, Cambridge, Mass. 1950.

30 L. Trotsky, *History, op cit.* pp. 1206–7.

31 Eurocommunists have tried in the interests of their strategic dogmas to expunge the revolutionary movements of European labour, or to minimize their importance and strength. In *'Eurocommunism' and The State*, Carillo argues that revolutionary movements with socialist objectives existed in Europe at the end of the Great War but not after. Claudin believes, by a curious reversal of perspective, that the movements of the 1930s and 1940s were powerful and ambitious, but not those of the Great War. Hodgson, *op cit.* ignores Spain and the Resistance movements and distorts the history of the German Revolution.

32 Some writers on the subject, following de Tocqueville's analysis of the background to the French Revolution, argue that revolutions occur after a

that millions of people previously lukewarm towards politics find that the dangers of revolutions appear less terrible than the evils that are certain to occur if those currently in charge of the country are left in command. Here, incidentally, is where the moral objections to revolutionary action lose much of their force. The casualties of the German November were numbered on the fingers of one hand, those of the slaughter it brought to a close were innumerable. Even the bloodier uprisings of the Resistance, in which thousands perished, helped to destroy a tyranny that took the lives of millions.

For thirty years most Europeans have enjoyed prosperity, peace and democracy. It is an exceptionally sunny age. Would a social revolution now be given a uniquely gentle passage? Workers' parties often reach power by the ballot box. They might nationalize industry quickly and pay compensation over several decades. For with industry operational, no famine, and no armies of occupation to appease, a socialist government in present-day Europe would have tremendous advantages over the Bolsheviks. It may not escape rightist conspiracies, but a legitimate government with popular support would have no trouble in defeating rebels by arming the people. The revolution might then triumph with little loss of life, possibly without a civil war.

On the other hand, experience suggests that without the alarm and fanaticism created by some great peril the parties of labour are unlikely to win general elections or sustain parliamentary majorities on a socialist programme. This only means, however, that future attempts to build a socialist society will be made when the next calamity breaks. Then we or our children will go about things the hard way. Frightened and desperate people will push their parties to power by the most direct but most hazardous path, and even if the parties agree to take power in that way, as they did in Germany, they will inherit a broken and possibly starving country where the difficulties of a socialist reconstruction are enormous and when the temptation to sell out socialism in return for foreign aid is overwhelmingly strong. Who can even contemplate the nightmare of making revolution at the onset of the next world war? Or in its aftermath? We do not know war,

period of improvement in the material conditions of the people; followers of Marx tend to take a different view. Examples can perhaps be found to support both sides. My point here, however, concerns simply the outbreak of revolution.

conquest, famine. We do not wish to make their acquaintance. But one suspects that if socialism ever comes to Europe it will come by the more perilous track.

II

Revolutions will happen for as long as nations are badly governed. Yet, in view of all that has happened in Russia and other post-capitalist countries, it is legitimate to ask afresh whether the revolutions of the future *should* be taken to a socialist conclusion. Should they tarry with the existing social system or cross to the other shore? Experience seems to show that for the successful rebel to go on to expropriate property and communalize the life of a country will involve further bloodshed and a regime which Leninists call the 'dictatorship of the proletariat'. If the road to socialism lies that way, is it worth taking?

Orthodox Leninists often say that the phrase 'dictatorship of the proletariat' has no really sinister implications: after all, Lenin referred to any regime as a dictatorship. In their eyes, a parliamentary republic expresses the rule of the bourgeoisie, and is therefore a 'dictatorship of a sort[33]; those who grumble in Mitterand's republic are living under a 'dictatorship of the bourgeoisie' just as surely as those who endured under Hitler's Third Reich; and those who live in Castro's Cuba are under a 'dictatorship' of the proletariat, as perhaps were those who languished in Stalin's Siberia. The wisdom of this usage may be doubted. To confuse the issue further, however, Lenin sometimes used the term 'dictatorship' in the traditional sense as well: to refer to a certain form of government. Dictatorship, he wrote, is 'rule based directly on force and unrestricted by any laws'[34].

33 '... these forms of government [monarchy and republic] ... are only variations of the bourgeois state, that is, of the dictatorship of the bourgeoisie', V. I. Lenin, 'The Proletarian Revolution and The Renegade Kautsky' in *Selected Works*, Vol. 3, *op cit*. p. 76. 'Dictatorship is not a form of government. That is ridiculous nonsense.' *ibid*. p. 79.
34 V. I. Lenin, *ibid*. p. 75. This makes no sense except as a description of a form of government. Elsewhere in the same work Lenin makes a distinction between dictatorship and the 'form' of the dictatorship (*ibid*. p. 105). R. Medvedev discusses Lenin's elision of state and government in his *Leninism and Western Socialism*, New Left Books, London, 1981, pp. 37–53. See also K. Kautsky, *The Dictatorship of the Proletariat*, Ann Arbor, Michigan, 1964: Kautsky wrongly assumed that a majority class with a

This is a description of arbitrary government, that is, a government prepared to silence its opponents and critics, ban opposition parties, dissolve parliament, take hostages and set the Terror into motion. Indeed, some Bolshevik writers relished all that[35].

In actual practice, it was not until the Civil War, which broke out in 1918, that the Bolsheviks adopted dictatorial measures of that sort against their enemies. Only to defend themselves against sabotage, assassination, rightist coups d'etat, massacre, and conspiracy with foreign powers, did they silence their opponents and resort to terror[36]. In any revolution, whatever its aims, there is a natural resistance to the creation of a tyranny, not only because dictatorships are notoriously difficult to dismantle, but because oppression runs counter to the generous spirit of every great popular movement. That revolutionary government is uncompromising is certain. That its enemies need forfeit their lives and freedoms along with their estates is not so clear. The rigour of revolution is, or should be, proportionate to the mendacity of the counter-revolution. But that counter-revolutions are mendacious can hardly be doubted.

Nevertheless, there is a great deal of uncertainty about these matters among revolutionaries themselves. Some display an indecent haste to set up a dictatorship in the conventional sense

---

majority of the votes in parliament stands in no need of revolution and that Lenin and his allies did not have majority support in Russia, but his point that dictatorship is a form of government, one suitable to a period of civil war, is rather well made. Trotksy followed Kautsky's usage in his *Terrorism and Communism*, Ann Arbor, Michigan, 1961. Hal Draper and Richard Hunt point out that Marx and Engels used the ambiguous formula only eleven times in their writings, mostly when engaged in a united front with Blanquists in which the phrase represented a compromise formulation: see H. Draper, 'Marx and The Dictatorship of The Proletariat' in *New Politics 1*, No 4 (Summer 1962), and R. Hunt, *The Political Ideas of Marx & Engels*, Vol. 1, Macmillan, London, 1974. For a defence of the standard Leninist usage see E. Balibar, *On the Dictatorship of the Proletariat*, New Left Books, London, 1977.

35 N. Bukharin and E. Preobrazhensky, *The ABC of Communism*, University of Michigan Press, Michigan, 1966, pp. 80, 130, 172, *passim*.

36 M. Johnstone, 'Socialism, Democracy and The One Party System' in *Marxism Today*, August– September–November, 1970. This three-part article shows that dictatorial measures which later became permanent under Stalin, were originally adopted under the pressures of the Civil War and intended to be temporary. Brilliant, thoroughly documented and deserves to be more widely known.

of the term. 'The workers' state', according to a publication of the International Socialism Group (now Socialists Workers Party), 'does not allow capitalist parties or capitalist newspapers', neither will it permit 'former capitalists and their supporters to vote'[37]. Lenin himself rejected assertions like those[38]. Other revolutionaries have promised to preserve the rights and liberties enjoyed in a parliamentary democracy: free speech, freedom of the press, universal suffrage, no hostage taking, and no revolutionary tribunals. Liberty will be suspended only if the enemy resorts to civil war[39]. This is a more statesmanlike approach, although no one has given a satisfactory answer to the question of what happens if a majority of the people turn round and vote against a revolutionary government: does it step down?[40] However, although generosity and sagacious diplomacy may reduce the ferocity of civil war, it seems unlikely that they could avert it altogether. Where there is civil war there exists dictatorship. If future revolutions are social, we shall doubtless have more Cromwells, Robespierres and Trotskys.

Stalinism and bureaucracy

The most disturbing question of all, however, is where such a dictatorship will lead. The government of Lenin and Trotsky was unquestionably a popular one, not only among the industrial workers but also among the peasants, without whose support the Civil War of 1918–21 would have been lost. That dictatorships are never popular is a fallacy. Indeed, in the early years of the Bolshevik dictatorship, the people actively participated in the work of government in ways inconceivable in a parliamentary democracy, and although this participatory democracy was undermined by the militarization of life during the Civil War, by the exhaustion of the industrial workers, and by the eventual

37 R. Rosewell, *The Struggle for Workers Power*, International Socialists pamphlet, p. 14.
38 V. I. Lenin, 'The Proletarian Revolution and the Renegade Kautsky', *Selected Works*, Vol. 3, Moscow, p. 91.
39 *Socialist Democracy and The Dictatorship of the Proletariat*, Fourth International, IMG Publications, London,
40 It was this question that led to the debate about the 'dictatorship of the proletariat' in the Western communist parties. The leader of the Militant Tendency, Edward Grant, argued recently on television that a socialist government would be so munificent that no one would ever wish to vote it out, 'TV Eye', 3 December 1981.

appearance of one-party soviets following the demise (partly by repression but mostly by defection) of the Mensheviks and Social-Revolutionaries, it bore little resemblance to the Stalinist regime of the 1930s. Stalin established something quite different: a government that ruled *everyone* by dictatorship and terror, including workers and Bolshevik militants themselves.

Modern revolutionaries, influenced mostly by the ideas of Leon Trotsky, explain this unhappy development by saying that those who were placed in positions of trust – political leaders, technical experts, managers, army people, and so on – gradually evolved personal privileges of their own, to preserve which they suppressed all criticism, above all by the workers, their most astute critics. Here is the essential meaning of Stalinism, which sent to the Gulag not only bourgeois conspirators, nor peasants who, rightly or wrongly, resisted collectivization, but almost the entire old guard of the Bolshevik Party, the Left, the Centre and the Right, along with any dissident non-party worker. Whence comes this 'bureaucratic caste' or 'bureaucratic class'?[41]

The fundamental cause of the bureaucratic degeneration of the Russian Revolution, according to the Far Left, was the extreme backwardness of the country. The Bolsheviks knew when they took power that no backward country could establish socialism unless assisted by the overthrow of capitalism in the West, where alone history had assembled the material preconditions for a truly socialist society. But their hopes of revolution in the West were dashed. Instead of becoming the granary of a socialist state of Europe, easing herself gently into the modern world, backward revolutionary Russia was straightway invaded and pillaged by her mighty industrial neighbours. She survived the wars of intervention (1918–21) in which many of the most idealistic communists were killed. In order not to succumb in future wars, Russia must now industrialize herself, largely by her own efforts. She must catch up with the West, accomplishing in a few years what the West achieved with more leisure at its

41 L. Trotsky, *The Revolution Betrayed*, New Park, London, 1973, is the foundation of the Far Left's understanding of the Soviet Union as a workers' state ruled by a parasitic bureaucracy. I. Deutscher, *The Unfinished Revolution 1917–1967*, Oxford University Press, Oxford, 1967, updates the analysis but, unlike orthodox Trotskyists, Deutscher was hopeful of reform. The Socialist Workers Party holds that the bureaucracy brought about some kind of capitalist restoration in the late 1920s and that there are no workers' states anywhere in the world: T. Cliff, *State Capitalism in Russia*, Pluto, London, 1974.

disposal. Marx had held that socialism presupposes plenty, whereas poverty and hardship sooner or later reproduce the struggle of individuals one with another. But how could the solidarity that marked the birth of the Russian Revolution survive the hardships that now lay ahead? The worker who did not perish in the Civil War wanted to return to the plough; nor did the peasant a few years later want to leave the land for the rifle, the shovel and the lathe. Year after year everyone struggled for bread, for a moment's rest from incessant back-breaking labour, for some meagre comfort. Inevitably, the public servant, the manager and the expert, shook themselves free of control in the struggle for personal advantage: to secure exemptions, to go to the head of every queue, to procure easy jobs for family and friends, lay hands on an automobile or a larger apartment. Thus did social inequality reappear once again. And where privilege is odious to the people – it is especially odious to the people of communist countries – it can support itself by no means other than a totalitarian dictatorship. The Russian Revolution was 'betrayed', and socialist revolutions in other backward countries have suffered a fate made less severe only by the aid that fresh revolutions receive from those that went before, though social inequality and its repercussions are there for all to see[42].

Many revolutionaries hope to remove from power by a political revolution the communist parties of the East, and to replace them with incorruptibles who will abolish the privileges of officialdom and introduce a workers' democracy. But they also hope that socialism in the West will avoid bureaucratic degeneration. The West is rich. It needs no lengthy period of reconstruction. It needs no hectic bout of industrialization. Here, the revolution could follow the itinerary of Lenin's *State & Revolution* – from a 'dictatorship of the proletariat' (a state that is a 'thousand times more democratic' than a parliamentary democracy and already in the process of withering away) to a

---

42 This is why social democrats and Stalinists have generally believed that revolution in Third World countries should not take up socialist tasks but confine itself to the world of the 'bourgeois-democratic' revolution. Trotskyists reply that the European path of historical evolution cannot be transposed into the backward countries in the epoch of imperialist domination, and that revolutions everywhere should be given a socialist character even though not all countries will be able to move towards socialism with equal rapidity.

society which is self-governing and virtually or wholly stateless[43].

No one can say whether this optimism concerning the West is justified. Totalitarian rule exists today in Russia despite industrialization and comparative prosperity. Poland is not a backward country. Some critics maintain that collectivism is congenitally doomed to bureaucratization and totalitarianism: that planners in an industrial collectivism need the same despotic powers as those who administered the 'hydraulic societies' of the semi-collectivist world of classical India or China[44]. Then there is the argument from human nature itself: if human wants should prove to be infinitely elastic, the individuals will always be driven by insatiable appetites which not even the material prosperity of the West will assuage, and those playing prominent roles in society, those upon whom others depend, will sooner or later exploit their power for personal advantage. It is indeed noticeable that the sons and daughters of a revolution stand, in the moral scale, at the knee rather than on the shoulders of their elders. If all this is so, then it hardly matters how we arrive at collectivism, whether by persuasion or by force, by poll or by powder: corruption is ineluctable and the socialist dream is just another of the innumerable follies of mankind.

III

The obstacles to a revolution in present-day Europe are considerable. Europe is at peace, and since the war her peoples have enjoyed a spectacular rise in living standards. As class hatreds have subsided so political liberties have flourished. The contrast between the past three decades and the three that preceded them could scarcely be more complete. The only socialism so far known is hardly attractive. Not surprisingly, most people regard socialism with suspicion, and when millions vote for socialist or communist candidates they are voting for social reform. Those

---

43 V. I. Lenin, 'State and Revolution', *Selected Works*, Vol. 2, p. 334, *passim*. But see Trotsky: 'Just as the lamp, before going out, shoots up in a brilliant flame, so the State, before disappearing, assumes the form of a dictatorship of the proletariat, i.e. the most ruthless form of State, which embraces the life of the citizens authoritatively in every direction.' *Terrorism and Communism, op cit.* p. 170.
44 K. Wittfogel, *Oriental Despotism*, Yale University Press, New Haven, 1957.

proposing to introduce this suspect thing by a round of armed rebellion are greeted with disdain. Gone is the enthusiasm that once lifted the socialist orator. Gone too is the revolutionary culture so popular in many countries between the wars.

There have been some semi-revolutionary upheavals during the past thirty years, usually triggered by the occasional European or US involvment in wars in the southern hemisphere. Following its defeat in the Congo, Belgium experienced a general strike in the winter of 1960, during which youth began revolutionary activities, but these quickly petered out. France underwent a critical period during the Algerian war when Paris lived for a time in fear of a military coup[45], and again during the general strike of May 1968 when, after a student insurrection inspired among other things by hatred of US action in Vietnam, ten million workers struck and occupied their factories, some demanding the replacement of de Gaulle with a socialist regime[46]. But the Algerian-based generals did not rise, and in May 1968 there was no one willing to overthrow de Gaulle's government so that the general strike was doomed to end in a grand anti-climax. There was in 1968 no issue over which the French people wanted to risk their lives. In 1974–75, having endured forty years of fascism and the longest colonial war of post-war history, Portugal embraced socialist revolution for a whole year. Even there, however, the implacibility of the past was gone.

As a result of all this, the forces of the Far Left remain tiny, at least for the time being. How to increase their size and influence is the question that preoccupies and divides them. Clearly, it is not enough to sit back and wait for events. There is too much to change, above all in the minds of the workers themselves. This is why the Far Left support every struggle of the exploited and the oppressed – not so much for what the contestants may gain as for what they may learn. The Far Left is often the first to spring to the defence of workers' economic and political rights, to raise the alarm against sexism, fascism, racism, imperialism and rearmament, or to demand workers' democracy in the East. By these campaigns, usually conducted in collaboration with more moderate forces, the Far Left hopes to expose the true nature of the

45 P. Henissart, *Wolves in the City*, Paladin, St Albans, 1973, pp. 83–5.
46 E. Mandel, 'Lessons of May' *New Left Review*, 52, Nov/Dec 1968, p. 22; also P. Seale and M. McConville, *French Revolution 1968*, Penguin, Harmondsworth, 1968.

social system, prevent the rich from creating scapegoats, combat the unacceptable face of socialism, and all in all propagate the idea of a socialist revolution. Some build new political parties that promise to lead it.

'Transitional demands'

Besides this work, a large part of the Far Left seeks other ways of hastening the great event, notably by urging the labour movement to fight for what are called 'transitional demands'. These are generally associated with Leon Trotsky, but were also developed by the Communist International in its early years. Almost all the major groups and parties of the Far Left have been connected at some time or other with the Fourth International which Trotsky founded in 1938. Transitional demands include: a sliding scale of wages and hours, abolition of business secrecy, expropriation of big business, the formation of workers councils and workers' committees, the creation of workers' militia, and the setting up of a 'workers' government'.

Now, according to Trotsky, these demands form a 'bridge' stemming 'from today's conditions and today's consciousness of wide layers of the working class' and leading to the seizure of power[47]. Rather than a bridge, however, these demands seem to be the very tasks and measures of the revolution itself. The ambiguity did not trouble Trotsky, for in his day society was, as he wrote himself, already in a 'prerevolutionary' condition[48]. 'The multimillioned masses again and again enter the road of revolution'[49]. In his time countries were hardly able to catch their breath between one round of rebellion and another. In a land already pregnant with revolution, a vigorous campaign for one or other of those demands might easily arouse the people to yet another effort. But what might once have induced birth will not compensate today for an empty womb.

Campaigns for 'transitional demands' have yielded disappointing results. If we were facing 1920s-style inflation or the sort of economic chaos that followed the Great War, sliding

47 L. Trotsky, 'The Death Agony of Capitalism and The Tasks of the Fourth International', commonly known as 'The Transitional Programme', p. 75. All references are to *The Transitional Programme for Socialist Revolution*, Pathfinder, New York, 1973.
48 *Ibid.* p. 73.
49 *Ibid.* p. 73.

Socialist strategies

scales of hours and wages would be burningly relevant[50]. If we had to liberate our country or stop our government going to war, we should certainly need a workers' militia 'drilled and acquainted with the use of arms'[51]. Were the rich treasoning with hostile foreign powers, as they did in Russia in 1918 or in Eastern Europe under Hitler, everyone would instantly see the justice of a penal measure like expropriation of property[52]. Transitional demands are emergency measures; it is in emergencies that revolutions usually occur.

Where transitional demands have been acceptable, history has robbed them of their explosive character. Some trade unions have negotiated agreements to tie wages to the cost of living or to give workers a guaranteed wage during short-time working, but these agreements provoke no coup. Workers control is another popular idea, yet the recent legislative proposals on this subject by the British TUC are so mild as to compromise the independence of the trade unions were they to be made law; the demand that workers should be able to ban or veto managerial decisions, also popular, is often confused with less radical industrial practices[53]. Factory committees have existed in Britain for forty years, skeletal soviets for a century; but although our shop stewards committees are the envy of continental trade unionists, it would be fanciful to speak of 'dual power' in British factories[54], and our trades councils are scarcely the tumultuous assemblies of 1917. We have also seen 'workers' governments' in the sense that workers' parties have taken exclusive possession of the ministries. That was rare in Trotsky's time, when coalitions ('national governments' or 'popular fronts') were common. Yet

50 T. Sender, *op cit.* p. 107.
51 Trotsky, *op cit.* p. 85.
52 A euphemism is often used to refer to this policy: 'nationalization without compensation'. The phrase 'without compensation', however, is confusing, for it might refer either to the money paid in purchasing company assets, or to an additional sum paid to compensate the owners for their having been bought out compulsorily. The two things are significantly different.
53 K. Coates and T. Topham, *Guide to the Bullock Report*, Spokesman, Nottingham, 1977, pp. 79–81, and K. Coates and T. Topham, *The New Unionism*, Penguin, Harmondsworth, 1974, pp. 85–7. For a critical discussion of current ideas about workers control see my article 'The Enigma of Workers Control' in *International*, Vol. 5, No. 1, 1979, IMG Publications, London, 1979.
54 'From the moment that the committee makes its appearance a factual dual power is established in the factory.' Trotsky, *op cit.* p. 80.

Harold Wilson and Willy Brandt have passed by without causing substantial damage to the social order.

Nevertheless, these transitional ideas have immense educational significance. The labour movement absorbs in dilute form today ideas that will bring forth ripe fruit tomorrow. Some of these ideas have been widely disseminated. The notion of workers' control, for example, popularized by the Institute for Workers' Control, in which the International Marxist Group (IMG) once played a catalytic role, has influenced thousands of trade union militants. The Militant Tendency, the best-known of the four largest Far Left groups in Britain, has for years campaigned for the Labour Party to nationalize the 250 top monopolies with minimal compensation; so far without success. Although the response to them may for the present be disappointing, transitional slogans raise the eyes of the labour movement towards its great goal. One day millions will embrace these ideas – then the revolution will have begun.

The epoch

The difficulties over transitional demands are part of a more general problem. Through what sort of historical period has Europe been passing? Most revolutionary groups find it hard to accept that while the rest of the world may still be living through an 'epoch of wars and revolutions', Europe is no longer doing so[55]. Ultra-Leftism therefore abounds. The IMG, for example, in common with its sister groups of the Fourth International, held in the early 1970s that Europe was only three or four years away

55 According to Trotsky (*op cit.* p. 75) we are living in an 'epoch of wars and revolutions' when 'in general there can be no discussion of systematic social reforms and the raising of the masses' living standards', the situation is 'catastrophic', and the day-to-day work of socialists can be 'carried on indissolubly with the actual tasks of the revolution'. Most Trotskyists, at least in their economic analysis, have recognized the post-war changes. E. Mandel has written extensively about the 'long boom' (*Late Capitalism*, New Left Books, London, 1978), and the followers of Cliff (SWP) have argued that the permanent arms economy temporarily arrested the entropic mechanisms of capital. (M. Kidron, *Western Capitalism Since the War*, London, 1968). The SWP avoids crisis-mongering but rejects transitional demands, while Mandel has argued the implausible theory that revolution is possible without slump and war, *A Socialist Strategy for Western Europe*, Institute of Workers Control, Pamphlet No 10, Nottingham.

Socialist strategies

from either a 'decisive contest' or the 'strong state'[56]. The IMG's job was to bring about a general strike which, going one better than May 1968, would create soviets and open up a lengthy period of 'dual power' similar to that which existed in Russia during the summer of 1917[57]. From there, October is only a short hop away. Yet, such lengthy periods of dual power usually follow revolutionary uprisings like the February Revolution, which in turn are induced by happenings not seen in Europe for many years. The IMG seems unaware that in a general strike the workers' movement would be confronted directly with the question of power, and in its present condition the movement would recoil in alarm and disarray[58]. The 'strong state' has failed to materialize.

The misconceptions of the IMG are subtle; those of the Workers Revolutionary Party (WRP), formerly the Socialist Labour League, are thoroughly outlandish. Its leader, Gerry Healy, has proclaimed for two decades that the West stood only weeks or days from a 1929-style crash. For years we have been standing on the brink of a 'semi-fascist dictatorship'. The situation is 'revolutionary'. Sometimes, civil war is 'imminent'[59]. It is as if we were still living in Germany in 1930 or 1931. More sinister are the activities of groups like the Italian Red Brigades or the German Red Army Fraction. These militants believe that fascism has actually arrived. It is imperative to build a 'people's army', as though the Duce were still in Milan or Hitler in the

56 T. Potter, 'The Strong State', *International Socialism*, 2.4. Spring 1979.
57 'The Situation in Britain and The Tasks of the IMG', Theses proposed by the United Secretariat of the Fourth International, *International*, Vol. 2, No. 3, Summer, 1973.
58 '... every general strike, whatever may be the slogans under which it occurs, has an internal tendency to transform itself into an open revolutionary clash, a direct struggle for power.' Trotsky, *Whither France*, Merit, New York, 1968, p. 79. A campaign for a 'general strike to kick out the Tories', which the IMG demanded in 1973–74 and again in 1981, can mean nothing other than a call for armed overthrow of the government, though they seemed unaware of it; the IMG never calls for early general elections to remove the Tories. The idea that we might glide into a long period of dual power without an armed rising has been worked up into a systematic strategy by Ernest Mandel (*Revolutionary Marxism Today*, New Left Books, London, 1979, pp. 14–19); this is of a piece with his non-catastrophist theory of revolution, but it lacks serious historical or political foundation.
59 T. Whelan, *The Credibility Gap, The Politics of the SLL*, IMG Publications, London, 1970, pp. 9, 23, 29. Workers Press, 5.10.74. The imminence of civil war was a WRP theme during the general elections of 1979.

Chancellery. Thankfully, this particular lunacy has not yet arrived in Britain[60].

Another problem facing the Far Left is where to place its forces to maximum advantage. Should they build a new political party, pure in word and deed, or should they enter the mass 'reformist' parties in order to work as a vocal opposition? One view is that where mass parties already monopolize the field, new parties never become serious challengers unless they emerge out of a fission within the mass party during a revolution or a civil war; then they can expect to take a substantial minority or even a majority of the members. This is how the communist parties were born. Parties of reform adopt revolutionary phraseology in revolutionary times and even lead revolutions – in some cases *social* revolutions – and this is how they manage to retain command of their followers. Only at the very climax of events, and then only if words and actions diverge unmistakably, will a large enough number of militants be persuaded to form a new party, and only after a genuine bid for the leadership of the old. This is why many revolutionaries have followed the example of Rosa Luxemburg and Lenin, working as a fraction within the mass parties, perhaps for decades, in order to be in the best position to take control when the time comes[61]. Those closest to this approach in Britain are those of the Militant Tendency.

Some support for the policy of long-term entryism is provided, it must be said, by the early history of the Fourth International itself. Trotsky saw fit to form the Fourth in 1938 on the view that the parties of the Third International had compromised themselves hopelessly in Germany and Spain and would play an undistinguished role in the Second World War. In three or four years, prophesied Trotsky, 'millions' would flock to the banner of the new parties[62]. Yet the European and Chinese communists, far from becoming moribund during the war, led heroic struggles for national liberation and for socialism, winning the first in

60 *Documents from the Red Army Fraction*, Stoke Newington 8 Defence Group 1972. 'We, the Red Brigades' in *The Leveller*, No. 48, 1981, which romanticizes common criminals as a 'protelatarian vanguard'.
61 P. Frank, *The Fourth International: The Long March of the Trotskyists*, Ink Links, London, 1979, p. 97. K. Coates, 'Socialists and The Labour Party', *The Socialist Register 1973*, London, 1974: the case has yet to receive a serious reply.
62 I. Deutscher, *The Prophet Outcast*, Oxford University Press, Oxford, 1970, p. 426.

many countries and the second in several. The Trotskyists were left high and dry. In the most momentous war in history, the communists decided the fate of peoples, the Trotskyists railed, in obscurity.

Many revolutionaries believe, on the other hand, that entryism involves making too many serious concessions. The movement needs a 'Leninist party', which is supposed to exclude 'reformists' and 'centrists' from its ranks and operates a strict discipline alien to most modern parliamentary parties. It is not at all certain that Lenin formulated the idea of such a party; he wanted to introduce into Russia the party models then current in Western Europe. However, modern social-democracy has few of the virtues of the Second International, and even parliamentary discipline is not what it once was. It is also extremely difficult to conduct a principled opposition to reformist ideas within present day mass parties for long: either the left loses its ideological purity or it gets expelled. The Communists expel Trotskyists almost on principle, and it is not clear that the British Labour Party will tolerate the Militant Tendency indefinitely[63].

There is in fact no single transitional demand or party-building tactic that will miraculously induce a revolution or multiply the revolutionary forces. It is not given to every generation to mount the barricades. Tragically, however, the long years in the wilderness have produced so many splits – each faction clutching at the latest device for making the junction with destiny – that acrimony makes it difficult for the Far Left to fuse when a revolution arrives. That is surely one of the lessons of the Portuguese experience. Here, in the midst of a genuine upheaval, a dozen groups remained divided over matters of tactics and style that were trivial by comparison with the differences contained within the Bolshevik Party in 1917 or in the USPD a year later. Who in Portugal could take the Far Left seriously as candidates for power? The Portuguese paid the bill for thirty years of strife. A historic opportunity was criminally wasted.

Yet, whatever the shortcomings of the Far Left, these small forces remain the custodians of a culture whose time must surely return. They linger among its ruins, and with incantations culled from scroll and tomb they conjure for their incurious and

---

63 This approach is now being taken by the SWP and the WRP, but all the major groups have spent long periods in the Labour Party.

uncomprehending contemporaries the arts and powers of the past. Western labour has little interest in their strange teachings. But without mastering old mysteries afresh, the labour movement will surely be unable to build a new and perhaps better world.

Chapter seven

FEMINISM AND THE STRUGGLE FOR SOCIALISM

Sarah Perrigo

There is currently an increasing interest and debate over the relationship between socialism and feminism; a debate which has increased in urgency as both movements suffer the effects of economic crisis and political reaction. The destruction by the Thatcher Government of the Beveridge-Keynesian consensus which dominated post-war British politics, and the decisive defeat of the Labour Party in the 1983 election, have both served to highlight the need to rethink socialist strategies. There is a growing recognition of the inadequacy of existing models of socialism as embodied in the practice of both Western European social democracy and Eastern European communism. In the public mind, socialism is unpopular – it is statist, bureaucratic and remote, as well as dull and uninspiring. In the political space created by the break-up of consensus politics, socialists not only on the Far Left but also in the Labour Party and the trade unions, have begun to question some of their traditional ways of thinking and acting. Many are beginning to recognize that if socialism is to offer a viable and attractive alternative to present Tory hegemony it must find ways of overcoming its own fragmentation and disunity.

After a decade of its existence many in the feminist movement too are seeing the need for some critical self-evaluation. With the first wave of energy and enthusiasm waning, questions about future strategies and tactics are demanding our urgent consideration. Despite its considerable achievements it is widely recognized that the movement needs to reach out to a wider circle of women, and women in ethnic minorities, if it is to avoid gettoization and marginalization in its political struggles. It is clear that the initial gains won over the past decade are threatened by the present economic crisis and Tory cut-backs in public sector spending, the overall effect of which is to push women back into the home either through unemployment or to perform those services that the state no longer provides.

Both the labour movement and the feminist movement, both class and gender interests, are under attack at the present time. If the feminist movement is not only to defend itself but also to grow and move forward, many feminists, particularly those who identify themselves as socialist feminists, are beginning to see the necessity of some kind of alliance or co-operation with the socialist and labour movement; a need to enter some kind of dialogue with men that could potentially enrich socialism and provide feminism with a real root in working class life and experience.

Nevertheless, the road to a socialist–feminist praxis is paved with a myriad of obstacles – both theoretical and practical. Analytically, and historically, they are two distinct movements with different priorities, perspectives and aims. It would be naive, even dangerous, to deny the reality of the obstacles in the way of some unified socialist feminist strategy or to assume that there are easy solutions.

I would argue that the present period, with the opening up of a debate within socialism, offers a possibility (but only a possibility) of a transformed socialist project which integrates feminist ideals into its very being. Whether that ideal is translated into practice depends at least in some degree upon the willingness of feminists to take their ideas into the socialist movement in its various forms. It also depends on the willingness of socialist men to take those ideas seriously.

The aim of this chapter is to outline the history of the socialist and feminist movements particularly as they relate to Britain; to examine the ways in which contemporary feminism challenges orthodox socialist politics; and to tentatively suggest ways in which socialist politics must be transformed if they are to meet the feminist challenge.

SOCIALISM AND FEMINISM: THE PAST

Although present possibilities are not wholly determined by the past, if we are to grasp the problems involved in developing a feminist socialist movement, something of the history of the two movements and the ideas which have dominated them has to be understood, for the past still conditions in important ways the attitudes of both movements. Both movements have their origins in the nineteenth century, both are reactions to the development of industrial capitalism. The object of their concern has, however, led them in distinct, if at times, overlapping directions. The concern of feminism has obviously been with the question of sexual subordination; that of socialism with class relations. Socialism, as an ethical ideal, as a portrait of the good society, has always proclaimed allegiance to sexual equality as part of its project but, for reasons that will become apparent, it has tended to displace such a concern to the margins of its actual practice. Feminism, on the other hand, has displayed an ambivalence to questions of class and, at times, a hostility to the socialist movement.

Early socialist thinkers clearly saw sex equality as an integral aspect of the socialist vision. Barbara Taylor has written of Owenism, 'Feminism was . . . not merely an ancillary feature of the socialist project but one of its key motivating impulses'[1]. The so-called 'utopian socialists' such as Owen and Fourier wrote at the turn of the nineteenth century when industrial capitalism was still in its infancy. Traditional patterns of class and gender relations were beginning to be disrupted but new patterns of relationships had not yet become clearly established or fixed. To some extent this allowed these early thinkers to imagine possibilities of a total transformation of social life that seem to disappear later in the century as industrial capitalism advanced. They adopted what has been called 'a broad humanistic standpoint', subjecting all forms of domination to a radical critique, including the domination of men over women. To these early socialist pioneers it appeared obvious that the patriarchal family was as much an obstacle to the development of the socialist co-operative ideal as was the development of private property and capitalism. The family was perceived as the major site for the development of patterns of behaviour required for the effective operation of a competitive market economy. Within the structure of the patriarchal family, relationships of subordination and domination were formed and internalized. If harmonious social relations of socialism were to develop then such a family form had to be overthrown. These ideas of the early socialists suc-

1 Barbara Taylor, 'Feminism: utopian or scientific' in Ralph Samuel (ed), *People's History and Socialist Theory*, Routledge and Kegan Paul, London, 1981, p. 61.

ceeded in attracting a not insignificant number of women to the socialist cause, and allowed for a brief period of time a joint struggle of men and women against both capital and patriarchal authority. The rise of the organized labour movement and the development of Marxism both served in different ways to shatter the original coincidence of the socialist and feminist project.

Within Marxist theory, female subordination became understandable only within a context of class interests. According to Engels, dominant, private property owning, classes alone had a real material interest in sexual domination and patriarchal control. Within subordinate classes no such material interest existed. In fact, sex-antagonisms were non-existent within the proletariat whose 'interest', whether male or female, was the common one of overthrowing capitalist society[2]. Although Marx and Engels recognized that women experienced specific problems within capitalist society, it was asserted that those problems could only be solved with the overthrow of capitalist society and the institution of socialism. Only then could women be relieved of their domestic burden as those tasks were socialized.

Marx developed a penetrating critique of the ways in which capitalism distorts all social relationships. However, his analysis of the capitalist mode of production led him to place overwhelming emphasis upon the structural antagonism between capital and wage labour as the central site both for the development of class consciousness and for political struggle. The consequence was to effectively narrow the struggle for socialism to the point of production.

The denial of any material basis for sexual conflict within the working class, along with the Marxist emphasis upon production as the major arena for struggle, was to prove disastrous for women. It was to result in the marginalization of women from the revolutionary socialist movement. It was also to deny the need for, or validity of, any independent feminist platform within the socialist movement. Though the organization and participation of women was seen as important by Marxists, it was to be their organization as proletarians rather than women. An autonomously organized feminism was seen as dangerous and diversionary – a product of bourgeois thought propagated by bourgeois women. As such it had to be combatted as a threat to class unity and solidarity.

2 Frederick Engels, *The Origins of the Family, Private Property and the State* London, Lawrence and Wishart, 1973.

In the main 'classical' Marxist text on the position of women, Engels suggested that the major precondition for the emancipation of women was their participation in social production and their consequent proletarianization. Marxist analyses of the capitalist mode of production suggested that the development of capitalism would indeed draw more and more women into social production, thus providing the preconditions for their actual liberation. What both Marx and Engels failed to perceive was that the way in which women were drawn into social production was crucially mediated through the structure of the family and an ideology of a woman's role which served to place her in a subordinate and marginal position within social production and at times to keep her out of production altogether. They failed, therefore, to perceive the very real differential relationship women occupy in relationship to production *vis-à-vis* men.

The extraordinary tendency of the Marxist Left to view women opportunistically must be seen in this light. Women were either comrades no different from their proletarian 'brothers' or they were politically backward conservatives who required political education. No real attempt was made to explore women's differential experience of capitalist exploitation, or to theorize it into the political struggle. Lenin, for example, was clearly aware of the need to involve more women in the socialist movement. Yet, when women raised domestic concerns in political education meetings, he roundly condemned such talk as diversionary and a waste of time[3].

If Marxist theory marginalized women's oppression, the development of a less theoretical, pragmatic labour movement effected a similar result in practice. If Marxists failed to challenge the sexual division of labour within theory, the organized labour movement not only failed to challenge it but, for the most part, actually endorsed it. As we have seen, the fluidity of class and gender relations in the early nineteenth century allowed a joint resistance to capital and to proletarianization by men and women. As capital developed, both class and gender relations began to solidify into new and distinct forms. As the working class emerged as 'historical fact' it began to develop ideas about itself and what constituted its interest within the limits of capitalist society. The labour movement through the trade unions, and later the Labour Party, emerged to protect

3 Clare Zetkin, *Conversations with Lenin*, New York, International Publishers, 1974, p. 49.

those interests. In all essential respects this was to be the interests of working class men.

The organized labour movement developed into a context where the sexual division of labour was becoming far more rigidly defined. Bourgeois ideas about women which served to define them as wives and mothers rather than workers were becoming entrenched throughout society. For a series of complex reasons, male workers and many women accepted such a definition (though not without a struggle between male trade unionists and women workers). In the ideal world of the male trade unionist[4] women should not have to take part in wage labour but should be 'free' to fulfil her proper tasks – the care and protection of home and family. Thus, a major thrust of Labour's policy was the winning of a family wage sufficient to provide for a dependent wife and children. It is not necessary to impute men with evil or ulterior motives in pursuing such a policy; neither is it difficult to see why so many women supported such an idea. In a time when multiple pregnancies, child-rearing and arduous domestic labour left women old before they were thirty, even without the added burden of seeking paid work, such an objective must have been appealing. The effect however on women was disastrous, particularly when the struggle for a family wage was supplemented with a trade union policy designed to keep women out of wage labour, or at least out of the 'skilled' and better-paid sectors of it.

First of all, the objective of the family wage was never effectively realized. Few working class men have been able to provide adequately for their family without it being supplemented by a wife's earnings. The effect of a policy designed to keep women out of the labour force and out of the trade unions merely resulted in women being forced to take whatever jobs they could obtain, usually unskilled and badly paid.

Such a policy made no distinction between women: all women whether married or single, divorced or widowed, were placed in the same position of economic dependency and vulnerability. Not only did Labour and trade union strategy legitimate and maintain the sexual division of labour, it also served to develop and reinforce ideas about what constitutes 'real' socialist politics, reducing that to the perceived interests of male, particularly skilled, workers. The main objectives of struggle were to

4 See for example Henry Broadhurst, President of the TUC in 1877, *TUC Conference Report 1877*.

become centred around such issues as employment, wage bargaining and, ultimately, around control of production. These constituted the 'big' issues. Other areas, such as housing, education and welfare were seen increasingly as subsidiary and separate areas for struggle. This allowed women a 'legitimate' sphere of interest and influence but one that was distinct from men's and in practice secondary. Some areas of life were clearly not conceived as political at all, notably responsibility for child care and control of reproduction.

The uncritical acceptance of the sexual division of labour also meant that socialist men never had to consider the inter-relationship between home and work, between public and private, in developing a socialist strategy. It has led to the situation still prevalent today of 'tacking' so called 'womens' issues to the end of a shopping list of socialist objectives rather than identifying those interests as central to the socialist struggle to transform the quality of life and to offer a vision of transformed social relationships.

If socialism and the labour movement in general has been insensitive to the issue of women's subordination, the initial development of feminism was itself indifferent, if not hostile, to the idea of socialism. Though then, as now, there were different currents within a broad movement, feminism was predominantly a movement of middle class women formed in response to the intolerable position such women found themselves in, increasingly confined to the 'private' sphere of home and family, forbidden both legally and socially from participation in the expanding sphere of work and politics. This is not to suggest that working class women were not adversely affected too by the changes brought about through industrialization, but that it was middle class women who first experienced the effects of an intensified sexual division of labour and who had the time and energy to struggle against it.

These early feminists drew their inspiration and justification primarily from those liberal philosophers who emphasized notions of individual liberty and equality. Influential thinkers like John Locke had long argued that men are born with certain inalienable rights by virtue of their humanity. Such ideas had provided the inspiration for the French and American revolutions. They were to provide the moral arguments used by feminists in their struggle for equality. In an important sense, mainstream feminism in the nineteenth century stood with radical liberalism rather than with socialism; with Mill[5] rather than with Marx.

Though they were involved in a wide range of struggles combatting facets of patriarchal society, including exposing the hypocrisy of the sexual double standard, attitudes towards prostitution, and domestic violence, these early feminists conceived their primary struggle as one for equal rights. Thus, many of their most important campaigns were over issues such as suffrage reform, the opening up of universities and the professions to women, the granting to women of equal legal rights over property and children. Clearly, these demands were progressive and benefited women generally. They were, however, demands which were not conceived as incompatible with capitalism but were rather viewed as demands which when met would 'prove' the progressiveness of the liberal parliamentary democracy. Many feminists held to the optimistic belief that once women had achieved formal legal equality with men they would, in fact, be equal. This led them to neglect or underestimate other more powerful determinants of sexual inequality which would prevent all but a small minority of women from taking advantage of equal rights once they were achieved.

Neither their explanations of sexual inequality nor their demands led them to see any necessary connection between the struggle for socialism and the feminist cause. Indeed, it was the insistence by feminists on their demand for strict formal equality that led them into conflict with the organized labour movement and with the needs of working class women.

In categorically denying the need for any kind of differential treatment of women, they overlooked the real difference of interest of women of different social classes. In aggressively asserting the right of women to work and denying the need for any form of protective legislation, they failed to recognize that working class women always worked and often in intolerable conditions. Their ignorance and insensitivity towards the experience of working class women strengthened socialist beliefs that feminism was 'bourgeois' and antithetical to working class interests. The decision of the majority of feminist organizations to campaign for the vote on the same grounds as men rather than campaign with labour for full adult franchise further

5 John Stuart Mill, 'The subjection of women' in John Stuart Mill and Harriet Taylor *Essays on Sex Equality* (edited by Alice Rossi, University of Chicago Press, Chicago, 1970).

heightened the conflict between feminism and socialism. Though feminists had good reasons for distrusting male political parties, the overall effect was to increase the distrust of labour leaders towards feminism and, more importantly, to distance working class women from feminist organizations. Most working class women who actually campaigned for womens suffrage did so alongside men rather than in the female societies or in the militant Women's Social and Political Union (WSPU). The history of the struggle for suffrage demonstrates not just a difference of tactics between socialism and feminism but reflects the differential class composition of the two movements at the time. To have campaigned on a platform of adult suffrage would split the feminist movement wide open on class lines. By no means all suffragettes would have supported a full adult suffrage campaign; they wanted equality within classes not the abolition of class.

Richard Evans, in writing about the division between 'bourgeois' feminists and the socialist movement in Germany before 1914, has written:

Ideologically, bourgeois feminists were unable to support the wider aims of the SPD; they believed in reform not revolution, they were individualists not collectivists, they believed in individual moral autonomy as opposed to historical determinism, and above all at the centre of their system of belief was the conviction that the struggle between men and women overrode all distinctions of social class, a conviction which the social democrats, whose attachment to the interests of the proletariat was quite explicit, were unable to share.[6]

It is clear that similar sentiments divided most feminists from the socialist and labour movement in Britain in the same period.

WOMEN SOCIALISTS AND FEMINISM

Despite the failure of both the theory and practice of socialism to recognize any 'real' antagonism between men and women within the class struggle, the socialist movement did succeed in organizing a considerable number of women. In Germany, for example, by 1914 the Marxist Social Democratic Party (SPD) had already around 175,000 women members, published a

6 Richard Evans, 'Bourgeois Feminists and Women Socialists in Germany 1894–1914' in *Women Studies International Quarterly*, 1980, Vol. 3, p. 366.

women's paper, *die Gleichheit* (equality), and held annual women's conferences. Though the British socialist movement was, in comparison, less organized and advanced women were organized in the Womens Co-operative Guild, the Womens Labour League and in socialist societies such as the Independent Labour Party (ILP). In 1918, the new Labour Party constitution made provision for the setting up of womens sections in every Labour Party constituency and for women's conferences to be held annually. It also reserved places for women on the national executive committee, appointed a national women's officer and published a monthly journal called *Labour Woman*. By the late 1920s, around 68,000 women were members of Labour Party women's sections.

In many ways, socialist organizations made strenuous efforts in order to attract women members, and never more so than when the feminist movement was at its height as a powerful and influential force. In Germany, for example, in the period 1890–1914, feminism was an extremely influential movement involving at least 250,000 members. In the early 1900s, it tended to be a very radical movement in its ideas and practices, proclaiming strong opposition to the state and its patriarchal and authoritarian nature. The male dominated SPD, stimulated at least in part out of fear that the feminist movement might succeed in organizing working class women, made some efforts to encourage women to join the SPD. They were, however, very careful to distinguish socialist women from what they term 'the bourgeois feminist movement'. Clare Zetkin, a leading SPD activist and women's organiser, made regular and repeated attacks upon 'bourgeois' feminists who, she said, were only interested in gaining for themselves the freedom to compete on equal terms with men of their own class. She continually stressed that there could be no community of interest amongst women as a whole[7].

Arthur Henderson, in the foreword to a book edited by Marion Phillips on *Women and the Labour Party* in 1918 made a similar point when he wrote:

The Labour Party has always advocated the claims of women on the grounds of sex equality; the women of our movement have however consistently opposed every development of the feminist agitation which tends to emphasise the unhappy sex-antagonisms produced by the long and bitter struggle over the franchise . . . In the coming era of social

7 *Ibid.* p. 369.

reconstruction likewise the organised working class, which includes both men and women, has evolved a policy intended to promote the common interests of both sexes, and we believe that when this policy is properly understood by the bulk of enfranchised women they will recognise that separate sex organisations are fundamentally undemocratic and wholly reactionary.[8]

The Labour Party, as well as wishing to counter any feminist influence, was also clearly interested in mobilizing women after 1918 as some women became enfranchised, and thus needed to be appealed to as potential Labour voters.

In spite of the 'official' rhetoric of socialist leaders disassociating socialist women from feminism, there is some evidence that socialist women themselves were not always so willing to accept this view of the situation. Although we have seen that mainstream feminism kept aloof from the socialist movement, there were numerous women who supported both the socialist and the feminist cause. The propaganda and activities of the feminist movement had an impact upon the ideas and aspirations of many socialist women. At different times, both British and German women socialists found themselves in conflict with their male comrades. Women in the Co-operative Guild battled with men over the issue of divorce reform, socialist women in Germany clashed over a range of issues from the suffrage question to the right of women to control reproduction. Women in the Labour Party came into conflict with men over, among other things, the availability of contraceptive advice in local authority maternity clinics, and the issue of family endowment. They further demanded constitutional changes in the Labour Party so that women's issues could be more clearly reflected in Labour Party policy.

Sometimes, in their arguments and in their struggle, such women displayed a clear feminist awareness that what they were up against was not capital but male chauvinism and patriarchal attitudes. At the same time, it was difficult for socialist women to argue clearly in feminist terms. In order to be heard, and to avoid charges of attempting to divide the movement, many socialist women were careful to couch their arguments in terms that would not draw attention to differences of interest between men and women. Ellen Wilkinson for example, in a speech to the

---

8 Authur Henderson, in the foreword to Marion Phillips (editor) *Women and the Labour Party*, London 1918.

Labour Party Women's Conference in 1923, pointed out that the level of skill a woman possessed had nothing to do with the wage she received: Women received lower wages because they were women, irrespective of their level of skill. However, she failed to implicate men and the policy of the trade unions for this situation, but merely suggested that it was up to women themselves not to accept such a state of affairs. Similarly, women who fought to make contraceptive advice freely available and who argued for the importance of some system of family allowances paid to the mother, were careful to stress the ways in which children's welfare would be enhanced by such measures rather than argue in terms of women's rights.

Not only were socialist women very sensitive to charges of being diversive, many were the wives and daughters of socialist men. This made it difficult to assert that in certain matters the interests of men and women were fundamentally opposed. In the long run, the success of the socialist movement lay in solidarity, including solidarity between men and women – that was where the future lay. Given the overwhelming male domination of the socialist parties, it is not surprising that socialist women in the end drew back from any fully fledged confrontation with the men of their own party.

In any case, in the 1920s, feminist ideas began slowly to decline in importance. In Britain, feminists appeared to have won many of the legal rights they had been demanding. For many, including socialist women, it appeared as if the major feminist battles were over, that it was time to use the newly won rights in order to improve the general lot of women in society. At the same time, they were unsure of how to proceed: were women's interests to be identified with their role as workers or as wives and mothers? In practice, although they did, for example, support campaigns for equal pay and attacked the existence of a marriage bar in the professions, most of their energy was directed towards improving welfare provisions for mothers and children. For reasons that have already been mentioned, most socialist women accepted that married women's prime responsibility should be towards home and family. For this reason, socialist women saw their main priority as one of improving the material conditions of home and family life. As long as this did not interfere with male socialist priorities it was not likely that such activities would lead to any dramatic conflict with men.

Further, as the feminist movement receded to the background,

Socialist strategies

so too did the issue of women and feminism in socialist politics. Women's sections which remained active and vigorous in the 1920s and 1930s began to wane, only to be revived again with the advent of the so-called 'second wave' of feminism in the 1960s.

FEMINISM TODAY

Contemporary feminism differs in at least two important ways from its older sister. Firstly, its analyses of male domination are far more radical and critical of the structure and institutions of existing society. The failure of a substantial measure of legal equality to bring about any real substantive equality between the sexes, has stimulated women to search for explanations of the production and reproduction of sexual inequality which point to the need for a radical restructuring of society if the goal of equality is to be achieved. Thus many feminists today are aware of the incompatibility of their demands with the capitalist mode of production.

Secondly, the way in which feminism re-emerged in the late 1960s, and the reasons for this have led it to confront socialist theory and practice in ways that earlier feminism did not. The emergence of a 'new wave' of feminism in the late 1960s was the result of a combination of changes, demographic, economic and technological, which served to heighten contradictions between the ideology and reality of women's life and which forced many women to re-evaluate their position as women.

Early feminists and, indeed, socialist feminists, had been ambivalent about the kind of equality they wanted. Though they struggled for equal rights, they rarely seriously questioned the sexual division of labour within the home. They accepted that, whilst single women should be treated equally with men, married women ought to put their homes and families first. Though a small equal-rights feminism continued in the inter-war years, the majority of politically active women were much more interested in improving welfare provisions for women and children than they were in attacking ideological/cultural assumptions about femininity and women's place in the family. Post-war changes were, however, to place these issues firmly on the agenda. The economic growth and state expansion that followed World War II created the need for more labour; demo-

190

graphic and technological changes allowed women to respond to this heightened demand.

Post-war economic restructuring led to a shortage of labour that could only be met by encouraging more and more married women into the labour market. The expansion of the state's welfare services in the same period also created opportunities for women in education, health and the social services. At the same time, the trend towards smaller families which had begun earlier in the century had become clearly established in all social classes. This, along with the widespread availability of cheap and reasonably reliable forms of contraception, meant that women's child-bearing and child-rearing responsibilities were (potentially at least) lightened considerably in comparison with the past. For the first time, women could theoretically choose if and when to have children. All of these changes occurred within a political climate that emphasized a commitment to justice and equality of opportunity for all. In the 1950s and 1960s, higher education expanded rapidly, with the result that the absolute number of women with access to higher education increased dramatically.

During the same period, however, contradictory forces were being strengthened which prevented women from receiving the benefits of new opportunities. Women were still defined primarily as wives and mothers. Indeed the ideological arguments stressing the familiar duties of women were actually being more forcefully articulated[9]. Women were constantly reminded of the dangers of neglecting their children and families by selfishly pursuing their own interests or careers outside the home. The development of the welfare state constructed women as wives and mothers, located in a nuclear family and dependent upon a male breadwinner. Its system of social security benefits was built entirely around such a family model. It is doubtful if these assumptions actually reflected the reality of family life in 1945; by the 1960s, the discrepancy between them and social reality was glaring and causing increasing hardship and misery.

The intensification of contradictions between ideology and reality, and within ideology itself, was to result in an explosion of feminist consciousness in the late 1960s. The actual catalyst which finally triggered the development of a new wave of feminism in Britain varied from county to county; it also differed

9 See for example John Bowlby, *Maternal care and mental health*, World Health Organisation, Geneva, 1951.

for women of different social classes. For many educated middle class women, it was their experience in radical and socialist political activity which proved to be the crucial factor. As opposed to Stalinism and authoritarian socialism, the political radicalism of the 1960s stressed the importance of subjectivity, of feelings, to the emancipation of the individual from the alienating conditions of life in advanced capitalism. Yet, when women attempted to explore their own feelings of oppression within Left groups they were greeted with derisive jeers by their erstwhile male comrades. For many it seemed that they were involved in struggles to liberate black Americans, the Vietnamese, the working class, but there was no space for the liberation of women.

For many working class women, it was the intensification of wage struggles in the 1960s that was to spark off revolt. With the dramatic increase in the numbers of married women in the work-force, many more joined trade unions and became involved in labour struggles. In the process, they discovered that equality for women did not include equal pay or equal job opportunities. The strike of women workers at Fords for equal pay in 1968 was a sign that working class women too were prepared to question their subordinate position.

In many ways the development of feminism in Britain grew out of the inadequacy of the socialist and labour movement to reflect the interests and experience of women. In what ways then, has contemporary feminism challenged orthodox socialist politics? In what follows I shall attempt to examine some of the central arguments made by feminists as they apply to the future development of socialism.

Organization

The way in which the feminist movement has developed stands in stark contrast to the dominant forms of organization developed by the Left. Many feminists emerged from Left organizations convinced that it was the character of organization itself which inhibited the development of feminist politics. As Diana Adlam has noted, 'the dominant ways of organising and taking decisions were cited as crucial obstacles to the prioritiza-tion of feminist aims by those who from within socialist groups argued for an autonomous women's movement in the late

1960s'[10]. In the trades unions and the Labour Party, administrative procedure appeared to take precedent over any open political debate, and political debate itself appeared limited to making resolutions. Issues that were not readily amenable to resolution appeared non-existent, significant only by their absence.

On the Far Left, a continual reference to a Marxist-Leninist orthodoxy similarly denied women any space for effective intervention or impact. The women's movement thus set out self-consciously to avoid organizing in a hierarchical and bureaucratic manner: it eschewed formal membership, centralized decision-making and rigid constitutional practices. As Anna Coote and Bea Campbell have written. 'There would be no hierarchies, no lines of authority, no leaders, no stars, and by implication there would be no purges or palace coups'[11]. The women's movement attempted to decentralize power and decision-making as much as possible. The idea was that feminism should develop through the self activity of women themselves. Emphasis was placed upon the importance of small discussion groups where women could share their common experiences of oppression and develop a political consciousness around those experiences.

This difference in organization has been taken by some to be the most significant difference between soicialism and feminism. Sheila Rowbotham for example in her essay in *Beyond the Fragments*[12] has forcefully argued that one of the most significant ways in which feminism can contribute to the revitalization of socialism is for socialists to adopt feminist organizational principles. She argues that a major reason for the Left being so moribund, sterile and unpopular is because its organizational form stifles creativity, self-activity and the development of political consciousness, and makes it difficult for socialists to communicate with most people.

There are problems posed by Sheila's essay. It addresses itself almost entirely to one section of the Left – the Leninist-Trotskyist revolutionary Left, with little mention of trade unions or the Labour Party. Her critique is directed at vanguardism,

10 Diana Adlam, 'Socialist feminism and contemporary feminism' in *Politics and Power* No. 5, Routledge and Kegan Paul, London, 1982, p. 89.
11 Anna Coote and Beatrice Campbell, *Sweet Freedom*, Picador, London, 1982, p. 23.
12 Sheila Rowbotham in S. Rowbotham, Lynne Segal and Hilary Wainwright, *Beyond the Fragments – Feminism and the making of socialism*, Islington and Community Press, London, 1979.

democratic centralism, and a dogmatic conception of political truth. Many of her criticisms are clearly valid, though not as new as some feminists seem to have supposed. Arguments over such issues have been the subject of debate on the Left for as long as it has existed[13]. Libertarian socialists have consciously resisted these very organizational features. The Labour Party and the trade unions, although hierarchical and bureaucratic, have also never espoused such views.

It seems to me that the way in which the women's movement has organized reflects both its strengths and limitations. On the one hand, the ability to reach out and to transform the lives of so many women, to mobilize and campaign effectively around issues of importance to women, bears witness to the ability of a movement to grow and develop without the need for centralized direction, full-time officials and all the paraphernalia of bureaucratic politics. The women's movement has accumulated a wealth of experience in developing a diversity of organizational forms, from consciousness-raising groups to self-help co-operative enterprises, to the successful management of national campaigns which could be invaluable in the struggle to democratize and open up the Labour Party and the trades unions. Feminists, because of the way they have experienced Left organizations, are clearly more sensitive than most men to the ways in which power is exercised in bureaucratic structures. They are painfully aware that certain forms of organizations and bureaucratic structures serve to mask the real exercise of power in Left organizations just as much as they do in other non-socialist structures.

At the same time, there are real dangers in idealizing the organizational forms of the women's movement, in suggesting we have solutions to some of the perennial problems of effective organization. Karen Margolis has perceptively noted,

our inability so far to provide adequate conditions for open discussion and free exchange of opposing ideas led to the suspension of national conferences. We have found ourselves duplicating activity, stretching much needed resources, relying on gossip and personal networks, occupied with squabbles and sometimes paralysed with mistrust. We are

13 See for example Rosa Luxemburg's criticisms of both social democracy and Bolshevism in such articles as 'Reform or Revolution', 'Organisational questions of social democracy', the Junius pamphlet and 'The Russian Revolution'. For these, see Mary Alice Waters (ed) *Rosa Luxemburg Speaks*, Pathfinder Press, New York, 1970.

not yet able to project a public image that is attractive to women outside the movement; at times we appear closed and unwelcoming.[14]

There are deep divisions within the movement, based on class, race and age; there are theoretical divisions between radical feminists, revolutionary separatist feminists and socialist feminists, which the movement so far has failed to tackle effectively. We know that lack of formal organization does not necessarily mean that power is actually dispersed effectively, that power can also be exercised dictatorially by cliques and forceful personalities at times precisely because of the lack of formal organization[15].

On a host of particular, specific, issues women have achieved a great deal. They have effectively mobilized large numbers of women around the right to abortion, successfully developed a national network of refuges for victims of male violence, and have set up rape crisis centres to support and counsel women who have been subjected to rape and sexual abuse. On these and many other issues there is no doubt that feminist interventions have had a decisive effect.

At the same time, partly because the women's movement has eschewed formal organization, it has not had to face certain questions head-on. How, for example, to develop an overall strategy in relation to women's interests? How to prioritize or rank certain demands over others? These issues cannot be solved by organization alone but, clearly, they have organizational implications. Some feminists are today having to think through some of these problems in terms of how to respond to the initiatives of Left Labour local councils in their attempts to implement equal opportunity programmes. On the one hand, it is clear that those Left Labour initiatives would not have occurred without the feminist movement. On the other hand, the question of response raises vital questions about how women's interests are to be represented and who is to represent them. Has anyone the authority to speak for women? How representative is the womens movement? How far are women's interests divided by class and race? There are no easy solutions to these questions but they certainly have to be faced before feminism can claim to have

14 Karen Margolis, 'The long and winding road' in *Feminist Review*, No. 5, 1982, p. 95.
15 See for example Jo Freeman, *The Politics of Womens Liberation*, New York and London, 1975.

organizational solutions to either the 'making of feminism' or the making of socialism.

In an important sense, it is misleading to focus upon organization as the area of difference between socialism and feminism. To do so courts the danger of fetishizing organization, to see it as a panacea for solving what are, in effect, real political differences. One cannot discuss organization in a vacuum, without asking, Organization for what? Without a discussion of politics, activity, aims and objectives, a debate on organization is literally putting the cart before the horse. It too easily assumes that the objectives of socialists and feminists are fundamentally in harmony, that there are no real conflicts of interest to be grappled with. Underlying much of the debate on feminism, socialism and organization are more fundamental issues about the nature of politics and political activity and it is to those issues that we must now turn.

Feminist politics

As we have already implied, there are divisions amongst feminists on the question of the strategies women should adopt in order to further their own liberation. These divisions in strategy flow in large measure from different theoretical perspectives on the causes of women's subordination. There are, however, certain basic arguments about the nature of politics and political struggle upon which most feminists would agree. First and foremost, it is argued that a socialist conception of politics is totally inadequate unless it takes seriously the feminist insight into the political nature of personal life. Secondly, feminists are united in the view that womens oppression cannot be explained as a kind of by-product of capitalist exploitation for which men bear no responsibility.

1. *The personal is political.* In an attempt at understanding their own specific oppression within contemporary society, feminists have discovered that the structure of women's subordination cannot be comprehended without reference to areas of life usually considered to be non-political. Women's marginalization in the realm of 'culture', in waged labour and in political activity, for example, can only be explained by reference to a structure of relationships commonly thought of as private and personal.

V. Randall, quoting Sheldon Wolin, has argued that, 'forms of politics are not given . . . conceptions of politics reflect the power of those who hold them . . . definitions of politics are inevitably political'.[16] This observation is as true of socialist and Marxist concepts of politics as of any other. Though, in theory, Marxism has recognized some of the ways in which private life is determined, in practice Marxists have acted as though the social world were divided into two: a public world which is the proper terrain for political activity and a private sphere of home and personal life which is 'free' from political interference.

The central, pivotal challenge of feminist politics is to unequivocally argue that personal life is political. Social relationships in the private sphere, in family life, are for feminists clearly socially structured, just as much as are social relations in other spheres of life. Definitions of masculinity and femininity, ideas about sexuality, expectations about familial roles, for example, are not biologically or naturally determined, nor are they freely chosen by individuals uncoerced by social forces. Though feminists may disagree as to exactly who benefits from this public/private dichotomy, most feminists would agree that it operates to the detriment of women, that it serves to mask and justify the actual forces which structure women's subordination and to depoliticize what are, in effect, political issues. Not only does the public/private divide determine women's relationship to the world of waged labour and conventional political activity, its very existence allows men the freedom to live their public lives against a 'private' background provided by women.

Feminists have pointed to the ways in which the state and other public institutions operate to maintain and reproduce this situation, often in a totally inconsistent manner. The state, for example, interferes quite clearly in the private sphere through welfare provision to ensure that women remain economically dependent wives and mothers. It also intervenes to regulate women's reproductive functions through its control of contraceptive and abortion provisions. At the same time, it uses the idea of a private and purely personal sphere as a justification for non-interference in so-called domestic conflict which may result in sexual abuse and violence.

If feminism demands a reformulation of politics that recognizes that private life is a legitimate and important terrain for

16 Vicky Randall, *Women and Politics*, Macmillan, London, 1982, p. 7.

political activity, many feminists remain pessimistic about the ability of a male-dominated socialist movement to take such arguments seriously, because to some degree or other all men, including socialist men, have an interest in maintaining the subordination of women as wives, mothers and workers. In order to understand this claim, we must turn to the development of feminist theory and the concept of patriarchy.

2. *Patriarchy, sex and class.* As we have seen, in the attempt to theorize their own experiences of oppression in contemporary society, women could no longer turn to liberal theory as they had in the past. Though an extension of equal rights into spheres such as social security, and pensions and positive discrimination policies in relation to areas like employment and the training of women, are obviously important elements in a strategy for women's equality, equal rights alone cannot guarantee the emancipation of women. At the same time, feminists have also found traditional Marxist theory a totally inadequate tool for generating a coherent explanation. It is impossible within the scope of this discussion to give a satisfactory account of the various theories of patriarchy that have been developed. What follows is necessarily brief and schematic.

Though there is no consensus as to the precise meaning of patriarchy, it essentially asserts the existence of a structure of power relationships, economic, political and social, in which power is vested in the male, either as man or as father. Kate Millett was one of the first contemporary feminists to argue for the patriarchal basis of women's oppression[17]. In *Sexual Politics*, she argued that relationships between men and women were structured, systematic power relationships through which men control and dominate women for their own benefit. She further asserted that patriarchal domination is independent of, and prior to, all other forms of domination, including those based on class or race.

Politically, the concept of patriarchy has been very important to women. It has served to organize women's experience of oppression in a coherent and structured manner. It led directly to the focusing of attention on areas of political struggle hitherto neglected such as the family, reproduction and sexuality. Further, it provided a theoretical justification for the

17 Kate Millett, *Sexual Politics*, Abacus, London, 1972.

autonomy of the women's movement by pointing to areas of women's oppression that could not be collapsed into, or explained away as a by-product of class exploitation. Fundamentally, all theories of patriarchy serve to reveal the ways in which men are implicated in the subordination of women rather than capitalism. If feminist analyses are accurate, how can feminism collaborate with a socialist movement that is predominantly male?

The original development of the concept of patriarchy owes a great deal to those feminists who are hostile to, and deeply suspicious of, the socialist and labour movements as they have developed. For writers such as Millett, Firestone, and Delphy, patriarchy is the first, primary and most universal form of domination, it permeates all aspects of life and affects all women regardless of their class or race[18]. Revolutionary feminists like Firestone go further and argue that women form an oppressed class in relation to men in exactly the same way as wage labour forms a class *vis-à-vis* capital. Radical and revolutionary feminists differ to some extent in their theories of patriarchy and how it is maintained and reproduced. Millett, for example, sees the family as the fundamental unit of patriarchal society and roots it in the male's desire for power itself. Firestone explains male dominance in terms of women's reproductive capacity and men's control of that reproduction. Delphy, on the other hand, locates patriarchy in the institution of marriage, whereby men control and appropriate women's domestic labour for their own benefit. Despite these differences they are agreed that it is men who benefit materially from the sexual division of labour in all its forms.

The strategic implications of such analyses is clear. Women must organize separately and autonomously in order to combat male power; the focus of a feminist politics must be a struggle against men. Revolutionary feminists, basing themselves on Firestone's 'dialectics of sex', argue that women can only free themselves from dependency in their relationship to men if they withdraw from all relations with them until such time as male power has been totally destroyed. For such feminists, collabora-

---

18 Kate Millett, *op. cit.* Shulasmith Firestone, *The Dialectics of Sex*, Bantam Books, New York, 1971; Christine Delphy, *The Main Enemy*, Womens Research and Resource Centre, London, 1977.

tion with the socialist movement as presently constituted is clearly impossible.

The initial response of Marxists and Marxist feminists in the 1970s to theories of patriarchy was to attempt to show how both domestic labour and women's weak position in waged labour could be explained by the dictates of capitalism itself. Such attempts clearly failed, however, to answer the real questions that required explanation. It may be true that capitalism requires certain groups to perform domestic labour, and to act as a reserve army of labour; but it does not explain why it is women who fulfil these functions; neither can it explain the cultural construction of femininity, rape, domestic violence, and all the other manifestations of patriarchal power. At the same time, many feminists were unhappy with an analysis of women's subordination that locates it purely and simply in patriarchy, without reference to other structures of domination such as class or race. Nor could they accept a strategy that saw men as the only source of women's oppression. Such a position does not reflect the real experience of most women, whose lives are inextricably linked with men as fathers, lovers, husbands, and brothers; it also serves to isolate the feminist movement from most working class and black women for whom the daily struggle against capitalist exploitation and racism is as important, if not more important, than the struggle against male power. Further, a separatist feminist strategy which refuses to have anything to do with the labour and socialist movement fails to confront male power within those organizations; it leaves socialism untouched by the feminist movement. This is not to deny that, for all women, men constitute a problem, but is simply to suggest that the 'problem' will not disappear if it is not confronted. In order to combat the patriarchal aspects of male–female relationships, women must struggle against men in all situations and in all 'places' – in personal relations, at work and in political organizations. For socialist feminists, this struggle is impelled by their very commitment to a socialist future in which both men and women have a place. As socialists, socialist feminists cannot deny the centrality of capitalist exploitation. Yet, as feminists, they cannot ignore the reality of patriarchal power and authority.

In response to this dilemma some socialist feminists have attempted to elaborate theoretical models of how patriarchal sexual relations and capitalist class relations, conceived as two separate systems, articulate together to form a 'capitalist patriarchal society'[19]. For many feminists such an approach, postulating two modes of exploitation, had a certain attraction. Whilst not denying the importance of class struggle, it gave the feminist struggle against male power an equal importance. It avoided the inevitable down-grading of women's struggles which earlier attempts at incorporating feminism into Marxist socialism seemed to produce. It also retained the theoretical justification for the women's movement. I would argue, however, that such an approach does not provide a satisfactory basis for the development of a socialist feminist practice. It suggests that there are two independent and autonomous struggles to be fought simultaneously, one to be waged at the point of production, the other in the sphere of the family and personal life[20]. In the same way as a revolutionary feminist politics, suggesting that women withdraw from all relationships with men, leave men alone, untouched by the feminist movement, so too does an approach that conceives of two separate and autonomous struggles. It leaves male socialists free to continue to marginalize women's issues; it does nothing to transform socialist politics itself.

What is required, if a socialist feminist practice is to develop, is both a theory and a strategy which combines struggles around both production and the family life, which attacks both class and gender relations simultaneously. Recently, some socialist feminists have begun to argue in these terms and to assert that class and gender relations are not formed in different places (class relations at the point of production, gender relations at the point of reproduction) but that both are formed in both areas at the same time[21]. To the feminists they are saying that gender divisions cannot be comprehended outside of class dominated social formations; at the same time, they are asserting to the socialist movement that class struggle, its form and outcome, cannot be understood outside of gender divisions.

19 See for example Rosin McDonough and Rachel Harrison, 'Patriarchy and relations of production' in A. Kuhn and A. M. Wolpe (ed), *Feminism and Materialism*, Routledge and Kegan Paul, London, 1978; Lucy Bland *et al.* 'Women outside and inside the relations of production' in *Women Take Issue*, Centre for Contemporary Cultural Studies, Hutchinson, London, 1978; and Heidi Hartmann, 'The unhappy marriage of marxism and feminism' in *Capital and Class*, Summer, 1979.

20 This point is made by Veronica Beechey in 'The concept of patriarchy' *Feminist Review*, No. 3, 1979.

21 See for example Cynthia Cockburn, 'The materiality of male power' in *Feminist Review*, No. 9, 1981.

Feminism and socialism

It is clear from what has been said that not all feminists are willing to struggle within the socialist movement on a 'socialist feminist' platform. The history of socialism and their own priorities as feminists mean that many women are not prepared to expend their limited time and energy in fighting men in the socialist movement. Yet, without such a strategy it is difficult to see how feminist ideas will influence either men or the majority of working class women. At the same time, a socialist movement that fails to recognize its own patriarchal character and which refuses seriously to acknowledge the deep divisions that exist within the working class between men and women, will inevitably fail to generate the support of women for a socialist alternative to present Tory hegemony.

If the socialist movement is to take the claims of feminism seriously, then it will clearly have to transform its politics in a fundamental manner. It is not enough for the presently male-dominated socialist movement to claim to be on the side of women supporting 'them' in 'their' struggle as though those struggles were distinct from those of socialists. Neither is it sufficient to translate feminism into a demand for equal rights for women, in order that they can participate in an untransformed public world of men. Feminism seeks to transcend and transform the public world and the divisions between public and private life as presently constituted. As a first step, men in the socialist and trade union movement have to admit that there are conflicts of interest between men and women and that if they are to really support women they must critically evaluate their own relationship to ideas of masculinity and the maintenance of male power. As Michele Barrett has recently argued, 'No progressive movement can retain its integrity if it is riding on the back of an oppression conceived as someone elses'[22].

In more concrete terms, male socialists and trade unionists must recognize the real basis of women's differential relationship to production. Issues such as women's low pay, or their lack of skills, cannot be tackled purely and simply at the point of production without simultaneously tackling the problem of

22 Michele Barrett, 'Unity is Strength', *New Socialist* No. 1, Sept–Oct 1981, p. 38.

women's domestic resposibilities and the sexual division of labour in the home. Equal pay for women is bound to remain a dead letter if men continue to base their wages strategy around an outdated concept of the family wage, or if they fail to combat the deeply sex-segregated nature of the labour market. These issues all strike at the basis of men's domination of the socialist and labour movement, and it would be foolish to think they can be overcome overnight. At the same time, if they are not brought into the open and faced squarely, then both the socialist and the labour movements are bound to remain weak and internally divided.

Though feminist ideas have begun to permeate the socialist and labour movement, Labour's alternative economic strategy illustrates how far patriarchal political ideas still predominate. The alternative economic strategy takes as its starting point the need for economic expansion and full employment. It fails to ask what full employment means for women in a context where the majority of women work part-time. If full employment includes women, why isn't a consideration of child-care and domestic labour given priority right from the beginning rather than being postponed until such time as the economy has recovered and 'the country can afford it'. Anna Coote and Bea Campbell have written of Labour's economic strategy that it

takes men and women's relationships to each other as given, and proposes no change. It desexualises politics, and in so doing denies any political room for feminists. It is blind to the existence of children and domestic work and thus has nothing to suggest about transforming men's relation to children and child care. And it characterises the left's objectives in purely economic terms, so that the politics of sexuality and culture are beyond the pale.[23]

A feminist approach to the Alternative Economic Strategy needs to raise vital questions about the nature of work, the relationship of paid to unpaid work, and the distribution of society's resources between men and women. It is obvious that any alternative economic strategy will only be successful if it succeeds in creating mass support for its policies. It will necessarily fail to mobilize women if it fails to speak to their needs. In the long run, it may even fail to appeal to men as well. The Alternative Economic Strategy offers a return to the prosperity of

23 Anna Coote and Beatrice Campbell, *op. cit.* p. 242.

the 1960s, it fails to offer any vision of a socialist future in which the quality of human relationships are transformed.

Finally, the socialist and trade union movements still remain extraordinarily male-dominated institutions. Of around 9 million women workers, only around one-third are actually in trades unions. Women are conspicuous by their absence in the structures of policy and decision making, very few women are either full-time union officials or delegates to union conferences, even in those unions with a majority of women members. Similarly, women remain inadequately represented in the decision-making bodies of the Labour Party. Women delegates to Labour's National Conference in 1976 constituted a mere 11 per cent. At present, under 6 per cent of Labour MPs and only 15 per cent of Labour Councillors are women.

Women's participation in the socialist and labour movement is trapped in a vicious circle. Without policies designed to appeal to their interests, women will remain apathetic and disinterested in socialist politics. Yet, without the participation of women in the socialist and labour movement to struggle for feminist demands, socialists will continue to reflect only the interests and experiences of its male members.

IN CONCLUSION

Feminism has much to contribute to the revitalization of socialism. In an important sense, without a feminist dimension socialism will remain a remote materialist doctrine which fails to speak to the real needs of people. Feminism, by giving expression to the importance of private life and the need to organize around issues that affect personal life, offers a vision of future possibilities that present socialist politics lack.

The contemporary women's movement is far more sympathetic to socialism and class than was the feminist movement at the turn of the century. It is not their distrust of socialism as an 'ideal' that keeps so many feminists away from the socialist and labour movement. It is their distrust of a male socialist movement's ability to recognize its own patriarchal nature. The history of socialism demonstrates that the experience and interests of women will not be articulated or given expression in the socialist movement without a vigorous and autonomous women's movement. Men will not give up their entrenched positions of dominance in society generally or in the socialist and labour movement without a struggle. In the long run, men have much to gain from relinquishing some of their power, but it would seem that the ideological battle to get them to see that has only just begun.

A GUIDE TO FURTHER READING

Women's history

There are several interesting accounts of women's lives and work in the past. Sheila Rowbotham's *Hidden from History*, Pluto Press, London, 1973, provides a good general introduction. Alice Clarke's *Working Life of Women in the 17th Century*, reprinted by Routledge and Kegan Paul, London, 1982, gives a fascinating account of women's work before industrialization. For the impact of the industrial revolution on working women see Ivy Pinchbeck *Women Workers and the Industrial Revolution*, reprinted by Frank Cass, London, 1977. Olive Shriner's *Women and Labour* is also recommended, republished by Virago, London, 1978.

Other books which bring to life women's lives at the turn of the twentieth century are *Maternity, Letters from Working Women* (1976) and *Life as We Have Known It* (1977), both republished by Virago, London. See also Hannah Mitchell's biography, *The Hard Way Up*, Virago, London, 1977.

Women, trade unions and the labour movement

There is little written generally on women and the labour movement or Labour Party. Lucy Middleton (ed) *Women and the Labour Movement*, Croom Helm, London, 1977, and Marion Phillips (ed) *Women and the Labour Party*, London, 1918 are both worth reading but fail to explore satisfactorily the tensions between women, the labour movement and the Labour Party.

A good general introduction to women and trade unions is *Getting it Together* by Jenny Beale, published by Pluto Press, London, 1982. Sarah Boston's *Women Workers and Trade Unions* published by Davis-Poynter, London, 1980 is also recommended. A general history of women in trade unions is Sheila Lewenhak's *Women and Trade Unions*, published by Ernest Benn, Tonbridge, 1977.

Marxism, socialism and women

The classical texts on women and socialism are Frederick Engels, *The Family, Private Property and the State*, Lawrence and Wishart, London, 1973, August Bebel, *Women in the Past, Present and Future*, London 1885, and V. I. Lenin, *On the Emancipation of Women*, Progress Publishers, Moscow, 1965. See also Leon Trotsky, *Women and the Family*, a collection of Trotsky's writings on women published by Pathfinder Press 1970. For a feminist critique of Engels see Rosemary Delmar, 'Looking Again at Engel's Origins', in J. Mitchell and Ann Oakley (eds) *The Rights and Wrongs of Women*, Penguin, Harmondsworth, 1976. The writings of the Russian revolutionary, Alexandra Kollantai provide a very interesting account of the problems of women in socialist revolutions. Amongst her writings to be recommended are *Love of Worker Bees*, Virago, London, 1977, and *An Autobiography of a Sexually Emancipated Woman*, London, 1972. See also Alexandra Kollantai, *Selected Writings*, edited by Alix Holt, London, 1977. For a broader history of women and revolution, Sheila Rowbotham's *Women Resistance and Revolution*, Penguin, Harmondsworth, 1972 is extremely readable.

On utopian socialism and feminism see Barbara Taylor, *Eve and the New Jerusalem*, Virago, London, 1983. On socialism and feminism at the turn of the twentieth century see Jeffrey Weeks and Sheila Rowbotham, *Socialism and the New Life*, Pluto Press, London, 1977.

Feminism and the women's movement

There is a vast and fast growing literature on feminism and women generally. The following are recommended because they relate to the current socialist/feminist debate. For a reasonably up to date guide to the literature see *Work on Women*, edited by Mary Evans and David Morgan, Tavistock Publications, London, 1979. Compendium Books, Camden High Street, London, also produce a comprehensive bibliography of women's studies.

Olive Banks' *Faces of Feminism*, Martin Robertson, Oxford, 1981, provides a general introduction to feminist ideas in both the nineteenth and twentieth centuries. On nineteenth century feminist ideas see, Mary Wollstoncraft, *A Vindication of the Rights of Women*, reprinted by Dent, London, 1970, and John Stuart Mill and Harriet Taylor, *Essays on Sex Equality*, edited by Alice Rossi, Chicago University Press, Chicago, 1970. For a very readable account of the early feminist movement see Ray Stracy, *The Cause, A Short History of the Women's Movement*, reprinted by Virago, London, 1977. For the Women's Social and Political Union, see A. Rosen's *Rise Up Women: The Militant Campaign of the Women's Social and Political Union, 1903–1914*, Routledge and Kegan Paul, London, 1974. For an excellent account of working class women's involvement in the sufferage movement see Jill Liddington and Jill Norris, *One Hand Tied Behind Us*, Virago, London, 1978.

Feminism today

Elizabeth Wilson's *Half Way to Paradise*, Tavistock Publications, London, 1980, is excellent on women in post-war Britain. Anna Coote and Beatrice Campbell's *Sweet Freedom*, Picador, London, 1982, gives an interesting account of the development of the women's movement from the late 1960s. For a very readable account of the development of feminist consciousness see, *Woman's Consciousness, Man's World*, by Sheila Rowbotham, Penguin, Harmondsworth, 1973. For those interested in the development of feminist theory Veronica Beechy's 'The Concept of Patriarchy', *Feminist Review* No. 3 provides a clear overview of the different theories of patriarchy that feminists have developed. For an extremely clear discussion on sex and class, see Ann Phillips, 'Sex and Class in Revolutionary Socialism' – *Big Flame's Magazine*, No. 6, 1980–81. Michelle Barrett, *Women's Oppression Today*, provides a wide ranging discussion on Marxist feminist analysis, (Verso, London, 1980), So too does Lydia Sargant (ed), *The Unhappy Marriage of Marxism and Feminism: A Debate on Class and Patriarchy*, Pluto Press, London, 1981.

On feminist cultural politics, a good collection of writings is to be found in Caroline Rowan (ed), *Feminism, Culture and Politics*, Lawrence and Wishart, London, 1982.

For a clear and readable account of women and their relationship to politics in general see, Vicky Randall, *Women and Politics*, Macmillan, London, 1982. For a discussion of Politics and personal life, see Eli Zaretsky, *Capitalism, The Family and Personal Life*, Pluto Press, London, 1973, and Marshal Colman, *Continuing Excursions: Politics and Personal Life*, Pluto Press, London, 1982. For a discussion of socialism, feminism and future strategies, see Sheila Rowbotham, Lynne Segal and Hillary Wainwright, *Beyond the Fragments – Feminism and the making of socialism*, Islington Community Press, London, 1979. See also discussions on *Beyond the Fragments* in *Feminist Review*, Nos 4 and 5.

The final chapter of Anna Coote and Beatrice Campbell's, *Sweet Freedom*, Picador, London, 1982, provides a useful summary of some of the important arguments. Journals such as *New Socialist, Marxism Today* and *Feminist Review* regularly have stimulating articles on socialism, feminism and the future.

Chapter eight

COMMUNITY POLITICS AND DIRECT
ACTION: THE NON-ALIGNED LEFT

Richard Taylor and Kevin Ward

I

In many ways, the post-war period has been one of decline, stagnation and frustration for the British Left. The Labour Party's membership and its share of the popular vote at general elections, have both declined dramatically. Its performance in office and its ideological commitments have also been profoundly depressing for socialists, though some might argue that the current Alternative Economic Strategy marks the beginning of an ideological breakthrough. Similarly, despite numerous and important developments, the Marxist organizations of the Far Left have failed to attain political credibility or a real mass base in the working class. Whilst the major concern of socialists (and of the other chapters in this volume) has been quite properly the study and analysis of these 'formal' socialist organizations, there has been a separate and important dimension to the politics of the Left during this period. The last thirty years has seen an unprecedented growth in extra-parliamentary, radical, politics. These movements have been numerous and diverse in their objectives, methods and levels of support. Moreover, they have by no means been wholly socialist or libertarian in outlook. Indeed, like all single-issue campaigns, their ideological and class diversity has been their major weakness, as well as their major strength. Many of these movements have, however, mobilized mass support and popular involvement in a way that the orthodox labour movement has failed largely to do and, arguably, *some* of these movements have attained at least *some* of their aims.

Our purpose here, then, is to look at some of these movements and their ideas, in as much as they relate to socialist politics in

Britain. In particular, we look at the nuclear disarmament movement and the rise of 'community action' politics, examine the ideological positions, implicit as well as explicit, underpinning these movements, and draw some conclusions about the advantages and disadvantages of extra-parliamentary politics. We concentrate on the peace issue and 'community activism' because we believe they have the potential for developing into struggle for socialist change on a wider front. This is not to deny however that there are other extra-parliamentary 'movements' in recent years which have been fundamentally important. Obvious examples are the women's liberation movement, the growth of ethnic minority activism and, to a lesser extent, the development of alternative cultures and lifestyles. Each of these areas needs, however, a full consideration rather than a passing reference and so we have deliberately concentrated on peace and community action, areas in which we have personally been involved for more than a decade.

Before beginning this analysis the whole process must be put in its proper context. Above all, this means a discussion of the relationship between extra-parliamentary politics and the state. For all socialists the state has assumed, in late twentieth century capitalism, an importance unimagined by Marx and the early socialists. The debate on the Left over the analysis of the modern state has been one of the most central and significant in recent years, but only recently has a serious attempt been made to link the theoretical analysis to the practical microcosm of political action. Further developments on this front are essential: both the nuclear disarmament movement and the varied community politics campaigns have had, as their prime target, opposition to the state and its politics. In the case of the nuclear disarmament movement, a significant proportion of protesters has been opposed not only to the specific nuclear policies of successive governments and their ancillary 'defence' aspects, but to the whole 'warfare state' structure which has produced the insane waste of the arms race. For the majority of nuclear protesters the primary motivation remained on the moral plane[1], but among those who were politically motivated, there was a sharp theoretical division between those who saw the 'warfare state' as being

1 This has been confirmed by all surveys of nuclear disarmament campaigners, most recently by Richard Taylor and Colin Pritchard, *The Protest Makers: the British Movement for nuclear disarmament 1958 to 1965, Twenty years on*, Pergamon Press, Oxford, 1980.

the ultimate expression of an authoritarian, irrational and bureaucratic process of centralized and depersonalized power structures, which had been accelerating since the beginning of the industrial revolution and, on the other hand, those who analysed the contemporary state in more orthodox socialist terms, as being centrally related to the core socio-economic structure of capitalism.

That perspective which focuses exclusively on the authoritarian and bureaucratic nature of centralized power has strong links with anarchism. Formal anarchism in either its individualistic or its communist form, has never been a major force in British political life. However, the general influence of libertarian ideology has been extremely important in Britain in a variety of contexts and over a long period. From the syndicalist and shop stewards' movement of the first two decades of the twentieth century to the women's movement of our own times, the concepts, structures, strategies and priorities of libertarian thought have been of major importance. Central to this perspective has been the notion that repressive and centralized authority – manifested increasingly through the state and its agencies – has been at the kernel of the system. Antipathetic to class analysis and to Marxism in general, libertarians have opposed bitterly both social democracy (as an incorporated and integrated aspect of the institutional apparatus of modern society) and revolutionary socialism (as embodying repression, centralization, bureaucracy and, ultimately, totalitarian control). Thus, for libertarians, freedom, decentralization, and direct action have been central values as well as organizing concepts. Not only is revolution to come through the free and spontaneous association of free men and women (as opposed to the organized working class movement, whether based on Leninist or other socialist principles), the practice of direct action in opposition to the forces of the state will of itself build a mass popular movement which will eventually become powerful enough to immobilize and eventually overthrow the repressive state.

In contrast to this concern with the central state, community activists have primarily opposed the actions and inadequacies of the 'local state' at the level of the practical implementation of policy, even though the local state's politics have been determined increasingly by central government politics. Community groups have certainly achieved some successes (discussed below) in the 1960s and early 1970s but the major cuts of the

last few years, and the hardening ideological line of the New
Right, on the local as on the central level, have entailed a sharp
diminution in the potential for immediate short-term advance
via radical community politics. The 1980 Local Government
Planning and Land Act gives central government much greater
control over local authority expenditure, and the 1981 Law
Lords decision against the Greater London Council's cheap
transport policies reinforces this trend. Community activists in
the 1980s must establish practical ways of opposing these trends,
and this can only be done in conjunction with Labour councils
and trades unions.

Some of the ideological complexities within both these movements are discussed below, but what must be emphasized here is
that extra-parliamentary political action on the Left, diverse
though it has undoubtedly been in numerous ways since 1945,
has taken place within parameters determined by the structural
and ideological constraints of the contemporary state. This is
not, however, to say that the state is a monolithic structure, a
simple political representation of bourgeois economic control.
As has been argued at length elsewhere, the contemporary state
is a much more complex structure, characterized above all by its
contradictions. On the one hand, capitalism has had to adopt or
accept a variety of at least potentially quasi-socialist innovations
in state structure. For example, as Michael Barratt-Brown has
argued[2], although the basis for the vast increase in state intervention in the economy may have resulted from the destabilizing and
polarizing effects of private capital accumulation, the form that
that intervention has taken has been largely the result of public
demand, predominantly from the labour movement, for publicly
provided services. Even here, however, there must be a qualifica-
tion. *In practice* the ways in which these public services are
provided and controlled do much to alienate working class reci-
pients. For example, the stigma attached to social security claimants, and the attitudes of some Housing Departments to council
tenants, are indicative of a deep-rooted cultural rejection of the
socialist principles of 'welfarism'.

Nevertheless, the whole range of state provided or instigated
legislation, from the creation of the National Health Service by
Aneurin Bevan and the 1945 Labour Government, to the employ-

---

2 Michael Barratt Brown, *From Labourism to Socialism*, Spokesman Books,
    Nottingham, 1972.

ment protection legislation of the 1974–79 Labour Government, must be entered on the 'credit side' as far as socialist achievement goes. There is, too, the whole ideological dimension: the very *concept* of welfare-oriented, public service, public sector society is inherently socialist in orientation and will, and has, encouraged to some extent the spread of socialist ideas as well as socialist structures. Not least among these developments has been the rise to prominence and influence of public sector trades unions in both working class and white-collar occupational groups, e.g. NUPE, NALGO, NUT, ASTMS *et al.* Whilst it would be quite false to see in this a wholesale public sector commitment to socialist politics, there is no doubt that this development has seen a marked growth, in some public sector unions, of both trade union *and socialist* consciousness.

On the other hand, both economic and political considerations congruent with the continued dominance of capitalism have underlain the expansion of the state. The increasing size and multinational nature of contemporary capitalism has necessitated far greater state involvement on the economic level than ever before. Moreover, the increasing automation of the industrial structure has led to a need for greater emphasis upon necessarily public sector services – in particular a greater investment in higher technological education has been crucial to realize the potential of technological development to increase productivity. On the political level, there has been, of course, a continuation of the process of capitalist 'accommodation' with the power of the labour movement – the realization that to secure political stability and continuity, a price has to be paid, in terms of both rising living standards and legislative protection of trade union and working class interests. Significantly, the Thatcher Government, in the context both of a deep recession and a far more explicit and extreme Conservative ideology than before, has been engaged in the attempt to reverse these trends and policies. Ideologically, too, modern state involvement has resulted in a marked increase in the permeation of capitalist values into every sector at every institutional level. Even a cursory examination of institutions such as the education system and the media substantiates this assertion, whilst at the same time illustrating again the contradictory processes at work within contemporary society.

What follows, then, is a discussion of extra-parliamentary politics in the context of this complex and contradictory state structure. The possibilities of socialist advance through movements of the type we discuss depends crucially upon the prior analysis of the nature of the state and the points at which its structure and ideology can be 'breached' by the oppositional forces of the Left. This in turn relates to the wider question of whether the existing system is capable of reform from within or whether some revolutionary initiative is necessary to achieve a socialist transition. This debate has, of course, been at the heart of socialist theory and practice from the beginning, and it is certainly one of the key issues dividing activists in the extra-parliamentary politics of this period. At one level the two movements we discuss are 'case studies' of these politics. Essentially, however, they both represent and subsume the wider and more nebulous extra-parliamentary movements since the war.

II

Until recently, nuclear disarmament was regarded as a 'dead issue', and the mass movement of the late 1950s and early 1960s was seen as of no more than historical interest. Barbara Castle noted, in her political diaries, 'that the spirit of CND no longer walks the land'[3]. Bruce Kent, the Secretary of CND, was, as late as 1978, of the opinion that the days of CND as a mass movement were over, unless a major nuclear disaster occurred[4]. Yet, since the coming to power of the hawkish Conservative Government in 1979, the rapidly deteriorating international situation and the consequent intensification of the arms race, involving an agreement to site US Cruise Missiles in Britain, and the proposed expenditure of *£7,500 million* on the Trident missile system, as well as the USA's decision to proceed with neutron weapons, there has been a tremendous resurgence of a mass nuclear disarmament movement. 'Nuclear politics' is once again very much on the agenda. The rapid growth of the Peace Movement since 1979 has provoked strong reactions from the Thatcher Government. Accusations of appeasement and neutralism have been combined with personal and political smear campaigns against leading CND supporters as Communists and pro-Soviet fellow travellers. In 1983, leading up to the General Election,

3 Barbara Castle, *The Castle Diaries 1974–6*, Weidenfeld and Nicolson, London, 1979, pp. 227–8.
4 See Bruce Kent, quoted in Postscript, Taylor and Pritchard *op. cit.*

Community politics and direct action

both the Labour and Conservative parties gave the defence/peace issue central importance and CND's own campaign figured prominently in the political debate. What has it been about the nuclear issue that has moved such large numbers to political involvement in the post-war period? Further, what impact has the socialist perspective had in the movement, and why has this failed, as yet, to gain the adherence of the mass of movement supporters? Finally, how does the nuclear disarmament movement relate to other extra-parliamentary movements from the late 1960s onwards?

The movement arose in the late 1950s in response to a whole range of specific issues and concerns, underpinned by a climate of mounting dissatisfaction with the perceived materialism, militarism and socio-political inadequacy of post-war society. Whilst both the specific and the general concerns had political connotations – notably the reaction on the Labour Left to Aneurin Bevan's 'defection' from the unilaterist cause at the 1957 Labour Party Conference – the overwhelming tone of the protest was *moral* in inspiration. Even those who were explicitly committed Marxists realized the genuine importance and relevance of the moral issue. Thus, Stuart Hall argued that the Campaign would be 'most effective if *kept* as a moral issue'[5]. Indeed, the very groupings that made up the socialist Left were, in their different ways, inspired to a considerable extent by moral objections to nuclear weapons. The Labour Left has, of course, a long history of morally based pacifist internationalism and the support for the nuclear movement in this quarter was firmly within this tradition. The invasions of Hungary and Suez in 1956 had a more profound and generalized effect than the turmoil inside the Labour Party, however. 1956–57 saw the exodus from the Communist Party of a very large number of influential Marxists who were not prepared to accept the brutalities of Stalinism or the authoritarian 'democratic centralism' of the British party. The Suez debacle aroused a whole new radical protest, and large street demonstrations were seen in Britain for the first time since the 1930s. In both these cases, the core of the protest was a moral humanism – a rejection, of capitalism certainly, but also of the rigidified, deterministic Stalinism of the Communist party. The ex-CP core of the 'New Left' was complemented and strengthened by the younger radi-

5 Stuart Hall in conversation with Richard Taylor, quoted in Taylor and Pritchard, *op. cit.* p. 54.

215

cal group around the journal *Universities and Left Review*. This group, although it included Marxists, was far more eclectic and less doctrinaire in its outlook. As Stuart Hall has indicated: 'it was a lot of tendencies and what held them together was a notion that it wasn't the post-capitalist era, and that on the other hand, the traditional Marxist analysis didn't account for all that had happened'[6].

This New Left was uniquely well-placed to fuse into the mass movement for nuclear disarmament *and* exert pressure and influence for the adoption of socialist perspectives and objectives. Unlike the other extra-parliamentary organizations of the Left, the New Left had a genuine commitment to and involvement in the movement. This was in part generational: the majority of New Left activists was in its late teens or twenties, and their involvement in the New Left was part and parcel of a commitment to nuclear disarmament, to a new politics and to a new lifestyle. Even more important, however, were the political and policy commitments of the New Left which were genuinely congruent with CND, in sharp contrast to all other socialist organizations. For the New Left, the abandonment of nuclear weapons made sense politically only if it were combined with the decision to leave NATO and espouse a thorough-going 'positive neutralism' in alliance with non-aligned countries throughout the world. Only in that way could 'socialist humanism' be brought to political fruition.

For the Labour Left, the campaign was seen both as a 'moral crusade' in the old ILP/pacifist tradition, and as part of the general attempt to push the Labour Party to the Left and oust Gaitskell and the Right from the leadership. The Communist Party, a late and rather unwilling convert to unilateralism, always construed the movement and its objectives as part of the general anti-US, and by implication pro-Soviet, campaign. The Trotskyists of the Socialist Labour League (SLL) believed, quite straightforwardly, in the 'Workers' Bomb' (i.e. possession by the USSR of nuclear weapons). The smaller quasi-Trotskyist groups, notably the International Socialists (IS, now Socialist Workers Party), had more interesting and more original Marxist perceptions of unilateralism, but their influence both organizationally and ideologically was minimal in the campaign.

In a very real sense, therefore the New Left gave political coherence and realism to CND's emotive rejection of nuclear

6 *Ibid.* p. 68.

weapons and its passionate commitment to unilateralism. The potential here, from a socialist view, can hardly be over-estimated. For perhaps the first time since the 1920s, a mass movement and a socialist ideology had the potential to come together to create a serious alternative to the parliamentary labourism which has effectively contained the socialist potential of the British labour movement during the twentieth century. Moreover, the New Left did manage to persuade CND to adopt policies of leaving NATO and adopting positive neutralism in the early 1960s. Yet, unquestionably, the New Left did not convert the nuclear disarmament movement into a socialist movement: its impact on the 'rank and file' was minimal and it was powerless to redirect CND's politics in its crisis years of the early 1960s[7]. Equally important, it did not manage to build ideological and political bridges with the more libertarian direct actionists of the Committee of 100. With the exception of one or two individuals (e.g. Alan Lovell) there was no unification on the Left of the movement; there remained a profound gulf between socialists and libertarians.

Central to the New Left's failures were three crucial weaknesses. First, there was an almost total lack of working class or labour movement involvement: it was exclusively a middle-class intellectual movement with little commitment to, or ability for, the hard slog of building a base in the working class. Second, there was both an inability and an unwillingness to communicate its ideology in everyday terms and language. Dominated by university people of outstanding intellectual ability, its politics and propaganda resembled the post-graduate seminar more than the political meeting, and reinforced all the deep cultural prejudices of one of the most anti-intellectual labour movements in Western Europe. Finally, and perhaps most important of all, the New Left remained essentially wedded to *labourist*[8] assumptions

7 Despite CND's formal commitment to Britain's leaving NATO and to a foreign policy based on positive neutralism – both of which were achieved largely because of New Left pressure and influence – the movement as a whole never became committed to New Left perspectives.

8 The terms 'labourist' and 'reformist' in this context refer to the prevailing and fundamental belief within the mainstream of the British labour movement, that socialist change can and must be brought about *exclusively* within and through the conventional electoral and parliamentary institutional structures of existing bourgeois society. This has carried with it the strong and specific rejection of any attempt to mobilize a socialist, working class movement to achieve political change outside the parliamentary context.

and *labourist* politics. Despite its many 'New' Left tendencies it was anchored in an 'Old' Left concept of socialist politics. The political naivety and conservatism of the New Left contrasted sharply with its intellectual sophistication. As Peter Sedgwick observed, as early as 1964: 'What is particularly staggering is its failure to imagine that it might be outmanoeuvred: pursuing a tactic of total theoretical entry, all its eggheads have marched into the single basket of Left reformism'[9].

There were inherent and major problems for a socialist movement working within the context of a deeply conservative political culture and structure: radical progress at any level in Britain has been notoriously problematic, particularly since the turn of the century (although of course there have been periods when radical change and even 'revolution' have been on the agenda), but the potential of the CND/New Left alliance was considerable. This was fatally undermined by the weakness of the New Left indicated above, *and* also by the predominantly apolitical nature of the nuclear disarmament movement. However, there was one major strand of political activism which, at one level, was far more significant within the movement than the New Left. The direct action politics of, first, the Direct Action Committee and, after 1960, the Committee of 100, embodied the radical style of the movement and certainly involved large numbers of people in extra-parliamentary politics. This is not the place to explore in detail the complex ideology of the DAC activists. Formed in 1957 from within the radical Gandhian wing of the pacifist movement, to make a specific protest against nuclear testing in the Pacific, the DAC soon developed a pattern of militant but passive civil disobedience at rocket bases and other military installations throughout Britain. The DAC, which, among other imaginative national and international initiatives, planned the 'first' Aldermaston march in 1958, rapidly attracted major attention from the media. Moreover, its young and totally committed activists were able to exercise an effective 'ginger group' function on the more conservative and traditional CND leadership and organization. It was, however, ultimately ineffective: the selfless and disciplined techniques necessary for its demonstrations and the willingness to undergo repeated imprisonment or heavy fines discouraged all but the

9 Peter Sedgwick, *The Two New Lefts*, in David Widgery, *The Left in Britain, 1956–1968*, Penguin, Harmondsworth, 1976, p. 151.

most committed. More important was the ideological and political isolation of the DAC: for all its radicalism it remained firmly in the predominantly individualistic, *pacifist* culture, always a small minority in Britain. Moreover, it had no contact with, nor understanding of, the labour movement or the working class. Its central focus was the individual's moral responsibility to oppose nuclear weapons and, in the long term, to reform radically the whole structure of defence thinking. Despite its rhetoric, DAC was never seriously interested in creating a mass movement, let alone a *socialist* mass movement.

With the creation of the Committee in 100 in late 1960, a mass movement *was* created. Through 1961, the Committee of 100 mobilized tens of thousands of people prepared to commit civil disobedience for the cause of nuclear disarmament. Some of those centrally involved had a revolutionary perspective. Ralph Schoenman, the young American who persuaded Bertrand Russell and the Revd Michael Scott to take the initiative in establishing the Committee, had an uncompromising and insurrectionary orientation. Writing in *Peace News* in the summer of 1961 he argued that:

The model for our objective shall be, The General Strike . . . we are not a political party, we have no intention of providing a Civil Service or an alternative body of administrators. We have precise demands which must be pressed upon authority. They will acquiesce or face national disruption. There shall undoubtedly be a host of political consequences of our resistance. We must not be deluded by them. If we hand over our consciences to any political party we will be betrayed. There is no party, no bureaucracy, and no authority which may not outrage our most fundamental values[10].

This typified one strand in the Committee of 100: strongly libertarian and revolutionary, but not 'formally' anarchistic, and certainly not Marxist (although with some Trotskyist inclinations in terms of language and tactics, rather than ideology, as Stuart Hall has pointed out).

This was, however, only one component – and a minority one, at least through the years of the Committee as a mass movement. The Committee of 100 was a far more diffuse and eclectic movement than DAC had been, but the hard core of DAC was very

10 Ralph Schoenman, 'Resistance in Mass Society', Peace News 25th. August 1961.

much at the centre of the Committee (most notably, Michael Randle, the former Chairman of DAC, became secretary of the Committee of 100 at its inception). There were at least three other identifiable groups of importance: those who believed, with Russell, that the primary objective of the Committee was to stimulate and promote 'public opinion' to oppose nuclear policies; those who were attracted by the glamour and excitement of cocking a snook at authority and whose commitment was at best superficial and short-lived; and those who, like Stuart Hall, 'were not *philosophically* into Direct Action and Civil Disobedience but who were into it *politically* . . . into it as a *tactic* rather than a *principle* . . .'[11].

The Committee, despite its disparate nature, hung together through its year of hectic and accelerating success, from approximately October 1960 to October 1961. Numbers at demonstrations rose rapidly, culminating in the huge Trafalgar Square sit-down of September 1961 (where 1,314 were arrested). Some, like Schoenman, believed 'that 10,000 or 100,000 people could swing the course of British politics'[12]. But even at the height of the Committee of 100's success, the enormous task confronting a populist extra-parliamentary movement was so formidable as to be virtually impossible, given the inability of the Committee to relate to the organized labour movement in any way. The Committee of 100, divided and confused over its *long-term* objectives as it was, declined as rapidly as it had arisen, following the Wethersfield demonstration. It emerged, in 1962, as a more unified and anarchistic body, committed not only to nuclear disarmament but to a whole gamut of decentralized libertarian issues. *But* it had, of course, lost its mass support: its activities attracted hundreds rather than thousands and, despite a partial resurgence in 1963, it declined progressively, finally disbanding in 1968.

The nuclear disarmament movement, as a *mass* movement, had thus disintegrated to all intents and purposes by 1963–64. And the Left (i.e. the extra-parliamentary Left) had failed overall to imprint its ideology on the movement. However, although the nuclear disarmament movement failed to achieve its specific political objectives and, equally important from a socialist view, the Left failed to create a mass extra-parliamentary socialist

11 Stuart Hall, quoted in Taylor and Pritchard, *op. cit.* p. 82.
12 George Clark, commenting on Schoenman's view, in conversation with Richard Taylor, quoted in Taylor and Pritchard, *op. cit.* p. 82.

movement, it has been argued that the whole episode marked an important stage along the road to the radicalization of large sections of the population. In other words, it is argued that the movement marked a 'half-way house' between the 'Old Left' (whether Labour Party or CP) and the Marxist New Left ('the second New Left') of the late 1960s and early 1970s. Whilst there is some evidence that a substantial minority of nuclear disarmament activists went on to become active in the anti Vietnam war movement[13], there was relatively little correlation between support for the nuclear disarmament movement and membership of/support for the various organizations of the quasi-Trotskyist Left post-1968 (International Socialists, International Marxist Group, *et al.*). The notion, therefore, that the nuclear disarmament movement 'radicalized a generation' which then 'matured' into Marxist politics, is untenable. In fact, as is predictable given the orientations of the movement as analysed briefly above, movement activists either went on to other 'apolitical' single-issue campaigns or dropped out of political action altogether.

For the fifteen years or so from the mid-1960s to the Thatcher Government in 1979, the peace movement was very much a minority force: it became a small, well-informed, but relatively insignificant pressure group, and its days as a mass movement seemed at an end. President Reagan and Mrs Thatcher, operating in the context of a sharply deteriorating international situation, pursuing the most hawkish policies in the crudest manner, and in the midst of economic recession, proved the best recruiting sergeants that the peace movement has ever had. Throughout Europe, the movement grew at an unprecedented rate and, by 1982, had developed into an international mass movement on a scale dwarfing the earlier campaign.

In some ways, the new movement has progressed significantly, and not only in terms of size. Perhaps most important of all there is a new realization that *international* concerted and co-operative action is essential if the objectives are to be achieved. In Britain there has been a greater acceptance of the need for a Europe-wide initiative, a correspondingly greater emphasis upon the END perspective, and a realization that a British unilateralist policy alone and of itself would have little lasting impact. The notion that CND must link the unilateralist initiative into the political demand for withdrawal from NATO, and the establishment of a

13 See *ibid.* pp. 46–50.

nuclear-free Europe, 'from the Atlantic to the Urals', has been accepted enthusiastically by most of the CND leadership.

Equally important, in the domestic context, has been the awareness that the movement must link in to the industrial labour movement and must concern itself with both the economic and political dimensions of working class and labour movement involvement. There is now a greater involvement of rank and file trade union members in the peace movement than was the case twenty years ago. The commitment of the trade union and labour movement to unilateralism is more firmly rooted with rank and file activists than was the case in 1960, when the block votes of the trade union bureaucracies were largely responsible for the Labour Conference victory.

All this, and more, must be adjudged on the credit side for the peace movement in the 1980s. Yet, the fundamental political problems remain unsolved. At one level, of course, the substantive problem must never be forgotten: the cause of the resurgence of the peace movement has been primarily the horrific escalation of the arms build-up and the increasing danger of nuclear holocaust. In this context, as E. P. Thompson and others in the movement constantly stress, the alternative to the success of the movement is nuclear annihilation. Against this grim backcloth, however, urgent and fundamental political and ideological problems remain. The mass of the movement, *and* the majority of labour movement support, is still mobilized primarily on an emotive, moral, single-issue basis. There remains no widespread understanding of the necessarily *political* context of the unilateralist movement's objectives. This is exemplified in a variety of ways – from the overwhelming rejection in 1981 of the resolution at the Labour Party Conference to withdraw from NATO, to the 'single-issue ethos' which predominates in the large majority of local peace groups. Intimately related to this apolitical approach is, of course, the whole question of the relationship between peace movement activism and structural societal change. The movement is no nearer now than it was twenty years ago to solving the problem of *agency*, that is, Can its objectives, which are ultimately revolutionary, be achieved within an essentially reformist and labourist structure? If not, should the movement merge into a broader 'New Left' of some sort, working largely in an extra-parliamentary frame of reference? Or would this merely ensure that the bulk of the 'single-issue' supporters melted away? Even assuming that this transition *could* be made, what would relations be with the 'orthodox' Left, and how, if at all, would direct action fit into this schema?

Until it can answer these and related political questions, the movement is unlikely to attain any but the most limited and short-term of its objectives. The fundamental task and the fundamental problem thus remain as they were twenty years ago: How, and in what ideological direction, to politicize an apolitical mass movement, at present focused around a single issue, without alienating its mass support? That the socialist perspective is essential for the movement's long-term success cannot be doubted; and the embryonic 'New Left' within today's peace movement has at least the advantage of being able to learn from the mistakes of both the New Left and Direct Action wings of the movement in the 1960s, and the failure of orthodox labourist politics over the decades of the 1960s and 1970s.

III

A separate but related complex of problems has surrounded the development of community action politics over the last twenty years. In this context, the central problem has been how to link, in both theory and practice, the locally based struggles on specific issues, to the wider ideological and political awareness which is essential if the capitalist structure which produces these problems is ever to be challenged effectively on a collective, class-conscious basis. It is thus to an examination of these issues that attention is now turned.

In 1960, a major rent-strike was organized by council tenants who were opposed to dramatic rent increases in St Pancras in London. Don Cook, Secretary to St Pancras' Tenants' Association was served with an eviction order for refusing to pay 28 shillings (£1.40p) per week rent increase. Together with other tenants, he prepared for a state of siege. Eventually, 2,000 tenants went on a rent strike which lasted until 22 September. A force of 800 police supported 28 bailiffs in evicting tenants' leaders Don Cook and Arthur Rowe who had been barricaded in their flats for over a month. The Home Secretary, Harry Brooke, declared a state of emergency at St Pancras and all public demonstrations in the Borough were banned. 1,000 police cordoned off the Town

Hall from 14,000 marching tenants, striking railwaymen and building workers[14].

These sorts of actions by local tenants were not new. For example, in 1915, women on Clydeside had organized a rent strike. The government granted an immediate rent freeze. Such tenants' action was important for a number of reasons. Firstly, it was women who organized the rent strike: in 'community' campaigns it is usually women who are most affected and who do most of the work although they are clearly not always (or even often) in leadership positions. Secondly, the government accepted the demand for an immediate rent freeze because it was worried about the possibility of industrial action during wartime on Clydeside, which was a major munitions centre, if tenants' demands were not met. This action thus showed the possibility of linking 'community' to industrial struggles; this possible linkage of 'community' and industrial issues is something which has attracted much debate, although limited action, since the mid 1970s.

After both World Wars, working class action groups had protested about the housing shortage, and squatting had taken place in a number of major cities and also in ex-army camps and air-bases. It was not until the 1960s, however, that working class struggles in the community seem to have become much more widespread. Tenants' Associations were formed in both the public and the private sector and action was taken about rent increases, housing repairs and lack of consultation over redevelopment and other housing issues; local action groups protested about inadequate facilities for themselves and their children and about other issues such as dangerous traffic.

Why is it then, that this sort of action seemed to be widespread in the 1960s? Obviously people were reacting against poor services and conditions but why at this particular time? To answer this adequately, it is necessary briefly to look at the relevant major structural changes which have taken place in the post-war British economy.

14 For details, see Widgery, *op. cit.* p. 454. The use of force on this scale was, at this period, most unusual. There are other examples of tenants action developing around this time. In May 1962, the tenants of 'Greencoats Properties' marched 26 miles from Bethnal Green to the Council Chairman's home, protesting about the exorbitant rent rises and demanding compulsory purchase of the flats. By October, the tenants campaign had achieved its aim: Bethnal Green Council took over the 1018 flats of 'Greencoat Properties'.

One important change has been that, as the rate of profit in manufacturing industry has declined, capital has been transferred to more profitable sectors of the economy, particularly construction and speculative development. This has increased the competition for land space, particularly in central urban areas and led to dramatic increases in land and property values and rents. In the private sector, redevelopment and increasing home ownership limited the amount of rented accommodation which was available. Tenants were faced with higher rents for less space as the pressure on this form of housing increased, and the 1957 Rent Act which abolished effective controls on rent enabled landlords to do this. In the public sector, councils were forced to borrow money on the open market at higher interest rates, land was much more expensive and the cost of building new houses increased dramatically.

It is not altogether surprising then that there was some reaction on the part of both private and council tenants to these developments which for them had led to higher rents, overcrowding, homelessness, and possible displacement without any consultation, to new and badly designed tower-block systems. There were also other factors linked to the formation and development of tenants' associations and action groups. In many working-class areas, the Labour Party was often inactive. Membership and active involvement in the Labour Party had declined, and, for many tenants, the Labour Party was either a hindrance or actually seemed to contribute towards their problems. No longer – if indeed they ever had – did many working class people expect the Labour Party to improve their lot.

It should also be remembered that the upsurge of working class tenants' activity in the 1960s coincided with the development of CND, the Committee of 100, and the re-emergence of forms of extra-parliamentary protest. It is interesting that some of the extra-parliamentary activists who had been involved in CND and the Committee of 100 became involved with local groups of residents who were developing spontaneous forms of community action as a response to the pressures outlined above. They were joined by other activists who also rejected the traditional Left and felt it important to start political organization from the perspectives and struggles of working class people. This linkage of disaffected middle class professionals and activists to working class struggles for improvements on estates and in neighbourhoods gave community action a visibility which it might not otherwise have had. This, in turn, gave it increased political significance in a climate of general protest.

The 1960s generally should be seen as a time of growing challenge and protest in this sphere. Some local groups obviously thought that if they organized and protested sufficiently strongly, their demands would be met. The daily reality of working class lives was very different from the image of an advanced welfare state, but at least many people still had rising expectations and a feeling that improvements or change could come about. Unfortunately for them, however, the endemic and seemingly irreversible decline of the British economy which had been evident since the late nineteenth century, reasserted its dominance in the 1960s. Always a weak link in the capitalist chain in the twentieth century, Britain was the first of the major capitalist powers to undergo the problems of declining profitability which were, later in the decade, to signal the beginnings of a worldwide and especially deep recession. In Britain this meant that social policies/reform were limited by immediate economic difficulties such as balance of payments crises, and the first major post-war public expenditure cuts came in the late 1960s. Spending in the public sector was then constrained by these factors. Almost all public services were subject to official government reports, enquiries, and reorganization throughout the 1960s and early 1970s. Water authorities, health, transport, local government (including housing and social services), the police: all of these were 'rationalized' and reorganized. Overall, this meant much greater political and economic control by the central state over those previously locally controlled (to a greater or lesser extent) services. In retrospect, it was obviously necessary in a political system supposedly based on local as well as national democracy for the central state in spite of its increasing control – to show concern for local democracy. One of the ways this was done was by stressing the vague notion of 'community' in the late 1960s and early 1970s and developing community projects, and participatory measures generally, in local areas. At the same time, the government knew that it had to respond to the unrest of the late 1960s and early 1970s. There was certainly concern about the increasing rate of juvenile crime in particular, as well as the political consequences of not taking any action about the social unrest of the 1960s ('spontaneous' tenants' action, concern over immigration and the black community, etc.)

It was for a combination of these reasons that the state became directly involved in setting up various kinds of 'community' programmes. Urban Aid was started in 1969, the Community Development Projects shortly afterwards; then various other schemes in the 1970s, culminating in the recent Inner City Programme (1977–78), which supposedly deals with 'economic and industrial' as well as 'social' problems.

Grandiose claims have been made by various politicians about these programmes – how they would solve the problems of poverty and deprivation. In fact, comparatively minute levels of expenditure have been allocated to them. In the early 1970s the whole of the 'Urban Programme' amounted to, at most, only one-twentieth of 1 per cent of total public expenditure. In 1978–79, money under the Inner-City Programme was approximately 1.5 per cent of the total Rate Support Grant which was available for local government spending. Most of these programmes have been small-scale 'pilot' projects and the major intention of the state in setting them up was to show *concern* over issues such as 'urban problems' rather than to undertake fundamental action to resolve them – an impossible task in a declining capitalist economy. There has, thus, been a classic public relations exercise: maximum concern at minimum cost. Clearly these programmes have done very little to help working class people improve the quality of, or gain control over, their lives. While these minute amounts of money and resources have been put into a very few localities, massive amounts of resources have been taken away from all areas both by the government cuts of the mid 1970s and beyond, and by the changes in the methods of financing local government.

The existence of these programmes has, however, meant that some working class groups have been able to take advantage of them, and some of the programmes have in fact caused problems – albeit rather minor ones – for the state. At a practical level, local working class groups have received resources for advice centres, community centres, play provision and many other facilities. This process obviously has contradictory results: the state encourages some forms of voluntary self-help (the present Thatcher Government in particular has been doing this), because it may save money and deflect attention away from cuts in services. On the other hand, many people have been involved in organizing and controlling some local venture – often, especially for women, for the first time – and have used these state resources (advice-centre information, for example) to attack the inadequacies and workings of the local state. Sometimes, this conflict has led to the withdrawal of state funds. An advice-centre in Batley, Yorkshire, had funds withdrawn in 1974 because it was causing too many problems for Kirklees local authority and the local Labour Party.

At an ideological level, some of the professional workers in state-funded community projects have published the origins and inadequacies of such 'experiments' and shown how working-class residents suffer from the workings of a capitalist economy[15]. Not surprisingly, these projects – the Community Development Project which were set up by the Home Office in 1969 – were closed down from 1976–78.

Overall then, working class community action groups have achieved some successes since the 1960s. Independent action developed by previously uninvolved tenants has pressurized the local state into various concessions. At the same time, some local groups and professional workers have exploited the resources and contradictions of state 'community' programmes. This has helped to change the focus of 'community' from a vague notion used politically by the state to get people to take responsibility for 'their' problem (i.e. blaming the victim), to an idea which stresses the potential of class politics through collective action in working class areas.

It is important, however, to refer to some of the limitations of the upsurge in community action which took place in the 1960s. Many action groups seemed quite naturally to regard the problems of their own localities as all-important. This means that they could engage in struggle against the local council and perhaps, because of their campaigning, receive priority treatment – this may have been at the expense of people in other areas who were not organized. This concentration on local struggles often meant that the groups were socially and politically isolated. Thus, at a time of increasing public expenditure, improvements could, after a struggle, be secured for specific areas but there was no guarantee that the improvements would be lasting. The classic example of this is housing repairs: many local groups have campaigned in recent years for more effective repair systems within local authority housing departments – often, after pressure, repairs in particular neighbourhoods are speeded

15 c.f. *The Costs of Industrial Change; Gilding The Ghetto.* CDP. 1977.

up and improved. One can almost guarantee however that in a few months or a year afterwards, the repairs system will be just as bad as it was initially. In other words, minor administrative changes may be temporarily made but policy remains basically the same.

Thus, in the long term, these localized struggles, because of social and political isolation, did not develop into cumulative mass movements capable of more fundamental change. However, the struggles against the Housing Finance Bill and Act in 1971–72 did show the possibilities of widespread local opposition to specific government measures. Certainly, demonstrations, publicity and a great deal of tenants' activity developed around this issue, not just in the major cities but also in areas which had not previously been noted for militant activity, e.g. Clay Cross and Batley. Without analysing the struggles against the Housing Finance Act in detail, a general point can be made that the activities (and often the non-activity) of the Labour Party, both locally and nationally, contributed towards the stifling of working-class tenants action.

As the effects of the cuts became apparent both practically and ideologically in the mid-to-late 1970s, many of the gains which community action groups had achieved were lost. It is not surprising that many local groups became disillusioned and activity declined. It was made worse by the fact that a Labour Government was implementing the cuts.

Under Thatcher, the cuts have not merely continued but have obviously got very much worse. There has been a massive extension of both the scale and the nature of the attack upon the working class generally. Just as industry is being 'restructured' to meet the needs of capital and big business, so the welfare state is also being 'restructured' to support private capital. The Tories have embarked on large-scale 'privatization' which has included creating new markets for private enterprise, (supporting private hospitals, encouraging private bus companies to compete with public services on profitable routes), and selling existing public assets to the private sector (such as council house sales). In addition, expenditure on all social services has been drastically cut and charges increased. To facilitate these developments, the Tories have mounted a major ideological onslaught on 'scroungers' and the 'work-shy', generally lowered expectations about what can be 'afforded', and attacked the rights of women to go out to work – their places is once again in the home and they are expected to brear the brunt of the cuts in services for groups like the elderly and young children.

In this context, the isolated protest politics of the 1960s and the early 1970s will achieve little. What then can be done in working-class areas about issues of collective consumption? Clearly, new forms of organization, strategies and tactics are needed if past failures are to be avoided. Many activists have obviously been discussing the limitations of past actions and ways of organizing, and there is a large measure of agreement about them. There is also a broad measure of agreement about what must be done to overcome such limitations in the future. Unfortunately the ideas which have been discussed are usually pitched at a very general level and, as yet (at the time of writing), only minimally tried in practice. There has for example, been much discussion about the necessity of building alliances between tenants, and public and private sector workers; of creating 'links' between 'community' and 'union' struggles. There is clearly an urgent need for local and national alliances which are capable of strengthening and bringing together the broad labour movement. Hopefully, Thatcherism, instead of leading to apathetic defeatism, may be just the factor bringing various groupings together, because there is no alternative. However, it is possible – some would say probable – that this logical fusion of the labour movement will not take place. In these circumstances it is necessary to work from general principles into the harsh reality of local situations. It is vital for socialists to work with struggles in the community, as well as the traditional focus on the work-place, (working class groups must however beware of relying on either the local Labour groups, or indeed on a possible future Labour Government to solve their problems). Similarly, members of political parties must not exploit groups and campaigns for their own party ends – as has sometimes happened in the past.

Many people would agree with these general principles, but how can independent struggles around such issues as housing be developed and linked into the broader labour movement? A concrete example may illustrate the potential and the difficulties. Leeds lacks a recent tradition of organized tenants' struggle (in spite of activities elsewhere in the 1960s and early 1970s, radical community action seems to have bypassed the city). In the last two years, however, the few active tenants' groups have made links with each other and also with several sympathetic shop stewards in the Direct Works Department of the council to form a Housing Action Group. In this forum, experiences and common problems have been shared. Pressure has been put onto the Labour Council to oppose government policies over such issues as higher rents, dampness and repairs. Pressure has also led to the council taking on more apprentices in the Direct Works Department. In this way, housing and 'community' struggles have been placed more visibly on the political agenda of the local labour movement. Community workers and members of groups have broadened their perspectives through educational activities (such as day-schools) and joint action (publicity and demonstrations at full council and housing committee meetings). This broad-based group is now attempting to develop direct action strategies which would have been unthinkable a few years ago – the encouragement of a city-wide rent strike against the new rent increases. (It should be noted, however, that there are many practical difficulties in doing this). It seems, from press reports and contacts in various parts of the country, that there is mounting anger and opposition to these increases. This opposition is clearly, in the first instance, defensive. It is possible, however, that the anger which is generated by this opposition can be used as a means of education and politicization about the connections between local everyday problems and the political and economic system which creates them, and the need for socialism. Members of the Leeds Housing Action Group then will pressurize the Local Council but will know that in reality it is Thatcher's Government which is imposing massive housing cuts. However, they will hopefully also be aware that public work, housing and land, creates profits for private capital and firms, and how the bulk of rents and rates go to pay off interest to banks and financiers. Democratic educative work then, is necessary to inform political demands. There is an urgent need for more relevant and locally accessible courses and events which should be based on local people's concerns and experiences. Local Workers Education Association (WEA) branches and adult education centres and departments should and could be much more innovative, and involved in these possibilities.

In the early 1970s, many community groups did believe that reliance on the Labour Party or local councillors would improve their situation. Collaborative reformist measures such as participation schemes were in vogue then, but there is little of that in the early 1980s. It should then, under the excesses of

Socialist strategies

Thatcherism, be easier for local groups to avoid the dangers of reformism. It is almost a case of direct action or nothing. Paradoxically, however, even though local groups may see through the limitations of reformism more clearly than ten years ago, there has been a massive increase in the repressive apparatus of the State – with increased expenditure on law and order, more police powers, and the use of the military in strikes, as with the firemen in 1977. This will probably mean that any direct action on a large scale by working class groups will be met by force and repression. This repressive action may intimidate people or it may indeed spark off further action and support within the labour movement. This assumes, however, that the labour movement sees the importance of local community struggles and is already involved in them – which brings us back to the importance of building ideological and political links which can unite the two within a common socialist perspective.

In the late 1970s, locally based trade union and community resource centres were established in about twelve cities in Britain (including Coventry, Leeds, Newcastle, London and Nottingham). These are attempting, through research, education and action, to develop the understanding of issues which people face in the work-place, the home and the community. Sometimes they work with tenants groups, and/or shop stewards groups, and/or sympathetic trades councils: local circumstances obviously determine what possibilities there are. The funding for these centres, usually from trusts and charities, is extremely precarious. They are, undoubtedly, an important development but this importance should not be exaggerated. They are not a substitute for political organization and direct action but, rather, a local resource for these things. Many of them attempt to do 'link work' but the local practical difficulties of this are often underestimated. Moreover, they are not wildly popular with the official union leadership. Indeed, it is interesting to note that in December 1981 Len Murray wrote to trades councils at local, county and regional level saying that 'no TUC body should proceed to establish a new resource/research centre' or even 'participate in discussions leading to the establishment of such centres' until the TUC General Council had completed a review of the TUC's regional machinery. He was concerned that, if centres are not 'fully accountable to affiliated unions and the TUC... there is a danger that alternative trade union structures' would begin to emerge 'and be used to drive a wedge between unions and their members'. By the Spring of 1982 the TUC had specifically ordered a halt to centres then in the process of being established in London and Birmingham with money from the GLC and the West Midlands County Council; and this development obviously has serious implications for the future relationship of these centres to local trade union organizations.

A group of women (and it usually is women) campaigning for the first time from a local council estate about housing repairs or lack of nursery provision do not magically and suddenly 'link up' with sympathetic active trade unionists in the local labour movement. Sometimes, after a process of getting nowhere with the local council, they may contact the trades council and ask for support; or one of the group's members with experience of union activity may take the issue to other parts of the labour movement. Perhaps an aware community worker may help broaden the group's perspectives and help in establishing relevant contacts. Alternatively, some unions have passed motions at national level against the cuts (NUPE, NALGO, etc.) and may attempt through active local shop stewards, to seek out and support local community groups. As mentioned earlier, the possibilities will differ according to local circumstances. However, these local possibilities have to be sensitively developed. Activists, particularly male trade unionists, have to develop new forms of organization and communication. Many women have difficulty in finding time and energy to attend or initiate local estate or street meetings over particular issues. It is even more difficult for them to make links with other community groups in other parts of the city or town who may be organized around the same issue: How is transport to be arranged? What about child-care? Does the husband object? These are all real problems. If, however, after all these difficulties, links are then made with, for example, a trades council sub-committee (and with most trades councils, meetings with 'outside' bodies such as tenants' groups are tortuous processes to organize), then further problems occur. The way meetings are organized and the processes which occur during them are often guaranteed to put off working class women, and it is the politically active male trade unionists who are usually to blame for this. All this is mentioned here, not as a lead-in to simple answers – there *are* no simple answers – but these practical, albeit fundamental, points have to be brought into the open and discussed fully if 'link-work' is to become a reality. There are, therefore, many lessons from the women's movement which are relevant to the difficulties of organizing in the 1980s[16].

There are important general conclusions to be drawn from the experiences of community action over the last 20 years. The limitations of localism and social and political isolation can be overcome; lessons can be learnt from the women's movement; 'protest politics' can be built on and extended – not opportunistically, but sensitively – into something much more potent. But if this happens, the repressive forces of the State – the police and the army – will be much more in evidence, and then it is anyone's guess as to what will happen.

IV

What then are the strengths and weaknesses of this whole tradition within the contemporary British Left? At the most general, but perhaps the most important level, such politics are an integral part of the indigenous political culture of British radicalism in a way that all 'orthodox' Marxist movements are not. As E. P. Thompson and others[17] have argued so convincingly, this is a rich and deep vein of genuine, humanistic socialism, which has emphasized liberty as well as equality, civic freedom as well as collective consciousness, and moral commitment as much as structural conflict. It is the great upsurge from within this tradition which have, over the last 200 or more years, often produced the most significant and fundamental social and political changes in Britain. In this sense, then, the mobilization over the supreme moral issue of nuclear disarmament was a mass popular protest in the same tradition as the great popular movements of the eighteenth and nineteenth centuries. It is precisely because of this, it can be argued, that the movement attracted such widespread and massive support. (Similarly, it is at least in part because they have failed to link in to this indigenous radical culture that Marxist groupings have made such relatively little

16 One of the most interesting discussions in this area in Sheila Rowbotham's, *The Women's movement and organising for Socialism*, in S. Rowbotham, Lynne Segal and Hilary Wainwright (eds) *Beyond the Fragments: Feminism and the making of socialism* London, Merlin Press, 1979.
17 See particularly E. P. Thompson, 'The Peculiarities of the English', reprinted in E. P. Thompson, *The Poverty of Theory and other essays*, Merlin Press, London, 1978.

headway in Britain.) Pursuing this historical perspective, it can also be argued that changes within Britain over single issues of major significance (e.g. extension of the suffrage, abolition of slavery, abolition of capital punishment, etc.) have often been accomplished only after lengthy campaigns – and often long after those campaigns have ostensibly ended. Also linked to this 'cultural' argument is the fact that such movements, again unlike the formal political organizations of the Left, involve 'ordinary' apolitical people, either on the basis of moral commitment (as in the strong protest of women against nuclear testing dangers in the late 1950s), or because their own immediate environment and/or families are affected adversely by state policies (as in housing campaigns in the 1960s). There is a genuine populism here which transcends class considerations, at least at crisis periods. Such single-issue movements also have the great advantage of mobilizing a very diverse cross-section of the community and yet maintaining, in the short-to-medium term, a dynamic unity because of support for the central issue. To an extent, at least, this minimizes dangers of sectarianism and bureaucratization. Moreover, such movements have, on the whole, managed to carve out a distinctive extra-parliamentary path, using the institutional system as and when appropriate but not relying centrally on the commitment (and ability) of such institutions to produce the desired political results.

A single-issue campaign gives specificity and focus to Left political movements. In contrast to the Far Left, which has traditionally presented analyses of capitalism and, similarly, prescriptive programmes for socialist restructuring, single-issue campaigns have confronted specific problems with specific solutions. And, of course, whereas to date all macro-socialist attempts have failed to overthrow capitalism, some single-issue campaigns have had some not insignificant successes.

Overall, then, single-issue movements have the potential to build into serious mass political movements, and to raise the consciousness of large sections of the population, initially over the particular issue at stake, but ultimately over the general nature of capitalist society. With the deeply-rooted, albeit minority, radicalism of British political culture, it is single-issue movements, *operating on an extra-parliamentary strategy*, at both the local and national level, that have acted as the catalyst for achieving radical change. Applying this perspective to the history of radical progress in Britain over the last twenty years, it can be

235

argued that most, though not all, significant change has come, not through the Labour Party (and most certainly not through the Communist Party), but through the whole complex of extra-parliamentary movements: to the nuclear disarmament movement and community politics must be added, of course, the women's movement, the anti-racist movement and many others.

If this is 'the way forward', in terms of style and structure as much as substantive political issues, why it is that such movements have failed to produce a new and socialist realignment on the left? There are, we would argue, three fundamental weaknesses in the notion of the extra-parliamentary, single-issue, direct action movement acting as the successful catalyst for a new socialist movement: organizational, political and ideological weaknesses. At the organizational level, such movements have been characterized by a high degree of inefficiency. Libertarians tend to dominate such movements, and often have little competence at or interest in the most elementary of administrative tasks. This defect relates directly to the decentralized structure of such movements and their necessary lack of co-ordination, authority and regularized decision-making processes. They are, in other words, characterized by a libertarian and spontaneous organizational attitude which is based on an ideological distaste for centralized authority, bureaucracy, and so on. These factors have constituted a continuing problem for such movements and have been a major contributory factor to their generally short-lived existences.

This links in, too, with their political weaknesses: their inability to co-ordinate *local* initiatives to *central* political struggles (or, in the case of single-issue national campaigns like nuclear disarmament, the inability to move from the single issue to wider political concerns). Paradoxically, given the specificity of many such movements, there has also been a tendency towards 'utopianism': a marked gap between the immediate short-term objectives (which are usually well-defined and agreed upon), and the long-term objectives of a 'transformed' society (usually ill-defined and utopian). The great weakness, therefore, has lain in the absence of any medium-term strategy: how to move from the microcosm of the local issue to generalized structural social change. In practical terms, this has meant the problem of *agency*. For 'orthodox' Marxists (whether Leninists, Trotskyists or Maoists) agency has been inextricably linked to the notion of the party. For the predominantly libertarian activists of these direct action movements 'the party' and all it has symbolized has been an anathema. Inasmuch as there has been explicit discussion of 'agency' amongst radicals in these movements, there has been an ill-defined and utopian belief in spontaneity, populism and de-centralized community action.

This major political weakness is of course intimately linked to the inherently flawed ideological frameworks of such move-ments. Fundamentally, all have at their core a complex of incom-patible ideological frameworks. Almost by definition there can be no long-term political unity, and therefore no ideological unity, beyond the specific issues involved, among the disparate groups. (This was particularly true of the nuclear disarmament movement composed as it was of public figures from the Church and the Arts, anarchists, '*Guardian* readers', Trotskyists, and so on). Not only has there been very little ideological *agreement*, there has been very little ideological *analysis* of the ways in which the issues involved have related to the macrocosmic structures. This has been due in part to the perceived pressures of action over particular issues[18], but it has also been a result of the fundamentally divergent ideological assumptions from which activists in the movements have operated. Not only have they been acting with different objectives in view, they have defined the issues themselves in conceptually discrete ways (compare, for example, the DAC view of direct action with that of the Trotskyists). The campaign has thus been characterized by an over-riding concern with the specific issue, considered in isolation from the environment which produced it. The concern has, therefore, been fundamentally superficial: an attempt to deal with effect rather than cause, with the *manifestations* of an irra-tional and immoral system, rather than with the system itself.

Collectively, these weaknesses have prevented anything but the most temporary of alliances, however effective these may have been over a short period. Yet, there has been potential for socialist advance through such movements. How, if at all, can this problem be overcome? What are the contemporary areas for relevant activism?

As the capitalist crisis deepens, the stakes of political conflict become ever higher. And of course this whole process takes place against a backdrop of mounting international tension and an accelerating arms race. The 'progress' in nuclear weapons tech-

18 As April Carter, a leading member of DAC, has testified. See Taylor and Pritchard, *op. cit.* p. 78.

nology, combined with consistently high 'defence' expenditure, and nuclear proliferation, has made nuclear holocaust not only *far* more likely than twenty years ago, but *far* more horrific. At one level, then, the cause of the peace movement must transcend all other political priorities. Class conflict and the struggle for socialism are predicated upon human existence. Yet, to attain the objectives of the peace movement is an essentially political task, and is inherently and inextricably connected with socialist politics[19]. Unless and until the movement becomes aware of the complex and inextricable links between nuclear armaments and the capitalist system – and the need to link the struggles against them – the prospects for success in the long-term are minimal.

Similarly, working class resistance to Thatcherism in the community, if it is to be effective in the long term, must not only link in with industrial struggle, (and this is very difficult in practice, particularly as many unions focus mainly on econ-omistic[20] demands), but must become positively socialistic in analysis and prescription, rather than remaining purely defensive and implicitly social democratic. This is, of course, easier to say than to achieve. But there can be no short cut to the achievement of the objectives. There is no easy solution, no alternative to the hard work of linking industrial struggles to single-issue campaigns, and of convincing activists in both spheres that the solution to their problems lies only in the establishment of a socialist society. Unless this ideological and political task is accomplished, these conflicts will result in defeat for socialist perspectives, with incalculable consequences. Priorities, and strategies of involvement, will vary accordingly to local circumstances, but overall there can be no more important task facing socialists in the 1980s than the linking-up, in both theory and practice, of industrial, community, and peace movement campaigns.

19 See Raymond Williams, The Politics of Nuclear Disarmament, *New Left Review*, No. 124, 1981.
20 In practice, this means an almost exclusive 'pragmatic' focus on pay and conditions at work, unrelated to any understanding of, or even concern with, the structural processes underlying the system which has produced inequality and class conflict. This attitude is symptomatic of the political assumptions which underlie many unions' official policies: most trade union leaders explicitly or implicitly accept capitalist structures as beyond challenge, and 'treat as irrelevant to trade union strategy whatever commitment they may have to another social order'. Ralph Miliband, *The State in Capitalist Society*, Quartet, London, 1973, p. 144.

CONCLUSION

Chapter nine

BASIC PROBLEMS OF
SOCIALIST STRATEGY

Robert Looker and David Coates

Let us begin with a reminder of the obvious: that the replacement of capitalism by socialism is a task of epoch-making proportions and of quite overwhelming complexity. If Marxism teaches us anything about the character of the historical process, it must surely be that these replacements of one mode of production and associated social forms by another are extraordinarily rare, involve considerable struggle, and are achieved only by the displacement of one whole set of class relationships by another (historically), or (in the case of socialism) by the end of class itself. So it should not surprise us, or discredit the project as a whole, to say that socialists in advanced capitalist countries have not yet found a successful route forward: for the task that we set ourselves is of a unique and enormous kind, to replace one social system by another, and to do so for the first time by the mobilization of an agency of change that is conscious of its task, democratic in its practices and mass-based in its character.

In the design of an effective strategy for such a transition, socialists have three general and interconnected requirements. To begin with, we need an adequate analysis of the logic of the capitalist system that can locate both its strengths and weaknesses, on the basis of which we can move from a merely reactive response to capitalism's problems into an assertive politics that can transcend them. Then, we need a clear identification of the possible agencies of change which are capable of sustaining a challenge to capitalism, and a grasp of how such agencies can be won to a perspective which identifies socialism as the only viable solution to the experienced oppressions, injustices and exploitations generated by capitalism. Finally, we require instruments – organizations, programmes, arenas of action – which can effectively translate the aspiration into the achievement of a socialist society.

Socialist strategies

Yet, if these are the most direct problems that must be resolved before the project for socialism becomes a viable one, then the experience of the past century and a half of industrial capitalism has demonstrated how complex and intractable they are. Even before we can begin to explore their possible lines of resolution in the immediate context of contemporary British capitalism, we need to examine how socialists have sought to resolve them over more than a century of struggle, and to locate the problems such resolutions have encountered both in theory and practice throughout that period. Three aspects of that historical experience deserve more particular attention. First, there is the fact of fundamental divisions and disagreements between socialists themselves over the logic of the capitalist system and the associated agencies and instruments for challenging it. Second, there is the way in which capitalism has developed, and the manner in which its absorption, accommodation, fragmentation and repression of opposition currents has challenged and frequently subverted socialist theory and practice itself. Finally, there is the profoundly ambivalent character of the legacies that socialist movements have bequeathed us in the late twentieth century. It is at least arguable that that legacy, far from rendering the goal of socialism a more realistic possibility that it was, has on the contrary come close to discrediting socialism even as an aspiration among those to whom it should most naturally appeal.

THE HISTORICAL LEGACY

Division on the Left

From its earliest days, industrial capitalism has evoked a wide range of hostile responses, most notably in the practical resistance of its subordinate and exploited classes and strata, but also in the form of a complex range of critiques of the ways of living and the values it embodies. Many of these critiques posed against capitalism the possibility of an alternative, socialist, society; yet the fact of the appeal to a common word – socialism – only barely disguised the fundamental differences between such critiques – differences over what was being rejected and why, the nature of the alternative society, and how it was to be brought about. As early as 1848, Marx and Engels felt it necessary to devote a sizeable part of *The Communist Manifesto* to listing and exposing the heterogeneous and contradictory range of ideas which marched under the name of 'socialism', before they went on to articulate what they saw as its only scientific form.

Thus, from the start, a common word has served to obscure fundamental divisions over goals and strategies. We cannot here even begin to list, let alone explore, the vast range of perspectives that have claimed the label since Marx wrote in 1848. But what we can do is identify the two broad left-wing strategies that have competed – in the name of socialism – for working-class loyalty in the twentieth century, and which are represented in this collection, in the contributions by Geoff Hodgson and David Bailey. First, there is the *reformist* perspective. This argues for a strategy of advancing towards socialism through a series of legislative measures which progressively constrict and restrict capitalism out of existence. The reformist commitment to achieving a total social transformation distinguishes it, at least in principle, from the rather different politics of *social reform* where the search for qualitative social change has been explicitly rejected in favour of a strategy concerned simply with the achievement of specific benefits for the labour movement. On the other hand *reformism* shares with social reform politics a commitment to pursuing its goals within channels made available by capitalist democracy and within limits broadly imposed by bourgeois notions of legality and constitutionalism. Down the years, reformists have differed over the extent to which the parliamentary search for a socialist society would have to be supplemented by industrial struggle and mass mobilization, or even by defensive violence by the working class against capitalist counter-reaction, but all have been at variance with a second strategy, Bolshevik in inspiration, which still sees the struggle for socialism in revolutionary terms. That revolutionary tradition continued to see the transition to socialism as involving industrial struggle and political mobilization outside parliamentary channels, and continues to look to the armed seizure of power, the destruction of the bourgeois state, and the dictatorship of the proletariat, an essential elements in the process. This tradition has been willing at times to participate in the parliamentary process, but never as the main channel for the achievement of political and social power. Of course, this debate between reformists and revolutionaries predated 1917. William Morris, for one, had a clear sense of the issues thirty years earlier. But after the Russian Revolution it found initial institutional

expression in the existence of different international organizations of socialists – the Second, the Third, and even for a while
the '2½' International – which fought each other as hard as they
fought the common capitalist enemy.

It is worth dwelling for a moment on this division within
twentieth century socialism, to examine in more detail the main
alternative conceptions of socialist transition that it contains. It
is clear that socialists have always been confronted with a choice
between rival strategies. That choice has been variously
designated, depending on which element of the choice was being
emphasized, as one between 'reform' or 'revolution', 'the
evolutionary' versus the 'revolutionary' road, or particularly
since 1917, the 'parliamentary' as against the 'insurrectionary'
route to socialism. But, however labelled, what has been at stake
in the choice has been a basic disagreement over the nature of the
critique of capitalism, the agency of change, and the role of the
state as a possible vehicle for this change. With that in mind, let
us now examine each alternative in turn.

One fruitful way of capturing the essence of the theoretical
perspectives underpinning reformism or 'evolutionary
socialism' is to focus on the essentially universalistic, humanist
and rationalistic character of its critique of capitalist reality. The
nature of that rationalism may vary – it might be an essentially
ethical rationalism which focuses on the injustices of
capitalism, as in the case of Bernstein, or it might be a technocratic rationalism which damns the system for its inefficiencies, as with critics as varied as Saint Simon and the
Webbs. Underlying this diversity of sources, however, there is a
common commitment to a strategy of critique – that capitalism is
to be judged and found wanting by reference to a standard, which
does not itself derive from capitalism but rather transcends it. In
this sense the standard is a 'universal ideal' which could be
vindicated by appeal to ethical or technocratic propositions that
have their basis in reasoned argument. It can be noted that there
are real tensions between these rival standards which manifest
themselves with some frequency in the theory and practice of
reformism. Ethical rationalism tends to be the dominant motif in
periods of opposition, but gives way rapidly to technocratic
rationalism when in office. This may be acknowledged however,
without denying that they also share a unity of approach compared with the revolutionary alternative, a unity which derives
from the manner in which such standards, for reformists, are

neither ideological nor simply a matter of subjective preference, but are instead grounded in some universal truths.

The appeal to such universally valid truths – and, at least in the secular versions, rationally demonstrable truths – already implicitly locates the agency which can bring about the transformation of capitalism into socialism. For reformists, it is those who have access to, and at least potentially share in, that common rationality: that is, all the sane adult population who make up the 'citizenry' in capitalist societies. (Such 'humanism', is not of course, incompatible with an accompanying elitism which locates the best articulators of that rationality in some minority intelligentsia.) Of course, particular classes, most evidently the working class, may already be predisposed to respond to the appeals of socialism by virtue of their direct experience of the multifarious oppressions of capitalism, but oppressions are not confined to class, nor are class interests more than contingently aligned to, or equatable with, the 'community interest' with which socialism is concerned. It is, after all, the particular defect of the capitalist class that it tends to put its narrow and sectional interest above that of the community as a whole, and under certain circumstances, even working class interests could, for reformists, be said to embody a similar sectionalist threat to the 'public interest'.

Given this appeal to universal truths, to rationalism and to an abstract humanism, the most plausible vehicle for bringing about the transition from capitalism to socialism is the democratic state itself. It is not only that it is the instrument which both determines what is to be pursued as the common good and possesses the resources to legislate it into existence. More than this, the democratic state in its very nature embodies the principle of the supremacy of the universal (citizenship) over the sectional (class).

Socialist politics on the reformist view, then, are primarily oriented to participation within the framework of a democratic state, not only because it provides the suitable means to achieving socialism but also because it is very much part of the end itself. It is through the rational debates between the community interest embodied in socialism and the sectionalist interests embodied in the views of their opponents, as much as through demonstrations of its practicability through a series of concrete reforms, that the superiority of socialism is to be demonstrated. The project of reformism is, thus, one where the forward march of reforms pushes back the frontiers of capitalism with each step and simultaneously builds the wider consensus between all sections of society, which expresses the ever increasing ascendency of community over class. Parliament in this context is thus not merely an instrument of power for achieving socialism. More importantly, it is the essential framework for generating the value consensus which socialist society presupposes.

In stark opposition to the abstract humanitarianism, rationalism and, ultimately, idealism that permeates the reformist perspective, the revolutionary tradition, at least in its dominant Marxist mode, has been historically specific, materialist, and class-anchored in its approaches to analysis and prescription. Capitalism is identified as a system of class exploitation in the process of material production whose ramifications are embodied in the multifarious experiences of domination, hierarchy, inequality and oppression at all levels of the system. Yet the system is inherently unstable. The contradictory logic written into the capitalist mode of production – the unplanned and uncontrolled accumulation of capital propelled by the logic of capitalist market relationships – ensures its continuing if historically variable vulnerability to local, regional, national and international crises and disruptions. At the same time, the system of exploitation creates a class – the proletariat – whose experienced problems are capable of resolution only through the transformation of capitalism into socialism, and whose response to those problems generates a class struggle which opens up the real and practical possibilities for achieving that transformation.

For Marxists, then, socialism is not an abstract, rationalist and supra-historical standard or set of values. On the contrary, it is a programme, historically situated in and generated by the experienced exploitation and oppressions of industrial capitalism, which specifies the conditions under which the self-liberation of the working class can be achieved. That the consequence of achieving socialism involves also the abolition of class as such, and thus the achievement of a genuinely 'human' society, must not obscure the fact that this would be the historical achievement of class struggle by the working class, and not the triumph of some rationalistic value consensus which subordinates class to community perspectives.

This equation of socialism with working class perspectives and interests, and the denial of any overarching abstract 'community interest', flows out of and reinforces the conviction of revolutionaries that the central fact of capitalist experience is that of class conflict. It follows that in that conflict there can be no neutral instrumentalities for the discernment of the 'common good', but only institutions which articulate and execute opposed class interests. More specifically, the state, even the democratic state form dominant in advanced industrial capitalisms today, cannot do other than act in the interests of the capitalist system. On this account, therefore, the transition to socialism requires the replacement of that state structure with institutions which embody the interests and will of the working class and their allies.

It might appear that such a perspective necessarily involves an insurrectionist model of revolutionary challenge to capitalist state power. Certainly, for much of the twentieth century and under the influence of the Russian Revolution of 1917, revolutionary theory – if not practice – has been strongly drawn towards variants of insurrectionism. Yet nineteenth century Marxists, at least, were much less inclined to polarize 'parliamentary' and 'insurrectionary' routes to socialism. Rather, they looked for ways to combine them as different facets of the same strategy. More specifically, they argued that the democratic form of capitalist state, though an instrument of the ruling class, offered real possibilities for agitation, propaganda and organization among the working class, and also for achieving concrete if limited gains for labour at the expense of capital. Such gains were not themselves the stepping stones on the road to socialism; they were not even permanently guaranteed defensive positions for labour within capitalism. They did however contribute powerfully to the self-confidence and assertiveness of the socialist and working class movement. Thus, in contrast to syndicalists who posed industrial struggle against political (including parliamentary) struggle, Marxists prior to World War I, and increasingly again since the erosion of Stalinist communism, have sought for strategies that combine the two forms of struggle. Indeed, many of the debates and divisions today between those who identify with the revolutionary and Marxist tradition turns precisely upon how political and industrial struggle can be fruitfully combined, and on what instruments are best situated to achieve it. The theoretical perspectives of Eurocommunism, the Marxist Left inside the Labour Party, and groups such as the SWP, are all regarded by their adherents – if not by each other – as pointing in the right direction on this crucial question of the relative weights of, and the relationship between, 'the political' and 'the economic' in the struggle for socialism.

Thus, the first central fact and problem for socialists is that they confront not only a capitalist enemy but also a spectrum of rival strategies which identify that enemy differently, and appeal to overlapping but crucially different constituencies and instruments. Many would-be sympathizers with socialism are scandalized and repelled both by the degree of division between groups calling themselves socialist and by the degree of vituperation that these divisions involve. It cannot be denied that the history of socialist movements in the past century or so has demonstrated the real costs of those divisions, reducing as they have the chance of success of either reformists or revolutionaries and contributing, in addition, to a widespread belief in the lack of credibility of any socialist project, however conceived.

That socialists and their potential sympathizers should react with regret, even outrage, to this situation is both understandable and desirable, to a degree. It points to the important fact that socialists do share a common point of departure. They are reacting to the experienced exploitations and oppressions generated by capitalism in ways which seek to both resist and transcend that system. Yet, even our cursory survey of the rival reformist and revolutionary perspectives has indicated how fundamental is the gulf that lies between them. What is involved is not only choices about strategies to achieve socialism and divisions over whether or not they are likely to succeed. It extends to divisions about the detrimental consequences of pursuing those strategies, whether or not the outcome is regarded as a success or a failure. To revolutionaries, the reformist strategy, whether or not it is evaluated by its adherents as having succeeded, results not in socialism but in a buttressing of capitalism. Reformists, similarly, regard the revolutionary road as one that leads almost inevitably to totalitarianism. Thus, each regards the other as a major threat to the project for socialism, and because this is so, socialists must accept, for the foreseeable future at least, both the fact of division and the costs that flow from it for the socialist project. This should not preclude comradely dialogue and united action where possible, as we shall argue at greater length later, but that dialogue is unlikely quickly to produce unity, since a

truly united Left can only result from an agreement on fundamental perspectives – of reform or revolution – that has not
materialized anywhere yet in the twentieth century socialist
movements. Attempts to evade the choice, or to pretend that the
two opposites can be combined in some new synthesis which is
neither reformist nor revolutionary, simply misunderstand the
nature of the issues at stake.

Sources of capitalist stability

To stress the fundamental character of the choice involved
between reformist and revolutionary perspectives is not, of
course, to argue that historically these alternatives have always
been expressed in separate and rival organizations. On the contrary, that is itself one of the historical outcomes of the collision
of the rival perspectives with each other and with a world
capitalist system which has itself proved remarkably resilient to
such socialist challenges.

Prior to 1914, the majority of revolutionary and reformist
socialists could just about survive together within the umbrella
provided by the Second International, at least partly because they
shared a common conviction that the superiority of their
respective strategies would be fairly rapidly demonstrated by
historical developments. If the test of theory was practice, then
the expectation of socialists of both camps was that the development of capitalism itself – either in the direction of emergent
consensus or revolutionary crisis – would progressively vindi-
cate one strategy and consign the other to the dustbin of history.
Marxists, for example, saw capitalism as a system that was inherently incapable of avoiding deeper and deeper crisis, and one
which lacked any political or ideological mechanisms able to
sustain anti-socialist explanations of increasing immiserisation
and market anarchy. Certainly, it was congenitally incapable of
frustrating the supposedly natural propensity for working class
political action to take an increasingly socialist form. Whatever
their differences over the dialectics of class and party, of consciousness and leadership, the Marxist section of the Second
International felt that history was rapidly moving their way
rather than in the direction of the reformists. They possessed an
enormous optimism that capitalism would create in its labour

force a sense of their common interests as proletarians, and would radicalize those interests through the experienced exploitation, alienation, instability and injustice it generated for the working class. Moreover, precisely because capitalism was unable to accommodate those radicalized interests within its own structure, it would compel the proletariat onto a revolutionary transformation of capitalism itself. Until 1914 at least, the optimism of 1848 was largely intact as the system appeared to be demonstrating that 'what the bourgeoisie . . . produces above all is its own gravediggers . . . Its fall and the victory of the proletariat are equally inevitable' (*The Communist Manifesto*).

World War I shattered both this optimism and the organizational unity of reformists and revolutionaries. Henceforth, in virtually every country of advanced industrial capitalism, those seeking for a socialist alternative to capitalism would find themselves faced with choosing between increasingly bitter rival claimants to the exclusive inheritance. The central historical fact of the twentieth century is that for most of the time and in most of the advanced capitalist nations, a majority have supported the parties and/or politics of reformism rather than those of revolutionary socialism.

If 1914 was 'the moment of truth' in the choice between reform and revolution, then this outcome would appear both puzzling and perverse. If nothing else, the carnage begun in that year was so demonstrable of the fundamental irrationality and barbarism of the world capitalist system that it should have banished forever the illusions of any abstract humanism and rationalism transcending the divisiveness of class. That it failed to produce this result is one indicator of the fact that 1914 was itself only a crystallization of trends within capitalism which led away from, rather than towards, any easy achievement of a socialist revolution. No longer could the simple fact that the system created the material base for a socialist society and a social force capable of bringing that society into existence be held to guarantee that the transition would in fact happen, or that if it did, that it would be an easily achieved and unproblematic process of social reconstruction. In place of the optimism of the pre-war days, Marxists in particular were driven to confront, both in theory and in practice, a capitalism whose structure and modes of operation were proving far more complex and more recalcitrant to challenge by revolutionary socialists than had been anticipated. Still worse, it created an environment in which the appeals of reformist socialism were to prove far more powerful than their own for the working class support that was required to translate that revolutionary challenge into victory.

At one level, the class structure of capitalism was to demonstrate only a very approximate fit to the bi-polar picture of bourgeoisie and proletariat that Marx had appeared to suggest. Both in terms of its structure and its processes of conflict it seemed unlikely to bring an homogeneous proletariat to the position of an unassailable majority as early Marxists had anticipated. To begin with, the divisions within the manual working class created by capitalism – by skill, trade, industry and occupation – were to prove deep-rooted and long-lasting. The processes of instability, crisis and technological change which Marxists had expected would erode the significance of such divisions for class consciousness, in fact, often worked in the opposite direction, producing sectionalist responses not simply within the wider class but against other sections of the class. Furthermore, the manual working class was increasingly only a part, albeit a substantial part, of a larger working class defined in terms of its relationship to the means of production and the material necessity to sell one's labour power. The concentration and centralization of capital and the expanding role of the state created a non-manual 'salariat' which, for a variety of reasons, failed to identify itself and its aspirations with the classic proletariat. On the contrary, it has buttressed the capitalist system in ways reminiscent of the older petty bourgeoisie in the nineteenth century. Again, beyond the working class, however defined, there remain even today in many industrial capitalist countries social strata (especially in the countryside) whose origins predate capitalism and yet whose consolidation into the capitalist system leaves them ambivalently located in the divide between capital and labour.

This very complexity of the structure of exploitation within capitalism posed different problems for reformists and revolutionaries. The former, with their emphasis on a community consensus transcending sectional class interests, found it much easier to adapt their attempts to win majority support to this situation, particularly since the very logic of their essentially electoralist politics already pointed in this direction. Marxists, by contrast, have found that the tensions between their commitment to socialism as the programme for the self-liberation of the working class, and the need to build an 'historic bloc' (to use

251

Gramsci's phrase) which unites behind that programme strata who are not, or who do not currently see themselves, as part of the working class, has continually threatened to drive them in one of two opposed directions. It has driven them either towards the isolation of purely defensive 'workerism', or towards a reformist practice cloaked in Marxist (often Gramscian) rhetoric. (Critics of Eurocommunism often discern the latter trend just as opponents of the Trotskyist Left have discerned the former. Whatever the justice of such accusations, they point to the very real problems posed by the class structure of capitalism for the revolutionary socialist tradition.)

The complexity of the class structure and, more crucially, its political consequences, are closely inter-related with another feature of the capitalist system that Marxists in particular were prone to underestimate: namely its ability, at least temporarily, to resolve its internal contradictions by innovations at the material, ideological and political levels. At a material level, capitalism has proved able, at critical moments in its historical development, to produce circumstances particularly cogenial to the fostering of reformist rather than revolutionary politics. In the latter part of the nineteenth century, in a period which proved crucial for shaping the labour and socialist movements of almost all the industrial capitalist countries today, the distinctive position of the skilled workers and their craft unions provided a crucial basis within the working class for rooting the perspectives and practical politics of reformism deep in those movements. (This proposition seems historically incontrovertible, whether or not one accepts Lenin's linkage of the process with imperialism as such.) Or to look at more recent experience, the prolonged, indeed unprecedented, period of economic growth of industrial capitalism in the quarter of a century after 1948 has had a crucial impact in undermining the readiness of workers to look for, and parties of the Left to offer, revolutionary strategies and perspectives. These decades of apparent deradicalization of both class and parties have clearly been of crucial importance for shaping the choices seen as open today on the Left, as we shall see later.

The material processes of capitalism debilitated and undermined the revolutionary implications which Marxists discerned in the class struggle in several other ways. In creating its own distinctive division of labour and imposing it at all levels from the home to the world system, capitalism has created new divisions or tapped into and transformed older ones – of race, of sex, of nationality. Though the overarching logic of these divisions, and the oppressions generated around them, are seen by socialists as being rooted in the capitalist system, they do not map easily or directly onto the divisions generated by class. The result has been two-fold: (i) further sources of division within the working class, as racism or sexism or nationalism sets one worker against another; (ii) struggles against oppression which, because their source of solidarity is not directly tied to class, often stand separate from and distrustful of, or indeed hostile to, socialist and working class politics and perspectives. Once again, Marxists, in seeking to demonstrate that only a socialist strategy offers a framework for generating a successful challenge to the global system, which is the source of all these oppressions, find themselves faced with real tensions: How to widen their understanding of the socialist project to encompass the trans-cendence of the complex patterns of oppressions generated by capitalism? How to assert the hegemony of socialism and the primacy of class struggle without denying the reality of the oppressions of race, sex and nationality, or the importance of the challenges to capitalism that struggles against them pose? Or, alternatively, How to participate in often autonomous struggles without ending up dissolving the socialist core – both perspec-tive and organization – into the fragments? The fact that most Marxists see such a core as the only instrument which can combine the power of these disparate struggles within an 'historic bloc' does not make the problems of actually bringing it about any easier. Indeed, the assertion is itself a source of dis-trust for many who are involved in the specific conflicts yet do not share a socialist perspective on them. Faced with such real problems, it is hardly surprising that a reformist *tactic* of isolated struggles for specific and sectional gains can very easily drift over into a reformist *strategy* and perspective. Such a path has the additional advantage of not exposing the reality of class tensions within each movement to serious critique. Once again, the very structure of the problems seems to predispose a majority to search for reformist rather than revolutionary socialist solutions: and once again this has been the historic experience of twentieth century capitalism.

This cursory consideration of the complexities of the material experience of capitalism has already implicated the ideological and political innovations mentioned earlier. Marx and the early

Marxists saw the source of legitimation of capitalism as anchored in a liberal ideology whose assertions of the 'dull compulsions of economic necessity' would be rapidly and progressively exposed by the class struggle itself, both in its successes and in its failures, by demonstrating the contingent and capitalist logic of such 'necessities'. Historical experience has proved the power of such 'necessities' to hold working class consciousness in thrall to capitalist 'realities', the more so when the very failures of the reformist movements which have enjoyed the majority support of the class seem simply to confirm them. But the ideological legitimations of capitalism have historically gone far further than predisposing the working class to reformist perspectives whose very failures serve to confirm the capitalist system. It has sought to implant themes of social hierarchy, of strident nationalism and racism, of sexism and religious bigotry into proletarian culture, both to compete with and to contaminate the rising tide of socialist consciousness. The ability of capitalism not only to blunt the appeal of socialism for the working class but under certain circumstances to actively mobilize sections of that class against socialism – for war in 1914, for Nazism in 1933, etc. – is testimony to the scale of the challenge which has faced revolutionary socialists in their struggle to bring about a decisive break with bourgeois ideology in all its manifestations in the consciousness of the working class.

In a similar manner, the development of state forms and political programmes in the countries of industrial capitalism have, in a variety of ways, served both to weaken the revolutionary impulse and strengthen the alignment of the working class to reformism. The very struggles of socialists and the working class, in the nineteenth and early twentieth centuries, to achieve representative and democratic institutions against the resistance of older autocratic and oligarchic forms of the early capitalist state, understandably resulted in a very strong working class attachment to those democratic forms which both fed into and was reinforced by the politics of reformism. The successes achieved in opening up the political arena to participation by mass working class based parties, and their ability to win incremental reforms which brought real if limited benefits for the lives of workers, reinforced still further the bond between the working class and reformist parties. Indeed, they reinforced it to a point where the linkage came to be seen as an inevitable and structural feature of capitalism rather than as an historically contingent nexus which could, under appropriate circumstances, be replaced by a fusion between the class and revolutionary politics. Further, on those rare occasions on which revolutionaries did threaten to expand their influence among sections of the working class in that direction, the coercive and often extra-legal power of the state could be deployed against such 'extremists' in the name of those democratic principles which reformism saw itself as embodying. Far from exposing the class repression intrinsic to capitalist state power, it simply served to reconfirm both the prudence and desirability of taking the parliamentary road to socialism. *In extremis*, of course, that state power could be deployed to destroy not only the revolutionaries but also the reformists and their democratic institutions, as in Italy in the 1920s, Germany and Spain in the 1930s, Greece in the 1960s, Chile and Turkey in the 1970s. But for reformists these always remain 'special cases' to the general rule that capitalism and democracy have a natural affinity. Certainly such 'exceptions' have not so far proved crippling to the plausibility of their conception of the instruments for achieving socialism.

Moreover, the very uneven development of capitalism as a world system – only partially perceived as its central global feature before 1905 – meant that, in the battle for political support, revolutionary socialism itself was weakened by the way in which metropolitan capitalisms were able to push out their own contradictions to the system's periphery (with consequently soothing effects on class tensions in the advanced capitalist centres) and by the way in which the resulting revolutions in the periphery (especially in Russia in 1917, but to a lesser extent too in China in 1949 and Cuba ten years later) then further confused both the image and the development of the revolutionary socialist current. These revolutions and their subsequent development confused the necessarily internationalist character of the struggle for socialism, of course, by leaving revolutionary socialists in the West open to the accusation that they merely served 'foreign' powers and peddled 'foreign' wares. They also complicated the history of socialism in the West because, in their isolation in conservative labour movements, revolutionary socialists so often did turn themselves into loyal subordinates of a Russian state, itself degenerating in its global isolation, and in the process created amongst large sections of the Western European proletariats an equation of revolutionary socialism with

Stalinist totalitarianism that eroded still further its limited popular appeal.

The legacy of reformism

If, from the start, socialist perspectives have presented divided and opposed agendas for the task of challenging capitalism, if in its evolution, capitalism has proved remarkably successful in attenuating, containing, adapting to or suppressing the challenges offered to it, what lessons and conclusions can socialists today derive from the actual practice of the various socialist parties and organizations that have sought to implement their agendas in the face of that capitalist response?

If we start by looking at the legacy of the reformist tradition, this according of priority is a direct reflection of the fact that it is this tradition which has managed to secure a majority of proletarian support at most times and in most countries of industrial capitalism in the twentieth century. Our previous analysis may have strongly suggested that this result has less to do with any demonstrable superiority of the analysis and strategies of reformism that with the ways in which the structure and modes of operation of the capitalist system has shaped and predisposed proletarian consciousness in this direction. For whatever reason, however, reformist parties have come closest to securing the kind of mass support which would enable their project for taking the evolutionary and parliamentary road to socialism to be put to the test, particularly in the decades of 'the long boom' of the post-war years. What lessons does their experience hold for us?

The first and most obvious thing to be said is that, while reformist parties have at times achieved substantial advances – in terms of welfarism, trade union rights, nationalization of private industry, etc. – nowhere have they come close to establishing a society which would meet even their own criteria of what socialism should be like. This simple fact already begins to point towards the central dilemma and core tension of the politics of reformist socialism, that the strategy of reforms appears to require and presuppose the healthiness of the capitalist system that those reforms are intended to transmute, if not subvert. Without exception – from the German Social Democrats in the Weimar Republic, through the Popular Front Government of the French Third Republic and the experience of seventeen years of office for the post-war British Labour Party – the picture is a consistent one. Even under the most favourable circumstances, in conditions of capitalist economic expansion, reformist socialists have found themselves obliged to devote at least as much attention to ensuring the maintenance of the conditions facilitating expansion as to carrying through the reformist measures which that expension sustains. In such circumstances, the tensions between the reformist strands of technocratic rationality and moralistic outrage at capitalist injustice could just be held in precarious balance. However, it has been the invariable fate of reformist parties to come to power not in such easy circumstances, but, instead, amongst those instabilities and crises of capitalism that Marxists have always predicted. Then reformists have discovered that there is no permanent rolling back of the frontiers of capitalism – no reforms, however well entrenched, that cannot be undone. Faced with such conditions, the tensions always present within reformism seem inexorably to resolve themselves in two opposing directions.

For left-wing sections of each party – as we shall argue in detail in a moment – the experience of such tensions is invariably radicalizing. But for the bulk of the leaderships of such parties, it is not. They characteristically discover that both the logic of their electoralist strategy and the logic of their perspectives on capitalism itself – their embodiment of the 'community interest' and their view of working class interests as sectionalist – lead them to policies which not only do not protect working class living standards and industrial strength but actually erode them in the interests of restoring capitalism to health. Such crises push the leaders of parties of reformist socialism into the position of open and explicit policemen of working class discontent in the direct service of capital.

Before we consider the alternative and more radical response to crisis within reformist parties, it is necessary to explore somewhat further the nature of the connection between such parties and the working class. Given that the central thrust of reformism is substitutionist – parliamentary parties legislate socialism into existence on behalf of their supporters – the primary nexus between the working class and the party is an electoral one, supplemented at times by organizational links with trade unions. Even here, the connections are ambivalent: the party appeals both to the working class and beyond it to 'the people'. Yet, while the appeal to the former is essential if the party wishes for an overall majority, it may well undermine its attractions to the latter – predominantly the middle class, in practical terms. The usual technique for closing the circle is to argue that the party's electoral and organizational ties with the proletariat enable it to 'deliver', discipline and control that class and, more particularly, its industrial power. In this sense 'social contracts' are the essence of the class–party relationship in the reformist current, and depend upon the institutions of the extra-parliamentary labour movement curbing and controlling direct manifestations of class struggle in return for some parliamentary-won reforms. Further underlining this 'division of labour' is the insistence, central to the reformist perspective, that direct class action or industrial strength must not be used for political ends.

The actual content of this relationship between the reformist party and its working class base varies, depending upon the larger rhythms of capitalism itself. Periods of economic growth of the post-war kind, where there is an expansion of working class living standards through industrial action, tend both to marginalize the significance of the electoral connection for at least the more industrially militant workers and may produce a fairly narrowly instrumental attitude on their part to the value or otherwise of concrete reforms. In such a context 'socialism' as a conception of a completely new social order is progressively drained of concrete content and becomes nothing more than a synonym for what the party leadership does. This in turn reinforces the technocratic tendency within the party itself to glide towards the posture of a party of social reform, regardless of whether or not this receives official ideological recognition. (The limited significance of the difference made by the defeat of the Clause IV revision by Gaitskell in the British Labour Party and the simultaneous victory of the Bad Godesburg programme in the German SPD is instructive in this respect.) In times of crisis and instability, on the other hand, the relationship between the reformist party and its class base becomes more indeterminate and unpredictable. As militant sections of the working class struggle to prevent an erosion of their industrial power and living standards, they may well find, as in Britain in the 1970s, that they confront a reformist party in power intent on enforcing that process of erosion. The resulting reaction of workers, in terms both of narrower organizational loyalties and wider political perspectives, is not directly given by this, and can move in many directions: apolitical cynicism and privatization for some, a shift to the populist Right for others, a shift to the Left for others still. But it is also the case that, under pressures of defeat on the industrial front, and facing an onslaught from a rampant party of capital in power, as with Thatcherism in Britain from 1979, at least some sections of the working class will look to the mass party of the Left to provide a radical, even socialist alternative. It is in this context that we can approach the second trend within reformist parties in a period of crisis, that of Left reformism.

It is probably fair to assert that, by the late 1950s, virtually every major reformist, i.e. social democratic, party had become in effect a party of social reform, both in its practice and in the openly expressed perspectives of its leadership. This was certainly the case with the British Labour Party. The term 'socialism', if used at all by the leaders of such a party, remained simply a rhetorical device devoid of any real content. Indeed, in so far as such parties had any socialist content at all, it resided in sections of their activist base who believed that the party either was at heart socialist or could be won for socialism if the existing leadership could be displaced. The sources of the political ideas of socialism amongst this vestigial Left were heterogeneous – a majority perhaps motivated by moral outrage at capitalist injustice, some committed to older theories of ethical socialism or revisionism, some influenced in differing degrees by variants of Marxism – and the real tensions between these rival views made effective and co-ordinated action within the party difficult. But the real sources of their weakness lay elsewhere and were two-fold: inside the party they faced a highly elitist and bureaucratized control apparatus which the party leadership could manipulate to ensure its continued ascendency; and more fundamentally, the challenge of the reformist Left to such leaderships proved feeble, precisely because they had no significant anchorage in the working class outside the party. They spoke for no-one but themselves.

Facing renewed crisis and instability, and the palpably anti-working class policies of existing leaderships, Left reformists of late have sought to resolve the tensions of their political loyalties and theoretical perspectives by seeking to win the support of those workers looking to the Left, to displace the existing technocratic-capitalist leaderships, and to present a far more radical and socialist programme to the country. In the process, Left reformist critiques of existing party practices have increasingly extended beyond issues of leadership and organization to encompass the 'evolutionary road' as such, and to reappraise the relationship between parliamentary action and class action. In this sense, recent developments on the Left of reformist parties have begun to approach a theoretical confrontation with the problems posed from the start by Marxist critics of reformism – those of the nature of capitalist resistance to socialist regimes and the class character of state power. Where such Left reformist rethinking still halts, however, and what keeps it within the reformist camp, is its continued commitment to the centrality of constitutional and parliamentary action in the transition to socialism.

Before we try to grapple with the viability of this strategy for Britain today, it is perhaps worth emphasizing that it is a conjunction that has occurred on several occasions and in various locations before in the history of capitalism. The history of the 'centrist trends' in post-1917 Western Europe typified by the politics of the USPD in Germany, and the majority socialists in France and Italy, of the experience of the Allende regime in Chile in 1973, or even the experience of Mitterandism in France today – all provide evidence relevant for answering the key questions confronted by the Left reformist strategy. Can they replace or displace existing anti-socialist leaderships within the mass parties of the Left? Can they take power and use the existing or modified state structure to implement the socialist programme? Can they overcome the resistances generated by capitalism to this process? As a vital prerequisite for all these steps, can they win the active support of the working class for the struggle for socialism? But before we can begin to suggest some possible answers to these questions, we need first to examine the legacy of the practice of the other major tradition of socialism, that associated with the revolutionary rather than the reformist road.

The failure of the revolutionary alternative

If the experience of the parties of reform has been that they have managed to secure the majority support of the working class at most times and in most places in the countries of industrial capitalism, then that of the revolutionary tradition is necessarily its obverse. The starting point for revolutionary socialists has been their experience as an often tiny minority locked in bitter battles within and with working class organizations – both parties and trade unions – which were either wedded to the politics of reformism by its promises and limited successes, or which had drawn lessons from the very weaknesses of that tradition that no total transformation of the capitalist order was either desirable or possible. On those rare occasions on which revolutionaries began – or even threatened to begin – to win important sections of the working class towards a revolutionary perspective, the very nature of the challenge that was posed frequently ended in suppression and defeat at the hands of a repressive state apparatus.

Yet against this has to be set the one core achievement of the revolutionary socialist tradition in our century, the fact that it gave leadership to the successful Russian Revolution of 1917. From then on, for better or worse, the revolutionary tradition in the nations of industrial capitalism has been largely identified with the communist parties of the Third International, and their fate has in turn been profoundly tied to the tragic unfolding of the contradictions buried at the heart of the Soviet system. Here we can only sketch the trajectory of Soviet degeneration: the progressive shift from proletarian democracy to authoritarian party control and substitutionism under Lenin; the escalating repression of dissent both in the working class and within the party to the point where even the limited protections afforded by 'socialist legality' were flaughted at the convenience of the party leadership; the culmination in the unbelievable barbarism of the Stalinist tyranny. To those who could not close their eyes to this process, the crisis of revolutionary socialism seemed to point in one or other of two opposed directions. Either the disease was endemic to the revolutionary strategy itself, encapsulated in the vanguardism and substitutionism of the Leninist party – in which case there was no hope for the tradition at all, and the future of socialism would have to depend on some radicalization of the reformist social democratic camp (or maybe on some 'libertarianism' that preserved its purity only by remaining ineffective). Or else, more credibly, the key to the problem lay in the isolation of the infant Soviet state within a hostile world capitalist order, where the imperative of mere survival first distorted, corrupted, and finally consumed and discredited the revolutionary socialist vision of proletarian democracy.

The problem of isolated national successes for socialism within a hostile world capitalist system, which the Soviet experience illustrated, poses horrendous problems for socialist strategy anywhere and its implications are still only partially acknowledged by socialists of any camp. For the moment, however, its more direct relevance here is to the negative fact that it asserts by implication. For, though the West has experienced many episodes of intense and violent class struggle, the moment of genuine revolutionary potential have been rare: in 1918–21 particularly in middle Europe; in 1944–46 in southern Europe, perhaps; in 1968–69 in France and Italy, maybe; and in Portugal in 1974. But for the most part, the working classes in the nations of the West have shown very little responsiveness to calls for insurrectionary action. The one exception in the inter-war years was in Spain in 1936, under the very different auspices of an anarcho-syndicalist leadership. In the post-war years the main instances have occurred in the Eastern bloc, most notably in Hungary in 1956, where the working class sought to overthrow precisely those 'socialist states' imposed by Soviet bayonettes at the close of the Second World War. Similar, if more muted, challenges to Soviet domination have punctuated the post-war history of Eastern Europe from East Berlin in 1953 to Poland in 1980.

In any case, by the 1930s at the latest, it would be very difficult to justify the appellation of either revolutionary socialism or insurrectionarism to the perspectives and leaderships of the Western communist parties. Strategy was by then entirely a matter of the foreign policy requirements of the Soviet Union, or of 'defending the socialist fatherland' if you prefer. From being the guide to revolutionary practice, Marxism had become no more than a secular theodicy, justifying the ways of Stalin to the working class. Bureaucratized parties allowed for only the narrowest kind of internal debate within the current orthodoxies, and dissent which even began to question them was met with anathema and expulsion. Behind the rhetoric of revolution, communist party political practice was in fact no more than a largely passive parliamentary oppositionism. Only on the industrial front, in their attempts to maintain a direct presence in the factories and the trade unions, did the communist parties reveal their historical roots; but even here, the actual character of party responses to industrial struggle and labour militancy was more demagogic and tactical than guided by revolutionary perspectives.

Under the circumstances, the ability of the communist parties to recruit, for a time at least, the majority of those who, in each new generation, were attracted towards the politics of revolutionary socialism, and also to acquire a substantial anchorage in the working classes of France and Italy, in particular, is a sad reflection on the times. Many factors contributed – the very flacidity of the social-democratic alternative; the continuing appeal of the carefully idealized Soviet fatherland; the commitment to antifascism (apart from 1939–41) and, after the war, to anti-US imperialism; and the very demagogery of its political rhetoric and industrial tactics (at least when it was not within reach of a share in parliamentary power, as in France and Italy in 1945–47). But the only contribution that this made to advancing the cause of revolutionary socialism was, in essence, negative. The very presence of sizeable communist parties offering themselves as the only revolutionary socialist alternative to reformist social democracy ensured a polarization of organizational commitments which for half a century after the Russian Revolution left no space for third alternatives, and certainly not revolutionary ones.

The contradictions between the appearance and reality of the communist parties could not endure for ever. Increasingly, in the post-war years, the character of the alternatives laying claim to the perspectives of revolutionary socialism began to develop new configurations. One strand, powerfully impressed by and attracted to the struggles against imperialism and for national liberation, redirected – usually vicariously – its aspirations for socialist revolutions away from the countries of industrial capitalism towards a variety of Third World socialisms – first China, then Cuba, for a while Algeria, then Vietnam, most recently Kampuchea. The politics of such groupings often proved very successful in recruiting a new generation, mainly of students, for revolutionary socialism. The obvious cost, from a Marxist perspective at least, was that it broke with the conception of socialism as the practice programme for the self-liberation of the working class upon the material base provided by capitalism, and substituted for it a view of socialism as a programme for mobilizing predominantly peasant populations for the tasks of industrialization and modernization. Whether this shift from proletarian class to proletarian nation is either conceptually or empirically justified is outside the frame of reference of our discussion. Its relevance for us is precisely the pessimistic and negative view it took of the prospects for socialism in industrial capitalism, since as such it offered no positive guidance to the struggle for socialism in Britain today.

Partially overlapping with this Third World socialist strand and partially distinct from it were a variety of different groups and parties who claimed some lineage with the Trotskyist opposition to Stalinism in the inter-war years. In essence, they represented an attempt to reassert the relevance of the revolutionary Marxist tradition to contemporary capitalism, and to disentangle it from its subsequent Stalinism contaminations. The sources of inspiration for post-war Trotskyism lay for the most part and in varying ways in Leninism and the Soviet Revolution of 1917. Indeed much of the source of division between the groups turned on the differing accounts they gave both of that 'Leninism' and of the causes and degrees of degeneration of the Soviet regime. Insignificant both in terms of numbers and influence before the 1960s, the Trotskyist groups have come in the past twenty years to acquire a following in a small but influential section of the working class in several industrial capitalist nations. We will, therefore, need to consider the relevance of their perspectives for Britain today at a later stage of our discussion.

For the moment, however, we need to consider the third, and in some ways the most spectacular, of the trends within the revolutionary socialist camp in the post-war years, the so-called 'de-Stalinization' of the Western communist parties and the emergence of Eurocommunism. The history of the process – Stalin's death, the Secret Speech, Hungary, the Sino–Soviet dispute, detente, the long boom, and the experience of isolation and marginalization of communist parties within their respective national contexts – is too complex to examine in detail here. The essence lies in the result: the attempt by the communist parties of the West to break out from both the 'political immobilism' of their practice in the Cold War years, to distance themselves from both Stalinism and, in different degrees, the Soviet regime, and to discover a viable socialist perspective and practice of their own. At different paces, and with varying degrees of conviction and opportunism, the main Western communist parties appear to be searching towards a strategy which pre-dates the Leninist insurrectionist conception and resembles if anything an updated version of the constitutional Marxism of the pre-1914 Second International. The paradox here is that Eurocommunism appears to be approaching from the Marxist revolutionary tradition a position which is very similar to that we discerned emerging from Left reformism. The unbridgeable gulf that we earlier established between the perspectives of reformist and revolutionary theory would seem to be in process of achieving an historical reconciliation among at least some sections of organizations whose roots lie on the different sides of that divide. As such we will be justified in treating them together in subsequent discussion.

But whether or not Eurocommunism and Left reformism are converging on a common position, it is abundantly clear that the cumulative impact of the two traditions from which they are emerging has left them with at least a common problem – namely a generalized antipathy in their potential constituencies to the idea of 'socialism' of whatever variety. This indeed must constitute the last and in many ways most telling legacy of the historical experience that we have surveyed for the likelihood of socialist advance in contemporary Britain – the general discrediting of the very idea of socialism by the experience of its pursuit over at least a century. As we move from our consideration of the history of socialist struggle to an examination of the contemporary situation on the Left in Britain, we will find not merely the reproduction within British capitalism of the sources of strength discussed earlier, and the reproduction within the dominant alternatives on the contemporary Left of the weaknesses of reformism and revolutionary politics that we have just discussed. We will also find that the terrain on which socialists now must operate has been made more difficult by the pattern of failure inherited from the past. For the legacy of social democracy and Stalinism on the consciousness of the mass of the Western working class has been little less than disasterous. The experience of the practice of the dominant reformist social democratic and Stalinist communist parties has progressively drained the very word 'socialism' of any vestiges of the visionary future society that earlier generations had found in it. For probably the vast majority of the working class today, 'socialism', if it has any determinate content at all, means either Soviet totalitarianism or the bureaucratized state ownership peddled by social-democracy in its time. Far from 'the inevitable victory of the idea of revolutionary socialism' predicted by the young Trotsky in 1904, the experience of twentieth century capitalism and of the socialist movements which claimed to challenge it has left the task facing socialists more onerous than ever: to find a strategy that can *re-establish the credibility* of the socialist idea both for themselves and in labour movements long immersed in the material and cultural deformations of capitalist 'realities', and all too conscious of the backruptcy of the earlier models of progress towards socialism. The task of socialists in seeking to win over the mass of the working class to socialism is now not only to argue for the credibility of their own strategy for achieving the goal, but simultaneously to argue for the credibility of the goal itself in the face of a legacy of cynicism, distrust and disbelief.

THE CONTEMPORARY SITUATION

Crisis and stability in British capitalism

Any socialist strategy for Britain must take its point of departure from the fact that the current world depression is not the sole or even primary cause of the crisis facing British capitalism today. Rather, that depression has served mainly to intensify and accentuate problems which are rooted in the structure and historical development of British capitalism – and, more particularly, industrial capital – over the past century. As chapter 2 made clear, the consequences of this long-term structural defect have been most evident in the post-war years when, even against the background of substantial and sustained growth in the world economy as a whole, an ailing and weakly competitive British capitalism found its share of the world market steadily diminishing. Thus, even before the current depression destroyed the ability of the world capitalist system to generate rising living standards and full employment in the advanced industrial capitalist nations as a whole, the long-term decline in competitiveness and profitability had already confronted the British ruling class and its various political agents with the urgent need to bring about a major restructuring of British capitalism. In a very real sense, the central issues on the agenda of British politics for the past quarter of a century have been about choices between rival strategies for accomplishing this programme of capitalist reconstruction and modernization. The current world depression has served mainly to underline the escalating political, economic and social costs for capital of failing to carry through such a programme to a successful conclusion.

Of course, the choice of a correct strategy for renovation and renewal depends to a large degree on a correct diagnosis of the sources of the problems afflicting British capitalism. One line of argument much favoured by the Left today – though its origins date back to the Wilsonian 'technological revolution' perspectives of the 1960s – has been that the roots of the problem lie in the very nature of the British ruling class itself. The particular weighting of finance capital within that class, the imperialist pretensions of its political representatives, and its recruitment from within a markedly restricted and inward-looking social milieu, have produced a formation which has proved singularly incompetent and ineffectual in coping with the problems of competing in a world economy increasingly dominated by ruthlessly efficient multinational corporations, where the criteria of success are profitability and productivity rather than social background and accent.

There is considerable truth in this line of argument, and indeed, if it constituted the whole truth, then there would be a certain amount of 'space' within British capitalism for the kind of 'modernizing' and 'reforming' programmes which have been the stock in trade of Labour leaderships from the time of Gaitskell and Wilson onwards, and which are, in suitably modified form, advanced by sections of the Labour Left today. However, the very experiences of the Labour Governments of the 1960s and 1970s – and indeed of the 'Tory reformist' phase of the Heath administration – have served to demonstrate how partial and limited such an analysis actually is, and how inadequate are the strategies for renovation which are built upon it. For, inextricably bound up with the weaknesses and inefficiencies of the British ruling class, both as a partial cause and as a major consequence of them, is the entrenched industrial strength of the organized working class itself. If the central issue confronting orthodox British politics – both Labour and Conservative – for the past quarter-century has been the need to create the conditions for sustained and profitable economic growth through a major restructuring of the manufacturing base of British capitalism, then the history of the period discloses that the central *blockage* to such a programme has been the organized labour movement. Its ability to resist cuts in real wages designed to restore profitability, its refusal to abandon the degree of defensive and negative control it enjoys over the work process, and its consequential ability to thwart managerial strategies for raising productivity and increasing the rate of exploitation in the interests of profit, have been the rocks upon which the 'modernizing' strategies of Labour and Tory governments alike have threatened to founder. Increasingly, the orthodox politics of the period have pivoted on the alternative strategies for overcoming the blockages to capitalist modernization constituted and maintained by the industrial practices of the organized labour movement.

In reality, the choices presented by the rival parties – and by rival 'Left' and 'Right', 'wet' and 'dry', factions within each party – have been about the ways in which three approaches are to be combined into alternative packages for 'dealing with the unions'. First, state legal coercion – from wage freezes and incomes policies to legal constraints on trade union bargaining. Second, market power – particularly relying on the bite of unemployment to undermine labour militancy. Lastly, ideological incorporation – the various attempts to foster a 'community of interest' between management and labour (whether expressed in the language of Labour's 'social contract' or Thatcherite 'new realism') which would facilitate the restoration of control by the former over the latter. Against the relatively less severe economic circumstances of the 1960s and early 1970s, successive Labour and Conservative governments struggled to evolve corporatist strategies in which the ideological incorporation of the trade union leadership, backed up by a strengthening of the state's reserve coercive power against rank and file militancy, would be sufficient to bring about some significant shift in the balance of market power from labour to capital. In each case, the defeat by organized labour of some crucial element in the strategy – the opposition to *In Place of Strife* under Wilson, the miners strike and three-day week for Heath, the 'winter of discontent' for Callaghan – served to precipitate the termination and subsequent electoral defeat of the governments concerned. In each case, organized labour posed no positive alternative programme to the corporatist strategies that confronted it. (Indeed, particularly at the level of the trade union leaderships, the complex processes of 'consultation' inherent in the corporatist approach were particularly attractive for their self-images, career prospects and degrees of influence and patronage.) What it did do was deny to British industrial and manufacturing capital the conditions necessary for the restoration of managerial control within industry upon which the ability to compete successfully in the capitalist world economy crucially depended.

The changed economic environment of the late 1970s and

1980s has, however, served to transform the problem from that of an ailing British capitalism facing relative decline within expanding world markets, into the stark threat of absolute decline and peripheralization within a continuing world depression. In such a changed context, both the pressure for a shift in the current distribution of industrial power between labour and capital, and the degree of the shift now required to restore competitiveness to British capital, have escalated. One index of this escalation is the move away from corporatist strategies towards an increasingly brutal reliance on the market force of mass unemployment, backed up by state coercion and ideological assaults upon trade unionism and the welfare state, as the favoured programme for achieving these interlinked objectives. In this context it is instructuve to observe that, while it has reached its apotheosis under Thatcher, this strategy was already in process of emergence in the later years of the Callaghan Government. Its roots lie, not in some theoretical aberration called 'monetarism', but in the escalating crisis facing British capitalism and its ruling class, as the need to defeat organized labour grows ever more urgent. In that crisis no 'space' exists for any 'renovation' of capitalism which does not attack the powers of organized labour.

At first sight, this combination of the continuing crisis of British capitalism with a heightening pattern of class conflict – for that is what we have been describing – might seem to constitute peculiarly fertile and propitious circumstances in which to make political advances for socialism. Yet, such easy optimism overlooks both the general problem of class consciousness – the historical discrediting of 'socialism' discussed earlier – and the very particular way in which the pattern of industrial struggle in post-war Britain has served to accentuate that decline in the perceived relevance of any 'socialist alternative' to capitalism.

The experience of steadily rising living standards through the 1950s and 1960s did not predispose leading sections of the British working class to political radicalism, and certainly not of a socialist kind. A whole post-war generation of workers emerged prior to 1973, particularly in engineering and shipbuilding, chemicals and motor vehicles, who were able to win significant degrees of control over their own work processes and advance their standards of living by industrial action at local level, and who in the process lost any direct concern even with the bulk of national trade union activity, let alone with political change of a socialist kind. The survival of older political loyalties ensured the return of Labour government in 1964 and 1974, but the performance of those administrations, culminating as each did in cut-backs in welfare provision, rising unemployment and confrontations with key groups of workers – including its traditional supporters such as the miners – over pay, only weakened still further these workers' already slender electoral allegiance to Labour, and left them increasingly vulnerable to the anti-socialist appeal of Thatcherite populism.

Nor could the Left in the traditional labour movement look with any confidence to the Labour Party's own institutions and practices to act as effective cultural counter-weights to this right-wing upsurge. On the contrary, the increasing reliance by the party leadership on a narrowly 'electoralist' connection between the party and its traditional class base coincided with a still further dimunition in the means of communication and propaganda required to consolidate that connection. This period saw the effective demise of any kind of labour press, and the triumph of a narrow oligarchy of conglomerate media companies controlling newspapers and commercial television. Two key consequences followed. On the one hand, the domain of public debate and public opinion became even more exclusively pre-occupied with attitudes, prejudices and perspectives which were either explicitly and crudely Conservative, or which served to provide a covert constituency and pulpit for a critique of socialism from perspectives dominant on the extreme Right of the Labour Party. On the other hand, the public space available for political concerns was further narrowed and constricted, as the transformation of large sections of the press from purveyors of 'news' into components of a mass entertainment industry accentuated the trends towards depoliticization and privatization among large sections of the working class. In such a climate, socialists within the Labour Party possessed neither a means of communication nor an audience for their uncertain attempts to assert some public distance between socialism as they conceived it and the policies – and policy retreats – practiced by Labour governments. Nor did any benefits flow to socialists outside the Labour Party who found the growing antipathy to labourism amongst sections of workers to be productive more often of cynicism, apathy and conservatism than of any active search by significant elements of the class for a genuinely socialist alternative. It is true that an activist strata remained within the trade unions, still anchored to a labourist (or, to a lesser degree, communist) politics, and capable of mobilizing large numbers of workers in public demonstrations on occasions, against 'industrial relations reforms' in 1971 or unemployment a decade later. But they too were unable to prevent either the waning of industrial militancy as the depression deepened, or the increasing shift of working class electoral support to the new party of the Centre or to the old party of the Right.

On a more optimistic note, socialists might hope to be able to mobilize the growing ranks of the white collar 'salariat' produced by the growth of state bureaucracies and private financial institutions in late capitalism. Indeed, their impact here was greater than elsewhere. A new generation of college-trained non-manual workers emerged in the 1960s, open to a significant degree to radicalism. From their ranks came many of the peace campaigners of CND, both in the late 1950s and the 1980s, and the bulk of the new activists who flowed into the previously moribund constituency structures of the Labour Party after 1970. Yet the bulk of the white collar salariat remained firmly wedded to traditional conservative values and institutions. They were unionized now to a degree never known before, but were still largely virgin territory for socialist agitation. Socialists do now have a radical constituency open to them amongst sections of this new salariat and amongst the activists in the unions of manual workers. But we still have to find a strategy and a programme that is capable of extending that active socialist support into the broad masses of a well-unionized but politically conservative labour force.

As socialists attempt to find that strategy and programme, the terrain on which we struggle is largely outside our control. The crisis of capitalism, and the rising tide of unemployment and poverty, creates the material base for the revival of a mass socialist party in Britain. Because there is no capitalist solution to that crisis that does not involve the intensification of work routines, the persistence of unemployment, and the erosion of welfare provision, governments pursuing capitalist strategies will have to work hard to legitimate their activities in ways which prevent that socialist upsurge. Yet the ideological material available for that purpose is enormous. Ruling class strategies are clearly going to continue to be either of a corporatist or an authoritarian/populist kind. The Centre and Centre-Left of British politics (including Labour governments in office) will

Socialist strategies

no doubt canvass a corporatist strategy that calls for common sacrifice behind a neutral state in the pursuit of national economic regeneration. That appeal to national solidarity and class collabortion will tap deep roots of popular sentiment in a labour force which lives with the daily reality of a world capitalist order that does indeed continue to mediate its contradictions through separate national structures. Authoritarian populism of the Thatcherite kind has its constituency too, in a petty-bourgeoisie and a salariat burdened by high taxation and conscious of dwindling differentials between them and unionized manual workers, and even with strategic groups within the manual working class who are open to a view of the state's budget as equivalent to a family's (in need of balancing), hit by inflation and desperate about jobs. The potential division of interests between manual workers in private industry and 'unproductive' white collar staff in public bureaucracies is all too potent a source of working class support for a Toryism of low taxation and restricted social services. In the face of such a range of ruling class initiatives, the task confronting socialists is immense.

Contemporary alternatives on the Left

Given the magnitude of the task in hand, how are the three alternative socialist approaches currently on offer in Britain today – a revivified parliamentary socialism, single-issue campaigning in the fragments, and attempts to build an independent revolutionary socialist party and politics – able to measure up to the tasks involved? Let us briefly review each of these strategies in turn in an attempt to discern both their strengths and limitations.

1. *Parliamentary socialism.* This is obviously still the dominant indigeneous tradition in contemporary Britain and its very dominance ensures that both its virtues and defects stand out with considerable clarity. The parliamentary route to socialism has clear strengths and attractions. It involves no break with what is undoubtedly still the dominant political orientation of the bulk of the British working class – that politics is about parliament, and that legitimate political action has to fall within its constitutional conventions. The main party of that tradition, the Labour Party, still possesses some strong institutional connections with the class, particularly links with the trade unions and with the class as voters. Yet, despite this, the problems of the

parliamentary route to socialism are, and remain, enormous. The whole tradition is characterized by a failure to confront the real limits to state power and parliamentary politics, long recognized by more Marxist socialists (who point to such things as the absence of actual parliamentary control over bourgeois state institutions, the material and ideological constraints of the wider capitalist system, the deep implantation of bourgeois modes of thought and practice that parliamentarianism consolidates, and so on). Nor has the Labour Party or the bulk of even its left-wing faced up to the problems of implementing socialist strategies without the prior mobilization of the working class which the party's parliamentarianism precludes (in the case of the Right and Centre of the party) or militates against (in the case of the party's Left). Moreover, the historic tendency of the Labour Left to move right-wards when in power (not least because of their failure to confront adequately the role of working class strength in precipitating capitalist crisis) means that the parliamentary route to socialism in Britain has invariably *hiccuped* in a confrontation between a Labour government and its trade union base, with a consequent discrediting both of Labour politics and of the idea of socialism amongst large numbers of workers.

Despite these undoubted weaknesses and limitations – ones, moreover, which have been recognized and pointed to by the Marxist Left in Britain for many years – we find today that significant sections of that self-same Marxist Left are being drawn back into the Labour Party. Given the scale of the current crisis and the costs of failing to pose some credible and immediately plausible alternative to Thatcherite Conservatism, many socialists have found themselves impelled into a Labour Party whose left-wing presents itself not simply as such an alternative, but also claims to possess a strategy for overcoming the defects hitherto discerned by Marxists in the parliamentary road. For the Left within the Labour Party has lately put together a programme (the Alternative Economic Strategy) whose coherence and content appears to enable it to offer an effective way of linking immediate concerns with the longer term project of socialist transformation; and its current preoccupation with party democratization constitutes a real attempt to prevent leadership betrayal of the conventional reformist kind.

The renewed attraction of the Labour Party now to many on the Left necessarily raises again the question of 'entryism'. As far as we can tell, no major organization on the revolutionary Left is currently proposing entryism of the classical kind, namely the quick 'in' and 'out' for the purposes of recruiting. Instead entryism now seems to be conceived by those who advocate it on the revolutionary Left as a long-term strategy that keeps the Labour Party itself as the main focus of activity throughout. Five arguments seem to underpin that position:

(1) That for better or worse, the Labour Party still manages to secure a far greater share of working class political loyalty than any other party on the Left.

(2) That the disillusionment with the record of Labour Government in the 1970s has radicalized the traditional Left within the party to the point at which it is winnable to a broadly Marxist perspective.

(3) That such a radicalized Left within the Labour Party will be ready, willing and able to sustain a successful challenge to the traditional right-wing parliamentary dominance, not least by transforming the institutional mechanisms within the party on which that dominance has hitherto rested.

(4) That such a successful challenge by the Left would enable the party to launch its programme – the Alternative Economic Strategy – which is capable of winning working class support and electoral victory as well as beginning the transition to socialism.

(5) That the struggle to successfully implement the AES will then provide a framework within which the electoral loyalties of the working class to a radical reformist Labourism can be transformed into a consciously socialist mass working class movement.

If these five assumptions were in fact valid, then the choice of strategy for socialists would now be clear and unambiguous. But the problem is that they are not. Rather, they seem to us fundamentally misconceived and misguided. The first three assumptions come together in the Labour Left's current preoccupation with internal party democracy, as though the dominance of the Right in the party is not simply manifested in institutional terms, but is in fact rooted there. Unfortunately, the dominance of the Right and Centre in the Labour Party is much more broadly based, in the inability of the Labour Left to speak for any mass socialist constituency. For that reason, the Labour Left are, and will continue to be, easily containable by their opponents within the party, subjected to the call for unity and moderation in the run up to general elections precisely because the Right are correct in their assertion that, in the present climate, stridency by the Labour Left and entryism by the revolutionary Left are electorally damaging. Since the Labour Party has built its electoral ties with its working class base on purely reformist terms – offering itself as an easy mechanism to economic prosperity and social reform – the Labour Left faces insurmountable problems in arguing for the transformation of that party–class relationship into one that requires more of workers than that they vote; and ironically, the very failure of Labour governments to deliver even those modest promises of prosperity and reform has weakened still further that already slender electoral tie between party and class, and has left the bulk of working class Labour voters sceptical of any kind of Labour promise, be it Left or Right. The insoluble dilemma for the Marxist Left inside the Labour Party is that the very thing that they see as the outcome of their strategy – namely the existence of a class-conscious working class mass movement geared to socialism – is in reality the precondition of their achieving any leverage there at all. Only with the prior consolidation of such a social force could the Labour Party be transformed; and in its absence, no amount of constituency activism within the Labour Party can begin to create it without short-term electoral dangers and inevitable party schism.

If attempts by the Left to transform parliamentary and reformist vehicles like the Labour Party appear to us to be doomed to frustration, failure and disillusionment, what other alternatives exist? Two possibilities currently present themselves.

2. Single-issue campaigning. One alternative, which for many of its practitioners has been bred precisely out of disillusionment and despair with all 'party socialisms', has been to operate as individuals or loosely co-ordinated groupings in a variety of movements and campaigns around issues which are not themselves directly or explicitly socialist but which mobilize sections of the population to action in protest against experienced oppressions and threats. This has taken the form both of campaigns on particular issues – most notably the bomb, but also housing, poverty and the like – or of broader agitations against the generalized oppression of particular social groupings, particularly women and blacks. The strength of both these responses has been their ability to mobilize large numbers of people whose experience of oppression does not map immediately and directly onto traditional class categories and concerns. There has, thus, been a resultant propensity to widen, enrich and rediscover the range of areas that a socialist transformation has got to encompass, and to reach constituencies not otherwise amenable to socialist politics.

In this sense, then, such activities can contribute much towards the construction of that Gramscian 'historic bloc' of which we spoke earlier. Yet that bloc is not going to be easy to put together. For the very breadth of these campaigns and movements is invariably predicated on a silence on the questions of class power and socialist transition. The uneven constituencies within them hang together only by concentrating on the immediate issue, to the exclusion of any agreement on the relationship which that issue has to the other patterns of oppression and instability against which the Left attempts to mobilize, so that when the question of socialism is raised within them, it is often rejected by many as parasitical and divisive. Yet in truth it ought not to be. What these movements have done is to assert to the Left that socialism has to have at its core the creation of a society free of sexism, racism and militarism as well as of class; and what the Left has to assert to the non-socialist elements of these movements is that their goals are incompatible with the maintenance of capitalism itself. There is no doubt that the actual relationship between the various facets of struggle is a complex one, open to varying interpretations, and that within any 'historic bloc' for socialism many socialists will want to create 'space' for autonomous organization and activity for those oppressed by race or gender. But that does not mean that these movements offer a route to an emancipated society on their own, devoid of any relationship to, and involvement in, the wider struggle for socialism. To hold that position, as many do, is to confuse oppression and agency under capitalism, to fall into the assumption that to be oppressed is necessarily to have the location and resources to be able to successfully challenge the source as distinct from the consequences and symptoms of that oppression.

For Marxists, who identify the working class as the core potential agency of revolutionary change in capitalism, this confusion can often block an otherwise fruitful exploration of the ways in which such campaigns can be combined with the class struggle in a process of mutual enrichment. For the working class is not an agency of change because it is the most oppressed section of society – it clearly is not. Nor is it simply an unthinking reflex to the fact of exploitation. Rather it is the system of exploitation itself which places the instrumentalities for overthrowing the capitalist system in the hands of the 'collective labourer' it has itself created. The class struggle is thus not one more conflict against capitalism to be set alongside other struggles. Though the validity of those other struggles is not in question, nor their potential contribution to building a socialist movement in doubt, socialists cannot evade their responsibility to argue against the tacit assumption that there can be fundamental reforms on these questions without achieving socialist transformation. The historic bloc requires, to be effective, if not a directing centre then a hegemonic core, and that core can only be constituted in, and through, the linkage established between socialist perspectives and the class struggle.

3.   *Revolutionary socialism.* What then of the revolutionary alternative in British politics? Its strengths arise in part precisely because of its critique of the parliamentary road, which gives it a sharper view of the tasks ahead. It gathers strength too from its anchorage at the point of production where the attack of the ruling class on working class industrial power is now at its heaviest and most obvious. The revolutionary tradition still draws its power from its refusal to accept the division between industry and politics central to labourism, and from its counter-assertion that socialism, far from being the product of a tiny parliamentary elite, will come only from the industrial and political struggles of an entire social class. But, of course, the perspective is weakened by the fragmentation inherent in work-place struggles at a time when the employers' offensive is increasingly centrally co-ordinated and state-directed. It has problems too, simply because of the sheer shift in loyalties and practices that it requires of the mass of workers, and because of the real ambiguities surrounding its notion of (and models for) the 'revolution'. These have a habit of slipping back into re-runs of 1917, with each different scenario on the events of that year and its aftermath producing a different revolutionary sect, whose very fragmentation and internal feuding help to discredit the whole strategy still further.

These objections have in the past persuaded many otherwise

sympathetic socialists that the project for an independent revolutionary socialist party will not work in Britain. Even if groupings like the Socialist Workers Party seem to have lifted themselves to a size and a pattern of politics that is removed from the worst excesses of Trotskyist sectarianism, and which appear to offer a distinct and plausible revolutionary alternative, the problem of 'credibility' still remains. Given the gap between the scale of the task on the one hand, and the resources available on the revolutionary Left in Britain today, how can the enterprise be taken seriously? After all, it was precisely the frustrations and disillusioning failures of such politics that has propelled many Marxists out of such groupings into the Labour Party. Yet the problem of 'credibility' is ultimately a false one for socialists, for it assumes that there is some more plausible and viable alternative available. Tragically, there is not.

The argument – that the Left should build now an independent socialist party – rests on the recognition that the Labour route is doomed, and that partly because of the character of labourism itself, what the Left faces in Britain is a long and arduous struggle against appalling odds. There is no short cut, no easy solution and, therefore, the choice of strategy now must turn on the longer view. It must recognize where we have reached, after over eighty years of labourism: a situation in which Labour governments have great difficulty in constituting even a vestigially defensive reformist agency for the working class, in which large sections of that class have been effectively depoliticized and in which, for the vast majority of workers, socialism no longer constitutes a viable and perceived alternative to the anarchy and brutality of capitalism. The consequence of the repeated experience of Labour in power has not been Lenin's 'hangman's rope' radicalizing workers away from reformism to a genuinely socialist alternative, but instead has left significant sections of even the working class vulnerable, as we have seen, to the appeals of Thatcherism. That four years of mass recession, cuts in public services and government attacks on working class organization and industrial power, has not radicalized the broad mass of workers to a reinvigorated socialism must stand as the most glaring indictment of the bankruptcy of reformism as it has been practiced by the British Labour Party this century.

As we have said, what we are seeing now is an attack on working class industrial organization and power across British industry – an attack on shop stewards and work groups orchestrated through recession and legal changes, and an attack which involves heavy costs to industrial capital too, through the depth of the recession it necessitates. Indeed, there are clear signs that the resistance of industrial capital to any further intensification of that recession is now growing and that we face, instead, and for the foreseeable future, a period of relative industrial stagnation and national political stalemate, which will again provide the context in which working class industrial power can begin, however tentatively, to be reconstituted. But whether the recession does deepen, or whether it eases, the first task of socialists is clear: to help to defend and extend working class power at the point of production, and to block any further erosion of the strength and confidence of work groups there. That task is dictated to us not because of any lingering faith on our part in the efficacy of any syndicalist solution to the problem of capitalism. On the contrary, the revolutionary Left is, and must remain, committed to the view that only a political challenge, through a mass based socialist party taking and transforming state power, will bring capitalism down. The primacy of industrial struggle now, however, arises from the recognition that such a political challenge is not within the capability of the Left in the immediate future, and will not become so unless and until we see the rise again of a self-confident and assertive movement of workers engaged in industrial struggle. Precisely because industrial struggles can rebuild the confidence of workers in their collective capacity to challenge the system, they remain the prerequisite of any viable strategy of socialist advance, and no amount of conference resolutioning in the name of a socialist working class can hope to succeed if it is not underpinned by, and indeed generated from, such a class itself. The creation of such a force, in the light of all that has gone before, is a task of truly Herculean proportions; but it remains the Left's only hope, because there is no easier alternative way.

The way forward

The task is clear, but is many sided and extensive:

(1) To clarify the nature of the socialist alternative to market forces, bureaucratic degeneration and bourgeois democracy.

(2) To widen the sense of socialism to also encompass the transcendence of other social divisions, most notably those of race and gender.

(3) To evolve modes of organization and practices on the Left that will consolidate this wider sense of socialism amongst Left activists themselves, so that the form of political practice adopted by socialists before the transition will not block, but instead will already be working to create, the social practices of a genuinely non-sexist and non-racist socialism.

(4) To win active support and involvement for this broader vision of socialism in the labour movement and beyond.

(5) To build, that is, in that wider labour movement a powerful counter-culture of ideas, institutions and practices that can answer, point for point, the rationalization of the status quo as the only and inevitable way of running a complex, modern society.

(6) To forge a programme capable of initiating that transition to socialism.

(7) To locate a strategy that will consolidate support and overcome opposition.

It is impossible to specify such a strategy adequately without putting at its centre the likely political problems of the transition itself. We have to break unambiguously with a tradition of politics (that of reformism) that buys votes with easy promises, and be prepared instead to face shortages and economic restrictions (and worse) from international capital. We have got to argue honestly against any notion of the gradual and unproblematic transition to socialism. It seems only too inevitable that the arrival in power of a socialist government, and the existence of a mass movement pushing for a total social transformation, will precipitate significant degrees of resistance from the capitalist class. That resistance will be many sided: administrative obstructionism within the state machine; media hysteria and distortion; economic sabotage and international financial pressure; the mobilization of popular counter-socialist forces amongst the petty-bourgeoisie; the possibility of military action and paramilitary terror. These are so central a feature of intense class struggle elsewhere, that their likely arrival here has to be faced – and countered – by the only force available to the Left for that purpose, a broad coalition of popular forces prepared in advance for this, willing to cope with sabotage and shortages, primed for defensive violence is this is necessary, and committed to the creation of new popular forms of democratic control to replace the existing institutions of the state.

Those tasks fall, in our view, to the Left outside the Labour Party. They alone are in an untrammelled position from which to build an organizational strength of the kind the project requires. They alone are in a position from which to repeatedly assert the nature of the socialist project, and the necessary hardship and struggles involved in its achievement. And they alone are in a position from which to repeatedly draw attention to the limits of labourism. Those who enter the Labour Party hoping to win it to a socialist project go in vain, for the political distance that they expect the party to cover (from being a party of social reform with right-reformist elements within it to one led by left-reformists in alliance with revolutionary elements outside) is just too great a distance for any party to move without disintegrating in the process. The job of the Left inside the party can only be to win the battle for policy commitments in opposition, and to slow the rate of retreat by a Labour government in power. Yet that second job at least can probably best be done from outside, through the creation of independent class-based forces not compromised in their opposition to Labour Government conservatism by any vestigial sense of loyalty to the party itself.

As far as we can tell, and as we have argued elsewhere[1] even Left-Labour socialism has an inherent propensity in power to degenerate into a corporatist reconstitution of capitalist profits at the expense of the working class, with a resulting danger that too close an identification of the socialist project with the fate of Labour governments can only discredit that project in the very audience it needs to attract. To go in to the Labour Party is to add to the voices of those democratic socialists conscious of the vacillations of their party leadership; but it is also to provide bogymen for those leaders to exploit, to create an impression of party division which renders the project of Left labourism

1 Some of the issues raised in this chapter have been discussed earlier in David Coates' exchange with Tariq Ali, Quintin Hoare and Geoff Hodgson in *New Left Review* 129, 132, 133 and 135: and in his *The Labour Party and the Struggle for Socialism*, Cambridge University Press, Cambridge, 1975, and *Labour in Power?* Longman, London, 1980. We would like to thank a number of people who commented on an earlier draft of this paper: Ray Bush, Gordon Johnston, Stuart Ogden, Dick Taylor, Danny Ridgeway, Steve Kibble, Simon Cliffe, Pat Winn, Louis Charalambous, Dennis Donnelly and David Stephen.

impossible for lack of electoral support, and to fall victim to the accusation that the form of politics socialists are advocating inside the Labour Party is not true to the spirit of labourism that has united the party down the century. Because that accusation is true, its denial by revolutionary socialists inside the party must raise serious questions about their general credibility as an alternative to the existing party leadership, and it must also serve to reinforce the very labourism that a genuine push for socialism in Britain must leave far behind.

For the moment we must recognize and accept the fact that socialists in Britain will continue to pursue alternative and even conflicting strategies. At the very least, however, we should be able to agree that instead of concentrating all socialist political energies on struggles inside the Labour Party, we need to recognize the necessity of struggle on many fronts. We need to sustain the struggles against sexism and racism, and to link them into the centre of the predominantly white male labour movement. We need to propagandize on every available platform for socialist perspectives, to construct a socialist 'common sense' in answer to the ruling ideologies of the day. We need to put intellectual effort into the clarification of a socialist alternative, and to link that to the more immediate practical struggles for survival (in the peace campaign) and economic security against capitalist threats (in the unions). We need to work for a broad unity on the Left. There is an immediate need for united front campaigns aimed at defence of shop-floor organization, protection of living standards and jobs, and opposition to state coercion – as different facets of an overall ruling class strategy directed against the working class. The Left must, with renewed urgency, explore the possibilities of creating a federal united Left organization amongst those to the Left of the Labour Party, to establish some minimum degree of organizational credibility and, hence, political legitimacy. Moreover, the Left inside and outside the Labour Party needs to turn outwards in a systematic way, to build international linkages with the parties and movements of, particularly, those in the advanced industrial capitalist sector of the globe, in an attempt to match the internationalization of capital with a renewed sense of proletarian internationalism. The choice before the Left is still as it was: to see capitalism slide into barbarism (and now, perhaps, into total nuclear holocaust) or to remobilize the coalition for socialist advance that alone can save humanity.

APPENDIX

Compiled with the help of Paul Hubert and Sarah Perrigo

SOCIALIST ORGANIZATIONS

Big Flame   27 Clerkenwell Close, London EC1R 0AT. Journal: *Big Flame*. Theoretical journal: *Revolutionary Socialism*.

Campaign for Labour Party Democracy   10 Park Drive, London NW11 7SH.

Communist Party of Great Britain   16 St John Street, London EC1M 4AL. Paper (daily): *Morning Star*. Theoretical journal: *Marxism Today*.

Communist Party of Britain (Marxist Leninist)   155 Fortress Road, London NW5. Paper: *The Worker*.

Independent Labour Publications   49 Top Moor Side, Leeds LS11 9LW. Paper (monthly): *Labour Leader*.

International Marxist Group   see Socialist League

Labour Co-ordinating Committee   9 Poland Street, London W1.

Labour Party   150 Walworth Road, London SE17 1JT. Paper (weekly): *Labour Weekly*. Theoretical journal: *New Socialist*.

Labour Party Young Socialists   150 Walworth Road, London SE17 1JT. Paper: *Socialist Youth*.

Militant Tendency   1 Mentmore Terrace, London E8 3PN. Paper (weekly): *Militant*. Theoretical journal: *Militant International Review*.

National Organisation of Labour Students   150 Walworth Road, London SE17 1JT. Paper: *Labour Student*.

Revolution Youth   P.O. Box 50, London N1 2XP. Paper (occasional): *Revolution*.

Revolutionary Communist Group   BCM Box 5909, London WC1N 3XX. Paper (monthly) *Fight racism, fight imperialism*.

Revolutionary Communist Party   BM RCP London WC1N 3XX. Paper (monthly): *The Next Step.* Theoretical journal: *Revolutionary Communist Papers.*

Socialist League (formerly the International Marxist Group) P.O. Box 50, London N1 2XP. Paper (weekly): *Socialist Action.* Theoretical journals: *International, International Marxist Review.*

Socialist Organiser Alliance   28 Middle Lane, London N8. Paper (weekly): *Socialist Organiser.*

Socialist Party of Great Britain   52 Clapham High Street, London SW4 7UN. Paper: *Socialist Standard.*

Socialist Society   7 Carlisle Street, London W1.

Socialist Workers Party (formerly the International Socialists) P.O. Box 82, London E2. Paper (weekly): *Socialist Worker.* Theoretical journals: *Socialist Review, International Socialism.*

Spartacist League P.O. Box 185, London WC1. Paper (monthly): *Spartacist Britain.* Theoretical journal: *Spartacist.*

Workers Revolutionary Party (formerly the Socialist Labour League) 21b Old Town, London SW4 0JT. Paper (daily): *Newsline.* Theoretical journal: *Labour Review.*

Workers' Socialist League (see Socialist Organiser Alliance) P.O. Box 135, London N1 0DD.

Young Communist League   16 St John Street, London EC1M 4AL. Paper: *Challenge.*

FEMINIST AND SOCIALIST-FEMINIST
ORGANIZATIONS AND PAPERS

Feminist Review   published 3 times a year from 65 Manor Road, London N16 5EH.

Link   Communist Party women's forum, published from 16 St John's Street, London EC1M 4AL.

Revolutionary and Radical Feminist Newsletter (women only)   published from 17 Kensington Terrace, Leeds 6.

Scarlet Women (women only)   journal of the socialist-feminist current in the WLM, published from 5 Washington Terrace, North Shields, Tyne and Wear.

Spare Rib monthly feminist magazine published from 27 Clerkenwell Close, London EC1.

Wires (women only) newsletter of the womens liberation movement published from P.O. Box 162, Sheffield.
Women's Studies International Quarterly published four times a year by Pergamon Press.
Women's Voice the journal of the women in the SWP, published from P.O. Box 82, London E2.
Other useful addresses Womens Research and Resource Centre, 190 Upper Street, London N1. E.O.C. Information Centre, Overseas House, Quay Street, Manchester 3.

OTHER JOURNALS AND ORGANIZATIONS

Campaign for Nuclear Disarmament 29 Great James Street, London WC1. Journal: *Sanity.*
Capital and Class published 3 times a year by the Conference of Socialist Economists from 55 Mount Pleasant, London NW
History Workshop twice-yearly journal of the Socialist Historians, distributed through Pluto Press, The Works, 105a Torriano Avenue, London NW5 2RX.
Leveller published occasionally, from 52 Acre Lane, London SW2.
New Left Review published 6 times a year from 15 Greek Street, London W1V 5LF.
New Statesman weekly socialist journal obtainable from W. H. Smiths and most newsagents, published from 14–16 Farringdon Lane, London EC1R 3AU.
Peace News – for nonviolent revolution published from 5 Caledonian Road, London N.1.
Politics and Power Biannual publication by Routledge and Kegan Paul.
Tribune weekly paper of the Labour Left, published from 308 Grays Inn Road, London WC1X 8DY.

INDEX

Index

Index

Nationality Act (1948), 58
New Communist Party (NCP),
 133–4
New Left, 215–23
New Left Review (NLR), 126–7
New Reasoner, 126
New Socialist, 145
New Statesman, 123
Newly Industrializing Countries,
 19
North Atlantic Treaty
 Organisation (NATO), 81,
 216–17, 221–2
Northern Ireland, 136

oil, 17, 28
Organisation for Economic Co-
 operation and Development
 (OECD), 32, 33–5, 45, 53, 55
Organisation of Petroleum
 Exporting Countries (OPEC),
 28, 39, 70
Orwell G. 123
over-production, 16–17
Owen D. 103
Owen R. 180
Owenism, 180

pacificism, 215
parliamentary democracy and
 revolution, 161–2
parliamentary socialism, 272–5
patriarchy, 198–201
peace movement, 81, 214–22
Peace News, 219
People's Jubilee, 134
Petrograd Soviet, 157
Phillips M. 187
Pinochet, 30
Plaid Cymru, 71
Poland, 29, 124, 151
police, 82
Political Economy of Women
 Group, 139
Pollitt H. 123
Portugal, 27, 153, 156, 170

Poulantzas N. 138, 146
Powell E. 71, 140
Prague Spring, 128
President Azana, 156
Prior M. 137–8
prefiguration, 143
productivity, comparative levels
 of, 34–5
profit, tendency of the falling rate
 of, 15
Purdy D. 137–8

radical feminism, 199–200
Ramelson B. 137
Randall V. 197
Randle M. 220
Rate Support Grant, 227
Reagan R. 221
reformism, 243–6, 265–6
 legacy of, 256–60
Rent Act (1957), 225
rent strikes, 223–4
Resistance movements, 153, 155
revisionism and the Labour Party,
 97
Revolutionary Communist Party,
 109
revolutionary feminism, 199–200
revolutionary socialism, ch. 6:
 148–77, 243–4, 246–9, 277–9
 failure of, 260–66
Rowbotham S. 193–4
Rowe A. 223
Rumania, 153
Russell B. 219
Russian Revolution, 150–1,
 156–9, 243–4, 247, 261
 and the Constituent Assembly,
 161–2

Saint Simon, 244
Samuelson P. 10
Sassoon D. 128
Scandinavia, 10
Scanlon H. 99
Scheidemann, 154